Churchill and Morton

Churchill and Morton

R. W. THOMPSON

The quest for insight in the correspondence of
Major Sir Desmond Morton and the author

HODDER AND STOUGHTON
LONDON SYDNEY AUCKLAND TORONTO

To Mel, my wife.

Acknowledgments

MY GRATEFUL THANKS TO MRS. GILLIAN PARKER AND TO HER STEP-brother Brian Franks, not only for their permission to publish these letters, but for their encouragement throughout.

I wish also to thank Colonel F. W. Deakin, D.S.O., for permission to use his most valuable letter in my foreword.

My thanks also to Dennis Wheatley, Sir John Peck and Martin Gilbert for their encouragement and advice.

R. W. THOMPSON,
BELCHAMP WALTER,
SUFFOLK.

Foreword

By Captain Stephen Roskill, C.B.E., D.S.C., Litt.D., R.N.

I FIRST MET MAJOR (LATER SIR DESMOND) MORTON IN THE SUMMER of 1940 shortly after the fall of France. I was then a Commander on the Naval Staff and he was a Principal Assistant Secretary in the Ministry of Economic Warfare, to which virtually the whole of the Industrial Intelligence Centre had been transferred shortly before the outbreak of war. I knew that Morton had worked for the Secret Intelligence Service in the 1920s and was the chief architect of the I.I.C., whose purpose it was to investigate and report on industrial developments, and especially those concerned with arms manufacture, in European countries. As the international scene darkened in the mid-1930s the I.I.C. concentrated its activities largely on Germany, and produced a series of reports showing how in that country preparations for the large-scale production of aircraft, tanks and all the weapons of war were very advanced—and that at a time when our own comparable industries had either closed down for lack of orders or had been unable to modernise their plant.

I also knew that Morton had long been an intimate friend of Churchill's, and as at the time of our first talk he had just moved from the Admiralty to Downing Street it was natural that our conversation should have centred on the two great issues of the moment—namely whether a serious invasion of this country (as opposed to coastal raids or the dropping of paratroops) was a practical operation of war, and what the basis of our Grand Strategy should be after we had recovered from the enormous losses of material suffered in the recent catastrophe on the European mainland. I recall that we were in full agreement that invasion on a large scale, using chiefly the slow and ponderous barges then assembling across the Channel, would end in a decisive defeat for the Germans; for their navy had suffered heavy losses in the recent

Norwegian campaign, we had some forty destroyers and many light craft concentrated in south-east ports with bigger warships in support, and Fighter Command of the R.A.F. was in command of the sky— which had not been the case in Poland, Norway, the Low Countries or France. Moreover Churchill's leadership had united the country and inspired a spirit of defiance of the dictatorships such as had been sadly lacking in the 1930s. On the strategic issue we were also in agreement that our expulsion from the Continent meant that there was no alter- native to the adoption of a predominantly maritime based strategy— using our sea power to land forces at places and times of our own choosing, as had been done by the elder Pitt in somewhat similar circumstances during the Seven Years' War (1756–63), and again in the Napoleonic War (1799–1815). I remember being much impressed by Morton's grasp of these great issues, which were of course the principal subjects under consideration by the Defence and Chiefs of Staff Committees at the time.

The war soon took me to waters far distant from those concerned with Home Defence and the development of our Mediterranean strategy, and a long interval elapsed before I met Morton again. In the 1960s I undertook to write the authorised biography of the first Lord Hankey, who had been Secretary of the Committee of Imperial Defence 1912–38, Secretary of the War Cabinet or Cabinet 1916–38 and additionally Clerk of the Privy Council from 1923 (3 vols., Collins, 1970–4), whose papers and diaries I found to be exactly as he had left them, and to which he had repeatedly refused access during his life- time. On going through those papers I discovered that Hankey had been a neighbour and close friend of Morton's, and that they had collaborated intimately in the work of the I.I.C. and in furthering British rearmament in the 1930s. I therefore asked if I could visit Morton at his charming house on Kew Green to discuss Hankey's work and character. Morton agreed readily to my suggestion—on one condition, namely that his name and the part he had played in events were nowhere mentioned in my work. I soon discovered that he had an ineradicable obsession regarding the secrecy of his own activities, and although he spoke very freely to me about them and also wrote me a number of interesting letters I felt obliged to respect his obsession until his death in August 1971 released me from that obligation.

Robert Rhodes James then wrote in *The Times* (10th August, 1971) describing how Morton had been allowed by three Prime Ministers (MacDonald, Baldwin and Chamberlain) to pass secret information about German rearmament to Churchill—'their most formidable critic'. He considered that, although after May 1940 Morton's close association with Churchill was very important to historians 'it is probable that history will place even greater emphasis on the importance of their relationship in the 1930s'—a conclusion which my study of Hankey has led me fully to support. Furthermore James considered that 'any study of Sir Winston's war leadership will be incomplete without Sir Desmond Morton's advice, recollections and wisdom'.

The present work by R. W. Thompson wholly confirms that Morton was, as James described him, 'a shrewd and imaginative adviser, to whom his countrymen owe much more than most of them realise'. Thompson corresponded regularly with Morton for more than a quarter of a century, and although he was pledged to the same secrecy as myself about their relationship he made great use of Morton's letters in writing his book on Churchill, *The Yankee Marlborough* (Allen and Unwin, 1963). Again like myself he has been freed of his pledge of secrecy by Morton's death, and the selection from their correspondence published in this book covers the years 1960-2 when he was collecting material for that work and feeling his way towards an understanding of Churchill's complex character, the motives which inspired him, and his methods of work during the war. Thompson described his book as being 'an attempt at an assessment of Churchill as a person and a personality, and his impact upon his times in that light' (to Morton 13th July, 1961).

This is not the place to proffer any judgment on Thompson's success or failure in that ambitious purpose; but what is beyond doubt is that the letters that passed between him and Morton provide a fascinating study of how the formulation of his views and opinions progressed. They also throw much light on Churchill himself. We see him at his best, as what Thompson describes as 'the VOICE—the right words to the proletariat perfectly timed, catching an heroic mood . . . a collection of sustained dramatic performances without equal' (to Morton 10th November, 1960); and we see him at his worst, as in his treatment of Wavell, which Morton described as 'the first time I ever deeply disliked Winston, and realised the depths of selfish brutality to which he could sink'—in order to demonstrate his power (to Thompson 21st–24th August, 1961). Virtually every distinguished soldier of the Second World War—Dill, Brooke, Alexander, Auchinleck, Montgomery ('obviously he should avoid putting pen to paper at all costs' remarks Thompson), Wingate ('a swashbuckler', in Morton's opinion and not 'the Clive of Burma' as Churchill described him) passes across the screen of Morton's mind in these letters. So do Churchill's chief intimates, whom Morton considers to have been Brendan Bracken and 'Barney' Baruch. The notorious Tizard–Lindemann feud is reviewed, and to my surprise Morton does not accept that 'The Prof.' had much influence in the adoption of the area bombing strategy. That dreadful error he attributes predominantly to Air Marshal Harris. We here read Morton's judgment of Churchill as 'a wild tactician, certainly; frequently a crackpot strategist' (to Thompson 8th September, 1961); but he considers Churchill was too often blamed for mistakes for which he was not basically responsible, and given too little credit for ideas which were right but which he could not get the Chiefs of Staff (or the Combined C.O.S.s after the U.S.A. had entered the war) to adopt.

The disasters which move Morton most deeply are the decision to send military help to Greece in 1941 ('many, including myself, thought it just short of lunacy at the time'), which deprived Wavell of complete victory in North Africa, the 'Unconditional Surrender' dogma enunciated by Roosevelt at a Press Conference at Casablanca in January 1943, by which, he declares, Churchill 'was completely taken aback', and 'that appalling Yalta Conference' of February 1945 when a sick and dying President virtually placed central Europe in Stalin's hands. Few will disagree with Morton's judgments on those issues today.

As regards Churchill's attitude towards his colleagues, Morton's final analysis is that he 'heartily disliked any person whose personal character was such that he could not avoid . . . feeling respect for that person', and that his 'over-weaning desire to dominate resulted in a feeling of inferiority in regard to anyone who was not in the least afraid of him' (to Thompson 21st–24th August, 1961). Such were Generals Dill, Wavell, Auchinleck and Slim; and I would add Admirals Sir Andrew Cunningham and Sir John Tovey. My only disappointment is the paucity of the references to our leading sailors in these letters; but as Morton was himself a soldier he obviously studied and understood military men better than naval officers. I hope I may in due course repair that omission myself.

What is beyond doubt is that, as Robert Rhodes James foresaw, the letters here published throw a great deal of new light on Churchill himself, on the political, strategic and tactical problems of the Second World War, and on a great many of the chief characters of that period. Though Morton's views, and Thompson's acceptance or modification of them, obviously will not command universal acceptance, the professional historian will gain much benefit from studying the correspondence, while the lay reader can hardly fail to be interested, even excited, by the shrewd comments, opinions and judgments which emanated when two highly intelligent minds were striking sparks off each other.

STEPHEN ROSKILL

A List of the Main People Referred to in the Letters

AMERY, Rt. Hon. Leopold, Tory politician, Secretary of State for India, Second World War.

ASQUITH, H. H., Rt. Hon. Liberal Prime Minister, gave way to Lloyd George, 1916.

ATTLEE, Rt. Hon. Clement, Labour Prime Minister after Second World War. Deputy Prime Minister in Churchill's War Cabinet. Minister, Mr. MacDonald, permission to talk freely to me and keep

AUCHINLECK, Field Marshal Sir Claude, C. in C. Middle East, successor to Wavell, and afterwards C. in C. India.

BALDWIN, S., later Earl, Prime Minister 1924-9 and 1935.

BALFOUR, A. J., later Earl, Prime Minister 1902-5.

BARUCH, Barney, U.S. Financier, close friend of Churchill from First World War onwards.

BEAVERBROOK, Max, First Viscount. Canadian, newspaper proprietor, friend of Churchill's, and Minister of Aircraft Production, Second World War.

BEGBIE, Harold, Foreign Office official, a man of great charm.

BLACKETT, Professor P. M. S., close worker with Professor Sir Henry Tizard on important Committees. Opponent of the views of Professor Lindemann especially in regard to bombing.

BONHAM CARTER, Sir Maurice, Secretary to Prime Minister H. H. Asquith, and later an adviser to Lloyd George.

BOOTHBY, Sir Robert, later Lord Boothby. Distinguished politician and friend of Churchill.

BRACKEN, Brendan, Minister of Information, Second World War. Protégé of Churchill's. Later First Lord of Admiralty. Viscount.

BRAND, Lord, 1878-1963. Created Baron 1946. Deputy chairman, British Mission, Washington, 1917-18. Financial adviser at Paris Peace Conference, 1919. Head of British Food Mission, Washington, 1941-4. British Treasury representative, Washington, 1944-6.

BROOKE, General Sir Alan, later Field Marshal Lord Alanbrooke, succeeded General Dill as C.I.G.S. until end of Second World War.

CADOGAN, Alex, The Rt. Hon. Sir Alexander Cadogan, Permanent Under Secretary, Foreign Office, Second World War.

CHAMBERLAIN, Rt. Hon. Neville, Prime Minister, resigned 1940.

CHATFIELD, Admiral of the Fleet Sir Alfred, later Lord, First Sea Lord.

CHERWELL, Professor F. A. Lindemann, close scientific adviser to Churchill. Created Baron.

CHURCHILL, Randolph, son of Winston Churchill, soldier, author, journalist, wrote biography of seventeenth Earl of Derby.

CLEMENCEAU, Georges, French Prime Minister, First World War, known as 'The Tiger'.

COOPER, Duff, Rt. Hon. Sir Alfred, later Lord Norwich. Member of War Cabinet.

CROWE, Sir Eyre, Senior Official Foreign Office. Prominent in foundation of Committee of Imperial Defence, and 'The War Book'. Minister Plenipotentiary, Peace Conference, 1919. Permanent Under Secretary, Foreign Affairs, 1920.

DEAKIN, Col. F. W., D.S.O. Distinguished service in Jugo Slavia. Assisted Churchill in 1930s on his *Life of Marlborough*.

DILL, General Sir John, later Field Marshal, C.I.G.S. 1940–1.

EDEN, Rt. Hon. Anthony, Secretary of State for Foreign Affairs, War Cabinet, Second World War, later Earl of Avon.

ENVER, Pasha, Turkish head of State, First World War. Placed Turkish forces under German General Liman von Sanders in March 1915 to combat British attempt to force Dardanelles.

ESHER, Viscount, chairman of committee on War Office reform. Immensely influential. According to Hankey neither Balfour, nor Campbell Bannerman, nor Asquith could dispense with him.

EVEREST, Mrs., nurse to Winston Churchill, to whom he was devoted.

FISHER, Jackie, Admiral Lord Fisher, brilliant and eccentric Naval Commander, First Sea Lord. A man of many obsessions as he grew older. Devoted to Churchill.

FREWEN, Clara, sister of Jenny Jerome, afterwards Lady (Randolph) Churchill, and Aunt to Winston Churchill.

FULLER, Major-General J. F. C., brilliant Staff Officer, suffered for his powerful advocacy of the Tank. A strategist and tactician of genius. Military historian.

HALDANE of Cloan, Richard Burdon, First Viscount. Secretary of State for War, architect of pre-1914 British Army and Territorial Army.

HALIFAX, Lord, leading Tory politician. First choice for Prime Minister when Chamberlain resigned, 1940. Was not acceptable to Attlee and Labour Party, who preferred Churchill.

HANKEY, Maurice, referred to as Maurice, Capt. R. M., later Sir Maurice and Lord Hankey. Secretary to the Committee of Imperial Defence. Devoted servant of Great Britain. His Memoirs, *The Supreme Command* (two volumes) dedicated to: Arthur James Balfour, Earl of Balfour, creator of the Committee of Imperial Defence, prototype of the Supreme Command; Henry Herbert Asquith, Earl of Oxford and Asquith who developed it for defensive purposes in peace, and in war, under various titles, for war direction; David Lloyd George, Earl of Dwyfor who perfected it in the form of the War Cabinet as an instrument of victory.

HARRIS, Sir Arthur, Marshal of the Royal Air Force, A.O.C. Bomber Command. Known as 'Bomber Harris'.

HEENAN, John C. (the late Cardinal, Archbishop of Westminster).

HOZIER, Blanche, mother of Clementine Hozier who married Winston Churchill.

INSKIP, The Right Hon. Sir Thomas (later First Viscount Caldecote), appointed Minister for Co-ordination of Defence, 1936. Distinguished career as a statesman.

IRONSIDE, General Sir Edmund, later Field Marshal Lord Ironside, C.I.G.S. 1940.

ISMAY, General Sir Hastings, later Lord Ismay. Special representative Winston Churchill, Chiefs of Staff Committee, Second World War.

JEROME, Leonard, U.S. Financier, father of Jennie, wife of Lord Randolph Churchill and mother of Winston.

KENNEDY, Major-General Sir John Kennedy, D.M.O.

KING, Fleet Admiral E. J. (U.S.), markedly antipathetic to the British.

KITCHENER, Field Marshal Earl, the greatest general of his time, Egypt, Boer War, later Secretary of State for War. Dominated War Office and Army Council; even seemed almost to dominate England in First World War.

LESLIE, Leonie, sister of Clara Frewen and Jenny Jerome, afterwards Lady (Randolph) Churchill, and aunt to Winston Churchill.

LIDDELL HART, Capt. Basil, later knighted. Distinguished strategist, master of armoured tactics, mainly responsible with Major-General Fuller and others for introduction of armour in British Army. Military historian.

LLOYD GEORGE, Rt. Hon. David, Prime Minister 1916, regarded as main driving force of Great Britain, First World War. Later First Earl.

MACDONALD, Rt. Hon. J. Ramsay, Prime Minister 1924 (Jan. to Oct.) and 1929–31.

MARSH, Sir Edward. Literary assistant to Churchill and devoted friend of Mr. and Mrs. Churchill. Sacrificed himself to devote himself to Churchill.

MARSHALL, General G. C. (U.S.) Chief of Staff, U.S. Army.

MARTIN, Sir John, principal private secretary to Churchill, 1933–45.

MESSERVY, Major-General (later General Sir Frank), commanded British 4th Corps in advance on Rangoon; later G.O.C. Malaya Command.

MORGENTHAU, Henry, United States Ambassador to Turkey, First World War. Author of well informed books on Turkey.

MORLEY, Lord John, Liberal Politician, late nineteenth century–early twentieth.

MORRISON, Rt. Hon. Herbert, later First Viscount, of Lambeth. Member of Churchill's War Cabinet, Minister of Supply. Distinguished Labour politician.

MOUNTBATTEN, Vice-Admiral Lord Louis, later Admiral of the Fleet, Earl.

NYE, Lieut.-General Sir Archibald, V.C.I.G.S., Second World War.

O'GOWAN, Major-General E. E. Dorman, M.C., Chief of Staff to General Sir Claude Auchinleck, First Battle of Alamein. Produced appreciation, July 1942, for Battle of Alamein.

OLIVER, F. S., one of close circle of Tory Imperialists surrounding L. S. Amery before First World War. Friend of Austen Chamberlain. Biographer of Alexander Hamilton, considered by many to be one of the greatest biographies ever written. Noted for his wisdom and wit, a man of great charm, and influence.

PAGET, General Sir Bernard, C. in C. Home Forces, Second World War, dedicated to return to Europe after Dunkirk, and architect of Plan Skyscraper which enabled General Morgan to produce 'Overlord', the 1944 Invasion Plan.

PECK, Sir John, Private Secretary to First Lord of Admiralty, worked in offices of War Cabinet. Ambassador, Irish Republic.

PORTAL, Marshal of the Royal Air Force, Chief of Air Staff, Sir Charles, later Viscount. Member of Chiefs of Staff Committee.

ROSEBERY, Earl, Liberal Politician, Imperialist, late nineteenth–early twentieth century.

ROSKILL, Capt. Stephen Wentworth, distinguished naval historian. Biographer of Lord Hankey.

SKYSCRAPER, Documents (see Paget). Ground-work and plan for re-entry of Allies into Europe.

SLIM, Major-General Sir William (later Field Marshal, First Viscount), commanded British 14th Army, Far East.

STOPFORD, General Sir Montagu, Commander in Far East.

TIZARD, Sir Henry. One of the most brilliant scientists of the 1930s, 40s and 50s. Served on Tizard Committee and improved Radar Defences of Britain. Tizard finally forced out by Prof. Lindemann.

WAVELL, General Sir Archibald, later Field Marshal, Earl, C. in C. Middle East, 1939–41. Viceroy of India.

WHEATLEY, Dennis, novelist, served on Joint Planning Staff, Second World War. Worked in offices of War Cabinet. Invented 'War Games'.

WIGRAM, Ralph, young Foreign Office official, friend of Churchill, to whom he was devoted.

Major Morton

and

My Search for Churchill

THIS CORRESPONDENCE RECORDS THE HEART OF THE STORY OF MY SEARCH for Churchill, and much else besides. Churchill is the heart and core of it. Churchill the war leader of course, but above all Churchill the man. What manner of man was he? In these letters of inspiration I sought to find out.

Everyone who wants to know what Churchill did may find out from scores of available sources, not least from the remarkable body of work in which he recorded his manifold deeds from youth to age, his personal memoirs of the two world wars in which he was closely involved, and in the last of which he commanded and directed the vast flood of the British endeavour. All a man's personal work is revealing, but Churchill is seldom more revealing of himself than when he writes of others, of his great ancestor Marlborough, of his 'Great Contemporaries'. In this book it is easy to see what he loves and admires, and what he hates. No seeker after Churchill can afford to miss a line of it. Martin Gilbert, inheriting the monumental task of building 'the Life' from the Churchill Archive, will provide all else. Or perhaps not quite all else. There are the innumerable comments of many of Churchill's contemporaries, hidden in personal memoirs, in potent asides. And much is lost. It is not a life in which it is possible to sweep up the last grain of dust. But these letters from the man who was closest to him over so many years, who was his trusted friend, his intimate throughout the 'Wilderness Years' at Chartwell, and the years of the Second World War, reveal much that would otherwise lie hidden.

Desmond John Falkiner Morton—Major Sir Desmond Morton, K.C.B., C.M.G., M.C., Croix de Guerre avec Palmes, Officier Legion d'Honneur, Knight Grand Cross of Oranje Nassau—was born in 1891 and educated at Eton and the Royal Military Academy, Woolwich. He joined his Regiment, the Royal Horse and Royal Field Artillery, in 1911, and fought through the First World War. Commanding the last battery to fire at Arras, a bullet entered his body at the base of his neck and lodged in his heart; miraculously surviving, he was selected by Field Marshal Haig as his Aide de Camp. It was in that capacity that he met Churchill, conducting the then Minister of Munitions on battle-field tours 'as close to danger as possible', as no one who knows any-thing about Churchill will doubt. The friendship between the two men was immediate, and there is no doubt that the young Major Morton had that appeal of the brave that Churchill found irresistible. Moreover Morton combined a kind of nonchalance with an underlying gravity and humour. He was always completely at his ease.

In his Memoirs of the Second World War, Volume ii, *Their Finest Hour*, Churchill paid tribute to his young friend:

Another of my close friends was Desmond Morton. When in 1917 Field Marshal Haig filled his personal staff with young officers fresh from the firing line, Desmond was recommended as the pick of the artillery. He had commanded the most advanced Field battery in Arras during the severe spring fighting of that year. To his Military Cross he added the unique distinction of having been shot through the heart, and living happily ever afterwards with the bullet in him. When I became Minister of Munitions in July 1917 I frequently visited the front as the Commander-in-Chief's guest, and he always sent his trusted Aide de Camp, Desmond Morton, with me. Together we visited many parts of the lines. During these some-times dangerous excursions, and at the Commander-in-Chief's house, I formed a great regard and friendship for this brilliant and gallant officer, and in 1919, when I became Secretary of State for War and Air, I appointed him to a key position in the intelligence, which he held for many years. He was a neighbour of mine, dwelling only a mile away from Chartwell. He obtained from the Prime Minister, Mr. MacDonald, permission to talk freely to me and keep me well informed. He became, and continued during the war to be, one of my most intimate advisers till our final victory was won.

In fact, Lloyd George and Sir Eyre Crowe had most to do with Desmond Morton's appointment to establish Industrial Intelligence, concerned to keep a close watch on German and Soviet industrial developments in particular. He detected well in advance German factories adapted for swift conversion to armament manufacture. He constantly provided Baldwin with facts Baldwin would sooner have been without. Providing evidence of Germany's plans for war was not very popular with either Baldwin or Chamberlain, but such evidence was vital to Churchill at Chartwell.

In his Memorial Service in Westminster Cathedral, conducted by Cardinal Heenan assisted by half a dozen dignitaries of the Roman Church, Heenan, who had been at Desmond's bedside to administer the last rites, spoke of him as the power behind Churchill, particularly in the vital ten years of the 1930s when Churchill, a back-bencher, was almost in the political wilderness. I write 'almost' because Churchill's privileges and his immense drive, his remarkable fascination rendered his wilderness more inhabited and more fruitful than the wildernesses of more ordinary people. These years were perhaps the years of Morton's greatest service, for without that service it might have been very difficult for even Churchill to take over the office of Prime Minister.

Before 1929 Morton had been a frequent guest in the Churchill home, but in 1929 Churchill began to prepare for war and for his role. All at once Morton found the new attitude inconsistent with his work in secret intelligence and as a servant of the country and of the Prime Minister. The talk at dinner at the Churchills, and the company at Chartwell were embarrassing in the extreme to a man with Morton's knowledge, and reluctantly he felt compelled to excuse himself. Churchill coaxed him, and as a result Morton went at once to Ramsay MacDonald, the Prime Minister, explained his predicament and asked what he should do.

'Tell him whatever he wants to know. Keep him informed,' said MacDonald.

'Be good enough to put it in writing, Prime Minister,' Desmond replied.

Whereupon MacDonald at once wrote the necessary permission on a sheet of 10 Downing Street note-paper. Through the years this permission was endorsed by Baldwin and Chamberlain. It is almost certainly true to say that without the constant briefing on affairs provided by Major Morton, Churchill would not have been in a position to grasp power when the chance came.

Thereafter Morton was Churchill's constant support and privileged, trusted family friend. Listening to Desmond reminiscing over many years, and studying his letters, I think of him, particularly in the war years, as Churchill's 'father confessor', among other things. Perhaps a reader will find some evidence for that in these letters. The friendship of the two men was unique, for apart from Desmond's vital service in providing secret intelligence, he was also a valuable adviser and helper on Churchill's writings, especially his life of Marlborough. His literary taste and judgment were impeccable, and he had been highly critical of Churchill's attitude to his 'great Ancestor'.

My first meeting with Desmond Morton is clearly printed on my memory. I had reported to the Intelligence Corps depot at Oriel College, Oxford, feeling despondent. I had returned prematurely from a tour of duty in the North Caribbean in the spring of 1943. I knew that a report I had written on the situation in Central America had alarmed and irritated my superiors. Anyway, it was a fine tonic when I found a letter in the rack bearing the legend PRIME MINISTER. My stock rose at once with my brother officers kicking their heels, as I was, between jobs. The letter invited me to call upon Major Morton at Great George Street forthwith.

I was shown into a spacious room, and sat down in an armchair at some distance from Desmond. He was at his desk and on the telephone to an American general. The talk seemed to amuse him greatly.

Finally he turned to me. 'That chap wanted shipping space for diapers for Arab babies! When he realised he couldn't have them he was astounded, "What will the mothers of Massachusetts say?" he groaned.'

The Allies had just landed in North Africa.

I don't remember what we talked about, except that my impressions of the situation in the North Caribbean came into it. 'Your report must have infuriated one and all. It was excellent . . .' I think we were together for the best part of an hour, and we must have established some sort of rapport, for from that day forward I went to see him whenever I felt like it.

I think we exchanged our first letters, apart from brief notes, in early 1947. I was free of the war by that time, and so was Desmond. He had opted out of Churchill's *cercle militaire* in 1945, and occupied the garden room in the Treasury when he was in England, until he retired. I believe he had disapproved very strongly of Churchill's refusal to call it a day after the war. In any case his own task was done, and he must return to the Treasury. He was greatly moved by Churchill's consternation at being rejected by the British people. His dejection was —for a short time—absolute. It was almost as if he had forgotten 'politics' and parties. He, Churchill, was—surely—the 'father figure'. There was nothing for him to do but to retire gracefully, to devote himself to writing, painting, living out his last years, revered and full of honour. But the old man could not do that. Politics was his life, and that was an end to it. As for Desmond he was glad that there was work ready for him, needing to be done in the aftermath of war.

Desmond had sold up his family estate 'next door' to Churchill, and purchased his lovely little house at Kew, salvaged some of his treasures, including many exotic shrubs for his small garden, and the rich Mandarin jewelled garments his father—or mother?—had brought back from China. He had installed two very ancient family 'retainers' and a cat called Jezebel, and was, I believe, a happy man. His life was very full, for upon his retirement from the Treasury in 1953 he became Governor of the Hammersmith group of hospitals and devoted himself to the task of making Hammersmith one of the finest teaching hospitals in the world. He loved theological discussion and confounding the Bishops. His devotion to the Roman Church was total. He had become a Roman Catholic in his early twenties, and was not, therefore, he said, a member of the 'Establishment'.

He enjoyed those occasions when he was guest of honour and principal speaker at banquets given by very senior soldiers and sailors. He was a fine speaker, full of humour and with an incisive wit and an immense store of anecdote. About once a week, and finally once a month, he lunched at the 'Senior' to talk with old friends.

He was a wonderful, tolerant, loyal and affectionate friend to me for the last twenty-seven years of his life. His affection embraced my wife also, and my youngest daughter. He had a great admiration and liking for women, but I did not attempt to intrude upon his private life. I imagine that he had not married because his life expectation must have been minimal, and by the time he had grown accustomed to a precarious existence, it may have been too late. I do not know.

Without knowing Desmond Morton the last third of my life would have been very different. Probably it would have been more successful in money terms had I not pursued my search for Churchill and some of the unacceptable truths of war.

Yet, regarding these letters, I was appalled by my ignorance of Desmond Morton. I had asked dozens of questions, but very few of them personal, and never personal in the matter of what he had done, what his position had been in the Churchill household in those years before the war. And then he had destroyed his private papers—a tragic loss to historians. His reticence, and his resolution to avoid all limelight were extraordinary. Captain Roskill remarks on his 'horror of publicity', and thinks it 'probably derived from his service in secret intelligence'. I doubt it, but have nothing much to offer as an alternative. He was always a soldier, and I know that he was always treated as a soldier by those who knew him well, Alanbrooke and Alexander and many others. He regarded almost all war books by senior soldiers with distaste, and I think he felt that 'private papers' were dangerous. Situations might arise when it would be a great temptation to 'look things up', but he was determined not to take part in any assessments of the war. It was over for him. Perhaps a certain reluctance is evident in this correspondence, yet it seems clear that Desmond enjoyed writing these letters. He felt that he could trust me absolutely not to involve him. He was quite adamant about that. Perhaps he found that he needed some sort of outlet for the kind of thoughts my letters stirred in him. He did his best to dissuade me from writing about Churchill, but when he recognised that I was going to attempt the task he accepted that. Indeed I had no option, and I feel sure that he knew that my work had led to that, however unfortunately. In any case he tried to steer me clear of errors.

In most of the books by politicians covering the years there are references to Desmond Morton, usually tantalising. In Captain Roskill's fine work on Lord Hankey, *Man of Secrets*, Morton's sustained loyalty to Hankey long after Hankey had been abandoned by Churchill, is very clear and admirable, and there are many footnotes and references to his indefatigable work for Industrial Intelligence, to his friendship with Churchill. Harold Macmillan was one of those very much aware of that friendship and used it whenever possible. Those who knew Desmond Morton through these years say, 'he knew Churchill's mind'. None wonders how this came about. Simply, it was so.

Desmond Morton was never a recluse, but he remains an enigma. He was a kind of refugee from the war, from all that had happened since 1917 when his front-line soldiering came to an end. Yet that cannot be wholly true. He was a man so full of enjoyment, so full of an underlying delight in life. Wherever he was, his humour and wit were noted, not least in his 'minutes' to Churchill and to the Foreign Office. He would enliven any gathering with his presence.

Ever since I had permission from Desmond Morton's heirs to publish these letters I have searched my mind for someone of importance who would remember him, especially in the days before the war. There were a few still living who might do so, and those few were very old. After many months and on the point of giving up I remembered that Desmond's letters quite often referred to his friend, Dennis Wheatley. I only knew Wheatley as a writer of successful crime thrillers. How then, I wondered, did he come to be a friend of Morton's. I looked him up in *Who's Who* and found ample reason. He had a very distinguished record of service; 'the only non-regular officer to be commissioned direct to the Joint Planning Staff, and worked for the following three years in the Offices of the War Cabinet. Invented War Games'. He was born in 1897, and was only six years younger than Desmond. I went straight to my desk and wrote a letter:

Dear Mr. Wheatley,
    Please forgive this attempted intrusion. I write as a friend of the late Sir Desmond Morton, in search of someone who knew him well over many years. I met Desmond in 1943. I was a Captain in the Intelligence

Corps, just returned from a tour of duty in the North Caribbean. Desmond wrote to me and asked me to come to see him at Great George Street. From that first meeting we corresponded, and met fairly often, for the rest of his life.

I do not know what, if anything, Desmond knew about me when he sent for me in 1943. He did know that I had written a number of books, mainly about South America, and that I had been concerned about the war in the Gran Chaco in 1935–36. Major Gwynne of the *Morning Post* had helped me on that, rather romantically. Perhaps Desmond knew about me through Gwynne in those years? I don't know.

Our correspondence grew and when, after the Korean War I wrote *Cry Korea* more or less at white heat, I knew and Desmond knew that for better or for worse I had to attempt to understand war and especially war in this century. I had seen a good deal of it, much of it with forward troops in many battles. Desmond, reluctantly perhaps, began to comment on my stuff and my ideas. In short he took my self-appointed task very seriously.

It is a long story, but after writing a book called *The Price of Victory*, I knew that I must attempt to understand Churchill. It was awesome, probably hopeless, but I had to try. I knew as much about his part in both wars as was possible from all available sources. I wanted to know about the man. I had felt in a curious way a kind of affinity with him. I had been fascinated by him from my childhood—d'Artagnan was one of my heroes too!

Desmond's letters in answer to my flood of ideas, questions, guesses, speculations were long and often marvellous—about almost everything under the sun as well as Winston—and full of humour.

When my attempt on Winston came out—it was called *The Yankee Marlborough*—it owed a great deal to Desmond, but I had promised not to say so. It brought a flood of great praise from many of those who had known and worked with Churchill—Boothby, Morrison, Archie Nye, as well as some top historians—and vitriolic hatred and personal abuse from some of those resolved to sustain a myth. According to Desmond it was not simply the best book about Churchill, but the only book about Churchill. Basil Liddell Hart and others rushed to the book's defence, but of course it was doomed. Poor old Winston had to remain a 'god'. He couldn't possibly be a human being!

Liddell Hart was one who urged me to seek permission to publish the correspondence, and rather to my surprise Morton's heirs wrote that they knew, of course, that Desmond had been very fond of me, and always meant me to have his letters. You know he hated publicity, and that he had destroyed his private papers.

In his letters he often mentions you, mainly to tell me what a fool I was to sweat myself for years to write books like *The Price of Victory* and *The Yankee Marlborough* for about fourpence. 'Now, my friend Dennis Wheatley is far more sensible . . .' he would say. And somehow now you stand in my mind as one of the very few survivors who must know a good deal about Desmond.

I have to write a really good introduction to the letters, but who the devil knows about Desmond? How on earth do I grab the attention of readers who have never heard of him?

Well, the response was immediate. A personal telephone call to me next morning invited me to meet him for luncheon with Sir John Peck. 'I'll tell you all I know, but John knows a great deal more.'

Sir John Peck had been British Ambassador to the Irish Republic. He retired in 1973 after a distinguished career. Born in Kuala Lumpur in 1913, he became Asst. Private Secretary to the First Lord of the Admiralty at the age of twenty-three. He did not look back. Peck is mentioned in Churchill's Memoirs, vol. vi, as secretary to an important committee. With Ismay he had been instructed to discover certain military facts. He was, of course, very young and very 'junior' in that hierarchy, but was an authentic inside member of Churchill's war machine. He made no secret of his admiration for Desmond Morton, and for a good two hours Wheatley and John Peck laughed together and exchanged memories of the man. The thing that struck me forcibly was their obvious affection for him. His humour had been infectious. Whenever he put in a rare appearance in 10 Downing Street for luncheon he was a breath of fresh air. He knew what was going on. His stories were nearly always humorous and slightly 'off beat'. He carried a great burden, a 'loner', relieving Churchill of much, dealing with all the foreign Governments, especially, of course, with de Gaulle. De Gaulle referred to him as Churchill's Chief of Staff, not, of course strictly accurately, but de Gaulle knew that very well. It meant that he spoke for Churchill, and de Gaulle, and all the other heads of Foreign Governments, Poles, Czechs, Dutch—finally Jugo Slavs, recognised that. Desmond Morton's word was good enough, and his decision. What Morton said was the authentic voice of Churchill, 'he knew his mind'. They all said that. The idea of union with France had grown in Desmond's mind. He had had a hand in the Dakar episode, and much else besides. At times—it seems unavoidable—'crackpot schemes' were Desmond's as well as Churchill's. They thought together.

As Peck and Wheatley talked, I had a picture of Desmond as one of the heads of the Secret Service, of the man behind S.O.E.—Special Operations Executive. But a man entirely without affectation.

Finally Peck said, 'get in touch with Bill Deakin. I'm sure he knew Desmond in the 1930s. He's retired now and lives in the South of

France. And write to Martin Gilbert'.[1] It seemed the obvious thing to do.

After a day or two I overcame my reluctance to intrude upon people I did not know, and wrote to Deakin. Col. F. W. Deakin, D.S.O., had a string of Jugo Slav honours for bravery. I wrote in much the same way as I had done to Wheatley.

Desmond, it seems to me, must have been a vital factor in enabling Churchill to assume power when the chance came.

I don't know how well you knew Desmond. He had been, as you know, a fine soldier, and he was, in a sense, always a soldier. He wanted to be forgotten after the war. He rejected all attempts to intrude upon his privacy, destroyed his private papers, and dedicated himself to his hospital work (and theology! He loved arguing with Bishops of all denominations). He made me promise never (while he was alive) to disclose the source of my information.

I have missed him badly since his death, especially as it coincided with the deaths of my two other friends.[2]

I must have at least 300,000 words of our correspondence . . . I think that if I can edit the whole thing decently and contrive a good introduction for somehow or other I must try to interest people in Desmond—such a book could be of value to the uninitiated in understanding the immense figure of Winston.

Colonel Deakin's response pleased me greatly. He wrote:

As a young man, I spent much of my time working with Churchill as a literary assistant, starting with his life of Marlborough. This brought me to Chartwell, almost continuously over the years 1935/1939, during which I was a member of the household. It was a special and private privilege, which induced a certain amnesia, which, having known Desmond, will not surprise you!

He had Churchill's absolute trust and confidence, and, as you say, this was both tacit and underwritten by No. 10. I was a fly on the wall during many such conversations, and have no memory of them. Churchill appreciated that Desmond's loyalty was without limits or reserve. I don't know exactly how they first met, but remember Churchill saying, by way of introduction, how Desmond had literally been shot through part of his heart during the First War and had reluctantly been posted to Haig's staff after recovery from his wounds.

The main theme of his talks with Churchill during the late 30s was,

[1] Martin Gilbert, M.A. Biographer to Churchill in succession to Randolph Churchill.
[2] Captain Sir Basil Liddell Hart, Major-General Eric Dorman O'Gowan (Smith).

of course, the extent of German re-armament and the inadequate steps taken in official circles to collect vital intelligence. Desmond's own channels of information were never revealed—at least in my presence—but I do remember that about mid 1938, he mentioned that, under the cover of the Board of Trade, Desmond was charged with setting up a skeleton organisation to specialise in economic intelligence—in liaison with the War Office, and I was touched that he should propose that I might join the team. In fact, I volunteered to serve with a Yeomanry regiment, and he saw at once the point!

His service to Churchill was immeasurable, and typically concealed by a determination to remain unrecognised in the wings. I did not know that he destroyed all his private papers, and this is a great loss to historians.

After 1939 I have no personal knowledge of his precise role as private adviser. He was, as you will know, closely involved with the Free French and one of those who drafted—in June 1940—the project of Anglo-French Union. He must have been in touch with S.O.E., and there is some connection, historically, with his Board of Trade section (mentioned above) in the setting up of this organisation.

In personal terms, I met him twice during the war, in Cairo in December 1943 when Jugo Slav affairs erupted into a major crisis, and in Algiers in early 1944. But these encounters are not historically important.

After 1945 we met again frequently at Chartwell when I was again involved with Churchill in helping with his Memoirs. This was a time of wide-ranging discussion into which Desmond injected his profound knowledge of events and personalities.

One concrete point occurs to me. The papers of the Prime Minister have now been deposited in the Public Record Office, and I know (under reference PREM) that there are a number of Desmond's minutes preserved. You might find an inspection of these files—which are well catalogued—quite rewarding.

It would undoubtedly be rewarding to anyone striving to construct a 'Life' of Sir Desmond Morton to spend the necessary days, weeks, months in the Public Record Office, but that is not my purpose. Looking through some of the papers I came upon a long one of Desmond's addressed to the Prime Minister. What struck me at once was its relaxed manner. 'You asked for my inexpert opinion. Here it is'—and there followed four pages of opinion. There was nothing stilted about Desmond and nothing stilted in his relationship with Churchill, or anyone else. He was a 'relaxed' man.

His unique value to Churchill grows in my mind. Those two *knew* each other. In letters from Martin Gilbert that much is confirmed.

Gilbert has a 'mighty pile' of notes about Desmond extracted from the Churchill archive covering the 1930s. I am welcome to see all that there is, but for my present purpose what I have written here must be enough to establish Desmond Morton.

I decided to attempt to write a book about Churchill on 1st May, 1960. On that day my wife and I talked with Desmond all through the day at his house on Kew Green. It was my wife's first meeting with Desmond, and it was memorable, yet I do not think we expected anything from our day except pleasure. I had just come to the end of a task and must face another. Perhaps I knew that it must be Churchill, for my work had led me to that.

There is an entry in Mel's diary notes of that day.

On Sunday (1 May) Tommy and I spent the day with Sir Desmond Morton in his Queen Anne House on Kew Green. I had never met him before and had quite a different picture in my mind from the tall man in casual clothes who opened the door to us and bade us welcome. He looked like a refined Victor McLaglen, pepper and salt moustache, keen eyes, and hair that was more sandy coloured than grey. I felt at ease—and we all talked straight away—though Tommy and I did a tremendous amount of fascinated listening . . . he told us story after story, answered question after question. I asked him about de Gaulle, whom he thought a great statesman and a magnificent writer, absolutely sincere. He also regards Adenauer as sincere . . .

And then gradually we got down to the things that interested and fascinated us most—his own life story, particularly from 1919 to 1945. Returning from the war, he was appointed by Lloyd George to start the Foreign Intelligence Service with emphasis on Bolshevist Russia (and soon on Germany also, the Balkans etc.).

When I asked him, he said that the time during which he was head of I.I. [Industrial Intelligence] he liked better than any other in his life. When during the 1930s he began more and more to realise that war would be inevitable—though Baldwin would not consider the possibility—he deliberately briefed Churchill on matters W.S.C. could not otherwise have known and which would enable him to grasp the leadership of Britain in the event of war.

I asked Sir Desmond if this had been his conscious intention.

He said, 'Yes. I can say without any inhibition that I deliberately set out to do this. I regarded Winston as the only man who had the qualities needed for the job.'

I asked him, 'Did you ever regret it?'

'No,' he said. 'Although I won't say that once in power Winston might not have used his powers differently and in a better way. I could write an essay on the three different Winstons I have known. The man who was aspiring, who had an ideal . . . The man in power, and the Churchill in the years of defeat and retirement.

'Churchill was all his life torn between his pride in his great Marlborough ancestor—his Marlborough blood—and his love for his Yankee mother. His overpowering ambition was to amalgamate the two; to be made whole through the emergence of one vast English-speaking people—the United States of America and England! Maybe this blinded him to Roosevelt's aim to overthrow the British Empire—in which he succeeded.'

Sir Desmond told us how Churchill, having bought Chartwell, became his neighbour in Kent . . . After that they met regularly, to dine and talk, sometimes with other cronies of Churchill's present, but more often alone.

And that began a phase of our correspondence very much about Churchill. Here it is . . .

Before our meeting at Kew Green on 1st May Desmond wrote on 20th April, 1960 stating broadly where he stood.

Certain general observations must be made. The first is that finally and without possibility of retraction, I shall never write my Memoirs. The reason—or the chief reason—is that I have never kept a diary nor any contemporary papers. No man can write Memoirs without these. I am well aware of the frailty of human memory especially on details, however important. So many things, seemingly of little importance at the time and therefore not impressed on memory at all, turn out later to be nodal points of fact. Moreover as one ages, the memory for certain things gets less reliable. As . . . you feel, Truth is above all and a worshipper of Truth must not force it on the base of unreliable facts.

. . . I can say that in certain circumstances, if it were considered to be of any use, I would be ready to offer such facts as I am sure I remember rightly, and above all such opinions as I have formed on those facts; with the absolute promise that my name should never be mentioned, or appear, or be deducible, from anything published. Of course I should not mind in the least if my own views on the matters in hand were rejected as unsound.

My reasons for this insistence on absolute anonymity are, I hope, honourable. Anyway, they can be stated and no sum of money would, I trust, persuade me to another course.

R. W. Thompson to Sir Desmond Morton   2nd May, 1960
You gave us both a true red letter day. We hope that we didn't tire you overmuch, and pray that we did not bore you. I can only say that our conversation matched the perfection of the garments of Office of the Mandarin. Mel enjoyed herself immensely.

One of the things you did for me yesterday was to breathe life into the remarkable figure of 'Winston'. I do not think I had ever truly seen him as a real person. It would be a pity if no one ever did—or could. But such things must wait.

From Sir Desmond Morton   3rd May, 1960
Delighted to learn that your wife and you enjoyed yourselves, though Heaven knows what time you got home. What a lovely and charming person your wife is. It is an honour to know her, and what a darned good wife she is to you; but you know that. It is a dreadful thought that your youngest son is alleged to look like me at about that age. Do please see he grows up to be something much more respectable.

I will be sending back the copy of the lecture[1] given by O'Gowan in January 1941, and his letter. The lecture is a good one and reveals his ability; but remember the date. There is no prophecy in it. His error consisted in his lack of knowledge of how this country was placed financially and economically at that time. Alas! When he ends 'We have got the cause, the time, the men, the money and a clear-cut target. We have world industry behind us,' he is unfortunately absolutely wrong save in the matter of 'cause'. We had none of the others whatever. *That* is the great clue to so much. The fact that we had no time, we had squandered it in the past; no men (trained men) in sufficient numbers to man *primarily* our industry (men cannot fight without arms, which were being produced still in limited numbers, as compared with Germany), no money, since the U.S.A. had bled us white charging wholly exorbitant prices for the very stuff of life, taking over British firms and capital in the U.S.A. at a tenth or even hundredth of their true value etc., while world industry, more than half of which was already in Hitler's hands, would not accept our notes of hand and demanded cash; while in addition not even the U.S.A. was 'tooled up' to produce armaments in the quantities we needed . . . is the cause of much.

After all that was my own subject, as Director of the Industrial Intelligence Centre. I had perhaps at last convinced the Chiefs of Staff and Cabinet in 1937 that INDUSTRY of all kinds was the limiting factor of modern war. They had begun to SAY, 'My God, the Man's right.' But they had not in peace time started to do what Germany had been doing, whereby piano factories had secretly been tooled up to make aircraft, plans had been drawn up and engineering factories given the tools, gauges and jigs to turn over to shells, guns, parts of submarines etc. etc., in a few months. It took America three years to do it with all her resources.

Winston, who, even if he did not understand in detail, saw the point in principle, had no power until May 1940, which was too late. A book could indeed be written about all this, but would have no sale nowadays.

Recall that Neville came back from Germany shouting 'Peace in our time'. Consequently little was done during the 'year of grace'.

Pray lay my respectful admiration at the feet of your wife.

P.S. Do you realise that during the 1939 war, there had to be between 12 or 13 TRAINED men or women in industry (i.e. nothing directly to do with the Armed Forces) for every 1 soldier, or sailor or airman in the fighting forces?

[1] Lecture delivered to United Service Institution of India, 1940, reprinted in U.S.I. of I. Journal, January 1941.

Arising out of our ever to be remembered day we both of us had some good ideas, and it is likely that I shall attempt to write an assessment of Winston in the light of all that we begin to know and to sense. I feel sure that you will give us all the advice you can, but we are anxious not to weary you either with our words or our company. The O'Gowan continues to write first class stuff to me, much of which I would be most grateful if you would read. For in your comments upon some of his statements there will be vital material. Liddell Hart, back from his Near and Middle Eastern adventures, promises all possible aid. Auchinleck, with whom I am becoming warmly friendly, is always ready to discuss my kind of ideas. In fact, at last I begin to know a great many people sympathetic in their views to me. It should be a great help.

Did you see Lewis Broad's latest tribute to Winston? It made me sad, and realise how much against the popular tide my own thoughts would lead me.

Your words of wisdom and your attitudes govern my own thinking and approach. I find Winston—and what I know about him must seem almost 'nothing' to you—as fascinating a study as this century affords. I approach it striving, not to prove anything, but to discover the man—'The Yankee Marlborough'. The O'G Irishly insists upon his greater likeness to Cromwell—but I do not see that—Cromwell seems to have been a good strategist and tactician. Admittedly he had the 'Rump' parliament, and Churchill had something pretty similar. But psychologically the Yankee Marlborough's the story.

Meanwhile my *The Price of Victory* looks very good, and should be published about the first week in August. I'll send you the first copy, not for reading but as a small token. I believe I have a book out in Germany this week, and a new big edition of another book in a few weeks in Holland.

From Sir Desmond Morton   12th June, 1960

Such advice as I can give is always at your disposal, nor do I care whether you take it or not. You may be quite wise not to do so. I shall not be offended if you don't.

You say you are seriously thinking of attempting 'an assessment of Winston'. In order to comment helpfully and fully, I should want to know what you mean by the word 'assessment' and how you propose to tackle it. 'Assessment' might balance heavily towards 'character', or be chiefly concerned with activities, actions (good and bad), success or failure, real aims, and a host of other abstractions. There is Winston the man, Winston the politician, Winston out of power, Winston in power, Winston as the British saw him, Winston as Roosevelt or

Truman saw him, Winston as others saw him, Winston as the King's enemies really saw him (as against the obvious wartime hostile propaganda), Winston as his friends saw him, Winston as his family saw him, Winston as his private enemies saw him, Winston as he saw himself, and Winston as God sees him. And that is to mention only a few.

Again there is an 'assessment' of the effect of Winston on the British Empire, his effect on the war and subsequent 'peace', as a political strategist, as a military (including naval and air) strategist, etc. etc.

One thing is certain. In the external affects of character, there have been different Winstons, so surprisingly different in their appearances as to evoke the idea of schizophrenia or multiple personality. Although, like the true and real psychological disturbances called by these names, all these different 'personalities' are actually part of a single whole and manifest differently because some parts of the whole personality are at times suppressed.

The truth about Winston cannot be approached without knowledge and consideration of ALL these 'personalities'. Most people only know one. People like Lewis Broad do not *know* any.

Truly fascinating, but I doubt if it can be done. He is certainly not really the 'Yankee Marlborough' though that is a happy phrase. He is even less like Cromwell. Cromwell's driving force in its pristine purity was a real belief in a God, whose nature and attributes he, himself, had thought up and of which he had become convinced. That Cromwell's faith in God as he imagined Him waned towards the end, has nothing to do with the issue—or, in another sense, everything to do with it. There is no evidence that Marlborough ever thought God worth considering at all, save as a superstitious survival of Man's primitive thoughts, and therefore worth using to his own advantage. Winston fits into neither of these basic concepts.

You can drag up meretricious and accidental features of the lives of both Cromwell and Marlborough which bear a superficial resemblance to incidents in Winston's. That is, of course, worse than childish.

Curiously enough, I have long toyed with the idea—only toyed with it, mark you—that there is a great resemblance between the *characters* of Winston and Henry VIII, with Winston handling his character far better than did Henry Tudor of unfortunate memory.

My news is pedestrian and of little interest, save that I dined at the Savage Club last week at a private party of eminent persons (excepting myself) to bid farewell to another eminent person just going into retirement. The Savage Club lived up to its name only by producing a very old wine waiter, who, before the dinner supplied those demanding sherry with a large glass full of brandy and those, including me, who asked for a pink gin, with an equally large glass filled with *pure* gin of exceptional strength. The dinner thus began in an alcoholic atmosphere more usually associated with the end of a carouse. It says a great deal for the calibre of those present that when we got to the speeches, everyone could stand. Three noble Lords, an ex-Cabinet Minister, an ex-chairman of the Chiefs of Staff, two chairmen of very big international businesses and a sprinkling of Professors Emeriti, all spoke with a wit and freedom to which they and their hearers were unaccustomed. Having poured my second 'pink gin' into an aspidistra, which turned scarlet by the end of the evening, the principal guest and I (two different people) were, I think, alone able to recall the gist of the speeches next day. We were all able, however, to recognise the old waiter at the end of the evening, as we found him stretched out, outside the door, dead drunk. By the way, no one save the principal guest and I noticed that the huge silver gilt loving cup produced at the end was (mercifully) filled with plain tap water.

The ex-Cabinet Minister, renowned for his shyness, decorum and lack of external enthusiasm (which is why he never got further in politics) marched out to our waiting transports, shaking hands with all the marble statues in the Hall assuring them that he had never had such a good time since he was at Oxford.

In spe cum amore vale

R. W. Thompson to Sir Desmond Morton   17th June, 1960
I am anxious to clarify as far as possible at this early stage my ideas about my Churchill book. I must say first that the title does not mean to imply that Churchill was (is) either a Yankee or Marlborough, or like them. It is a statement of reasonably legitimate fact. He arose out of those forbears. His awareness of these origins might be said to have various effects upon him. As to his many-sidedness, all of us, save the most simple, are multi-phrenic, if there were such a word and it is this great variety within us that blends into a coherent whole, balanced or not, as the case may be. Of course, I don't think that Churchill bore any resemblance to Cromwell, certainly not in the religious sense, and only perhaps in that he wielded a great power in this Island. But that is certainly the O'G's Irishness. What is odd—and very cheering to me— is your mention of Henry VIII. I swear I had been thinking along those lines. Did you ever read Hackett's *Henry VIII*? I liked it very much, and, much in the same way, I intend to begin by trying to put over succinctly the political and strategic background of the years in the immediate aftermath of the First World War, when Churchill, Hitler, Mussolini, Stalin—the main protagonists (for Roosevelt is then obscure? and not in *that* running) were all coming upon their various scenes in various ways. If I can show the stresses and strains real and imminent of those years, the early 20s, and put my main characters upon the stage

I shall have set the stage for Churchill. Recently it has been said that Churchill 'in the wilderness' in the 30s was in his 'finest hour'. There may be some truth in that. The climax is, of course, for me 1941–2. This is the vital period when . . . Churchill realised power, abused it, and virtually 'lost it' in terms of our Allies. It is the background of those two years above all—politically at home—that is my gap. Auchinleck, the O'G, probably General Fuller, Paget and Liddell Hart, (will) give me all possible aid on the military side. All agree that the story must be told; that it has never been told; that it is essential to an understanding of our position in the world today. Well, poor vessel though I be I am about to attempt it. I know I can count on you for all aid 'short of war'. Whatever I thought I meant by that, as it came out.

As for your gallivanting in the 'Savage' of all places, I am deeply gratified. I like to imagine you in that hall taking your leave of statuary. But what a drinking shop the Savage always was (and is?). I used to go there fairly often with Henry Williamson[1] and Tschiffely[2] (he of the ride) in the old days. I always wanted to join, but I am too married to be a 'Clubman', and strong drink in quantity accords ill with my insides. Pink gin can be magnificent or horrible, according to the maker, the setting. For me it goes with H.M. ships, and my rare meetings these days with admirals ashore. Otherwise I mix tonic with my gin.

But no more of this for now. Mel was offered a job last night by Grenville School, Clare, to teach Latin to G.C.E. aspirants and take a lower form in other things. She accepted. It may mean moving. I think that in teaching she will find her metier. I pray so. I am building up a lot of the O'G stuff and some of Paget's on which I propose to beg your comments. You were going to tell me, I think, why Alexander struck fear into Churchill?

There are so many things I want to know that I am not using a letter like this for the task. Paget says that Beaverbrook was the 'Satanic' influence, and that Cherwell with his graphs bemused Churchill, and Harris with his bombers was a buccaneer after his own heart. Harris said to Paget, re airborne troops, what's the good of dropping men, they don't explode when they hit the ground! Ah well, it may all be the stuff of yesterday, but today—and maybe tomorrow—are made out of it.

But for *The Price of Victory*, and my first strivings in this field none of this would ever have been. But it is.

We send our affectionate greetings, and hope to meet again all easy within and without in the near future.

[1] Henry Williamson, author, perhaps best known for his book *Tarka the Otter*.
[2] T. F. Tschiffely, author of *Tschiffely's Ride*, the story of his ride on horseback from Buenos Aires to New York. This staggering achievement brought him immediate world fame.

'For the record' to clarify and explain any possible misunderstanding arising in your first paragraph of your good letter of 17th.

You are, of course, absolutely right and completely following my own feelings in your regard, by trying by all means to obtain some paid bread-and-butter writing however distasteful that may be to your ardent spirit in comparison with what you really want to write. I need not elaborate that point.

Secondly, you must obviously write whatever your publishers or financial backers consider will pay dividends. That applies also to your major writing.

Thirdly, when about two years ago I advised you to eschew 'personal books' in preference to 'military history', which I admit I did and still do, I was guilty of lack of clarity in definition. I see that there are really three, not two, categories of books which you might write— apart from fiction which I do not think you have attempted and to which I am giving no thought. By 'personal books', I meant and still mean, only books like the one you wrote and which was not well received, about your personal life, apart from military history. But it seemed and seems to me that your military history books fall into two classes. In one class would come books dealing with military matters whereof you have absolute personal experience, e.g. *Cry Korea,* where you were on the spot for some part of the time and could add your personal observations from experience on the spot to the statements and accounts of others. In other books which would also be military history, your own experiences in person of the events and conditions of which you would write, would be far less than in the first type, or even relatively 'nil'.

That is all.

But over-riding everything must be, as said above, the question of which book or type of book your backers and you think will bring in the cash, here and now.

As your backers think the book to back would be *The Yankee Marlborough* and not *War was my Peace* the matter is *res judicata.*

We can forget the title of *The Yankee Marlborough* for the time being, using it only to make it clear what we are talking about.

Let us then talk about it.

I see from your letter some idea of what the book intends to say. It is thus essential, as you have in mind, to begin right back at least at the First World War. You may find it necessary to go further back still —not in detail, but in order to set the stage. Hitler achieved power in 1933, from being nobody; Mussolini marched on Rome in the early 20s but Winston began to achieve power as a very young man, before the First World War, then lost it. Why? Then regained it. Why?

You have, of course, realised that you will be writing *political* history, even in the case of Stalin; also Tojo, whom you do not mention.

'The Age of the Dictators' was an outcome of the First World War in every case. There are great similarities in the political careers of all the dictators, and equally great dissimilarities. A fascinating matter.

Although the political and military aspects are interlocked, the military aspect is in all cases the means to the political power and not the reverse.

I venture to suggest that your 'big gap' is not the political events of and around 41–42, but the political events during and immediately following the First World War.

All the dictators, however varying their characters, had in common an immense desire to wield power themselves. Not one of them 'had greatness thrust upon him'.

The one quality (I will not say virtue) which makes for greatness is self-confidence; and in those who achieve greatness, a self-confidence to a degree incomprehensible to ordinary mortals.

I would find it hard to agree with Paget's *obiter dicta*, save in regard to Max, and then only in that he was not a good influence, normally, on anyone. But to call him 'the Satanic influence' on Churchill is to flatter him. The Prof. certainly never 'bemused' Churchill *by his graphs*. Bomber Harris was certainly not after Churchill's heart. Quite the contrary in what matters most. Churchill was most unwilling to accept Harris's advice, and at the crucial time, would not have done so had Harris not been backed by the Chiefs of Staff.

My admiration at the feet of your wife and my hopes for both of you.

From R. W. Thompson   30th June, 1960
Your letter of the 21st was, as always, a great aid in my thinking. No one, surely, could approach the problems and character of Churchill without excitement. I bear in mind—and shall do so constantly—all your warnings. I seek neither to diminish nor to magnify this remarkable character, but if I can to regard him and his times from the particular angles and points I have found myself in during these last years of concentration. As you say, we can forget the title of *The Yankee Marlborough* for the time being. I agree, of course, about the First World War. I am already dredging in Haig's[1] Diaries. I shall, as old Thomas used to say, 'explore every avenue'—or all the ones you above all think most profitable. I have begun to build a research list, and have already—apart of course from the Churchill Memoirs, his First War *Eastern Front*, which I thought first class and reviewed at the time (1931, I think), *Great Contemporaries, The River War*, Kennedy's book,

[1] General Sir Douglas Haig, later Field Marshal, C. in C. British Forces, Western Front, First World War.

Chatfield's vol. ii, his own *Marlborough*, and all kinds of odds and ends reflecting patches of light (or shade) upon 'Our Hero'. I hope profoundly that I will not shock you if I say that above all I hope to have you, if only (but I hope much more) to be able to send (as I do now) various correspondence coming in from the O'G, Paget, L.H., and others. You are my absolute touchstone, but I hope and believe that largely owing to your constant aid in the past I am not particularly gullible. I have, of course, a view of my own.

One para in your letter alarmed me, but I recognise its validity to the business in hand—Tojo. Here is a gap I must strive to fill, indeed one of the major problems constantly looming throughout the work of the last five years has been the inevitable broadening of the canvas. I began with a worm's eye view of various fields of battle and politics (and an enquiring mind), and found myself reaching out to *The Price of Victory* (in which there is barely a line of personal experience) and I hope—with anxiety—that you are not going to consider it among my worst efforts. It is, in any case, the boldest—perhaps to the point of impertinence. For who am I to question from the then almost total isolation of my study and my own thoughts (no contacts then with anyone, and not daring to try out too much upon your long suffering mind and memory), to question what, until then, had been the unquestionable. But as the book developed I had to do so. It was not my original intention. I did not know—or even suspect—such conclusions as, in the end, I found unescapable. However, it will be in your hands soon. At best it may persuade you that I may not fail entirely in the new task ahead.

I, too, find it hard to regard Max B. as 'Satanic'. This seems an overstatement, and all your para is interesting on Harris, the Prof. How odd it is to have the many-sided ideas this strange man created in so many minds—of himself. Above all your remark about the overwhelming self-confidence of such men—the vital ingredient (perhaps?) —is of great importance.

Do you remember, when I sent you some of the O'G's first startling letters you said that you would like to go through them point by point or para by para ...? I now send you an exchange between him and Paget (with permission). I know it is a burden, but I hope an interesting one. Most of all I hope that you will believe me capable of using such knowledge as I gain to good effect. In my small way I seek to discover what may be true—or more true—a genuine view point, it could be an illumination of a scene of which too much remains in harsh shade because of the brilliance of the light shed by some of the principal participants. It may be early for 'final' assessments (it always is) but I may put forward some new ideas—clues—to aid later historians. That shall be my urgent endeavour.

My filing system is already becoming impressive, for correspondence plays a considerable part in this task. The O'G thinks I should meet
General Fuller. I should like to. I have been for many years an admirer
of his work. But now I must put a great deal of reading behind me, and
develop the framework of my theme.

My Aemilia sends her affectionate greetings, and is striving to earn
your admiration. Tacitus, Livy, Vergil, Cicero are on her desk. Dutch
grammatical terms clutter her mind. She has a task ahead before which
my own seems (and is) simple.

Please tell me anything I *must* read in my context, and defend me
from error. Today is truly a new beginning.

Extract from letter, Major-General Dorman O'Gowan   9th June, 1960
to General Sir Bernard Paget
About that R.U.S.I.[1] Lecture, I reckon it is really by Boney[2] out of
yourself, or vice versa—so please keep it for as long as you want. I
have a spare copy. Boney taught me to see, you to arrange my thoughts
into meaning: 'the habit of making appreciations'; do you remember?

Our tragedy of the last war was that the British Army really had a
first-class corps of middle-rank officers, thanks to folk like yourself and
Boney. The proof of the pudding was Sidi Barrani and O'Connor's[3]
flashing campaign to which nobody gave enough attention. I doubt
whether, all in all, the Army ever had a better set of general officers in
its history—at least not since Moore[4] and Wellington.[5] Alas that
'Churchill/Cromwell' so deeply despised his King's soldiers. I agree
that we were slow off the mark in 1939–40, for Gort's[6] mind had got
stuck in G.Q.C. and 1917, but the capacity was there if it had only been
given a chance and not been mucked about from Downing Street.

Perhaps our greatest mistake after 1914–18 was the creation of the
R.A.F. as an independent service with a 'bombing strategy' complex.
The Americans did not make that fundamental error. There is no such
thing, even today, as an independent air, or missile, strategy.

I know that it is generally said that Churchill did not in the last
resort go against the advice of his Chiefs of Staff, but is that strictly
true? For example, from 11th February, 1941 until 10th April, 1941

[1] Royal United Services Institution.

[2] Boney, military nickname of Major-General Fuller.

[3] General Sir Richard O'Connor, routed the Italian armies in the Western Desert,
culminating in victory at Beda Fomm, 1941.

[4] General Sir John Moore, 1751–1809, one of the most respected generals responsible
for reforms and improvements, victor of Corunna on 16th January, 1809, where he
received his death wound and was buried before dawn the next day.

[5] Duke of Wellington, contemporary of Moore and victor of Waterloo.

[6] Field Marshal Viscount Gort, commanded British Forces in France 1940 and
made possible the retreat from Dunkirk.

Dill and Eden were out of London with the worst possible results. Not only did this mission distract the C.I.G.S. from his clear view of the situation in North Africa arising out of O'Connor's decisive victory at Beda Fomm, as Dill afterwards realised sadly, but it resulted in Dill and then Wavell getting entangled in a Balkan muddle in which Eden's half-baked foreign policy dominated strategic common sense. As a reflex of that, when we could have taken Tripoli in March 1941 had the Chiefs of Staff concentrated all available sea, land and air power, towards reaping the fruits of O'Connor's victory, the Chiefs of Staff were rendered powerless by Dill's despatch to Cairo–Athens–Cairo–Ankara; so we jettisoned our victory, thinned out Cyrenaica, and did not land troops in Greece until the first week in April. A vital month went down the drain and we almost lost the Middle East.

Again, and also in that fateful April 1941, Churchill, on the 28th issued a Directive by the Prime Minister and Minister of Defence beginning, 'Japan is unlikely to enter the war unless the Germans make a successful invasion of Great Britain'. (Kennedy, *Business of War*, p. 108.)

It might almost be said that Churchill never went against Dill's advice because he never took Dill's advice.

On page 193 of Kennedy's book there is summarised the Chiefs of Staff advice on the defence of Malaya and Singapore and Churchill's contrary decisions. Certainly between August 1940 and September 1941 the Prime Minister consistently turned down the Cs of S recommendations—that is if Kennedy's summary is correct.

I think that matters were better when Brooke was C.I.G.S., but then it did not matter much because in effect Marshall and King dictated global strategy; the best the British could do was to effect minor modifications.

I fear that the trouble arose from the beginning of Churchill's regime, when Ironside left the job of C.I.G.S. to take over Home Defence. This seems to me to have been the moment when our best operational brains ought to have been reviewing the whole future of the war—and perhaps producing something like my R.U.S.I. India, August 1940 address, but with greater knowledge and experience. Instead, so it seems to me, the Prime Minister, as Minister of Defence, adapted the Military Wing of the War Cabinet Secretariat under Ismay to be a super 'Directorate of Operations' to which, in August 1940, he added the Joint Planning Committee. 'They will work out the details of such plans as are communicated to them by the Minister of Defence. They may initiate plans of their own after reference to General Ismay. All plans produced by the Joint Planning Committee or elaborated by them under instructions as above will be referred to the Chiefs of Staff Committee for their observations.'

In effect Churchill did push the Chiefs of Staff Committee out on to a limb. It was no longer an initiating body, its role became the defence of strategical principles rather than their application. And it seems that the War Office was the poor relation of this system because on September 3rd, 1940, the Prime Minister laid it down categorically that 'the Navy can lose us the war, but only the Air Force can win it. Therefore our supreme effort must be to gain overwhelming mastery in the air . . . the bombers alone provide the means of victory.' He added, in the same memorandum, 'The Air Force and its action on the largest scale must, therefore, subject to what is said later, claim the first place over the Navy or the Army.'

I find it difficult to believe that any Chiefs of Staff Committee containing Dill would have reached this conclusion. Nevertheless this Directive, plus another on priorities of October 15th, 1940: 'The A1 priority must remain with aircraft production for the purpose of executing approved target programmes' dominated British war policy until the U.S.A. entered the arena.

In fact, Churchill, taking into his hands powers of direction and decision greater than Cromwell's, for which he was by temperament and experience less well equipped than Cromwell, set himself an impossible task, particularly when he tried to influence minute operational details. Add to this his tendency to take advice from such curious types as Cherwell, Harris, Mountbatten, Wingate,[1] Beaverbrook . . . anyone indeed except Dill and his D.M.O., and it is small wonder that we proceeded disastrously from Dunkirk to Alamein 1 dropping Greece, Crete, and South-East Asia en route. Most of our major disasters between July 1940 and July 1942 were avoidable, such military successes as we obtained weren't followed up and the Chiefs of Staff were largely engaged in hunting will of the wisps (return to Norway, capture of Pantelleria, invasion of Sicily from U.K., for example).

And so we got the Prime Minister telling Parliament on July 2nd, 1942: 'We are at this moment in the presence of a recession of our hopes and prospects in the Middle East and the Mediterranean unequalled since the fall of France.'

As he said these words the tide was turning, but why should they have had to be said? I fear because the British School of Strategy never got a chance to express itself.

I may be wrong about all this—you may, with your great knowledge pin my ears back with a 'super-Raspberry' for thinking along these lines, but one cannot begin to write about what you describe as 'the higher conduct' of war and coordination of all the means of waging

[1] Major-General Orde Wingate, Commander of Chindit Expedition in Burma. His 'ardent spirit' appealed to Churchill.

war, including the political unless one gets this position at the very top in focus.

Are we now, at last, on the right lines with a Minister of Defence separated from the Prime Minister, and a Chief of Defence Staff besides the Chiefs of Staff of the Services, and did the failure to set up some such system during the Second World War throw us awry, strategically and politically?

Chatfield thought so for one, and he was a very wise person. 'Julius Caesar at his best and Napoleon could never have attempted to run a war of such magnitude, to conduct armies, navies and air forces as well. There should be a separate Defence Minister.'

Were Cherwell's graphs at the back of the whole thing? And how came it that Churchill did not know that Singapore had no landward defences, or that the Middle East commanders, early in 1942, had given up the idea of ever again holding Tobruk in isolation?

To deal successfully with detailed issues one should at least know the details.

But these are the sort of things which have to be cleared up . . . Of course, the personality of the Prime Minister affects the issue and for this there is no precedent—but Eden, during Suez seems to have tried to apply the 'Churchill System', disastrously—which is where your comment on precedent and obsessions is so wise.

And anyhow, dare anyone in our generation come out with such blasphemies about the 'Father figure'? . . . Reg would probably be horrified . . .[1]

From General Sir Bernard Paget, G.C.B., D.S.O., M.C.
to Major-General Dorman O'Gowan, M.C.   14th June, 1960

My dear Chink,

Once again I have to apologise in the delay in replying to your very interesting [letters] for which I thank you very sincerely, and also for your article on 'Land Warfare' of which I hope you have sent a copy to Boney Fuller. He might have written it himself. Unless you instruct me otherwise, I will keep your article which provides much food for thought.

We were terribly incapable of learning the lessons of the Kaiser's War, as we always seem to be and that is worthy of record; and we did not apply them until the Germans taught us a lesson and showed us how in 1940. It was later still before we learnt the vital need for integration between the Army and the Air Force. Even in 1943 the Americans believed it to be possible to carry out an opposed landing

[1] Colonel Sir Reginald Dorman Smith, younger brother of Major-General Dorman O'Gowan.

outside the range of fighter cover, as did Churchill in 1941 when he demanded of me that I should capture Trondheim. He never forgave me for my refusal to do so.

Though I agree with you that the war we fought twenty years ago is to a large extent obsolete, I am sure that there are very valuable lessons to be learnt and applied now and to the future, and that you are very well qualified to set them out because you think so clearly and objectively. These lessons concern mainly the higher conduct of war and coordination of all the means of waging war, including the political. There is much of the art of war in this.

Often I wondered during the war where Churchill got some of his more outrageous strategic ideas from. It seemed to me that he much preferred to seek and take advice from people like Cherwell, Wingate, Bert Harris, Mountbatten than of the C of S. But fortunately for us, unlike Hitler, he did not in the last resort go against the advice of the C of S.

Cherwell was an amateur who thought that military problems could be solved by means of a graph. He produced an album of them which gave Churchill an almost childish pleasure to peruse. But when I told him how misleading some of them were, he did not show me any more!

Bert Harris was the sort of buccaneer whom Churchill particularly liked, though Portal did not. He assured Churchill that he could win the war by bombing alone and that is what the P.M. hoped for instead of D-Day. Harris was not interested in anything but bombing. He had no use for airborne troops and I was never allocated more aircraft than for the lift of a battalion, though in 'Skyscraper' I envisaged five airborne divisions (two British and three American), as in fact we had available on D-Day. Harris told me it was useless to drop troops since they did not explode when they hit the ground. He had the full support of Churchill for his reckless bombing.

I also thought that *Beaverbrook* was a very evil influence on Churchill. We used to call it 'Satanic', though I have little proof of this.

Obsessions are always highly dangerous, and this applies particularly to the conduct of war. Admiral Fisher said that precedent is the grave-digger of independent judgment, but surely this is even more true of obsessions! Churchill was obsessed by his hatred of Hitler and the Nazis and it undoubtedly affected his judgment e.g. unconditional surrender and his relations with Stalin and Roosevelt.

I feel I could write pages more in reply to the stimulus of your letter, but it would be much better to meet and talk. So I shall be delighted, if you will come to see me, either here or in London, when you come over in September.

With all best wishes and do please write a book on the conduct of war.

P.S. Reggie was in very good form when I saw him a week ago.

From Sir Desmond Morton to R. W. Thompson   1st July, 1960

I have read through both your letter and the enclosures and shall take great delight in trying to comment at length in due course. Meanwhile, how vastly different it is to have the *two* letters, not only the O'G's, but also Bernard Paget's reply. The latter is a much more comprehensive thinker than is evidently the O'G; and, moreover, is suffering from no equivalent sense of personal grievance at any treatment he may have received from or because of the sayings and doings of W.S.C.

I have known Bernard very well and have much affection and admiration for him. A first-class General though not a first-class starred. When not temporarily affected by his blood pressure, he has a very careful and judicial mind. This is well illustrated by his reply to O'G.

I find the two together deeply interesting from several points of view, and hope in due time—not too long, I hope, to analyse the thoughts they invoke as well as I can. What one has to be so careful to do, is to divide what one believes to be correct from (what) one knows evidentially to be so. Anything of this kind must contain a large measure of personal opinion, but the second thing to do is to be sure to convey to the recipient as clear an idea as possible as to what is apparent fact, supported by evidence, and what is mere opinion, based on a deal of mental cerebration. Not that the latter is unimportant—far from it— and, sometimes, the opinion is of greater value than the apparently provable fact; but they are two different things.

In your letter you ask for books to read on your great subject. You must read Winston's *My Early Life*. You should also read relevant extracts from such political works as Leo Amery's Political Life and other political Memoirs which refer to Churchill—even some pages of Randolph's *Life of Eddy Derby*. You should get into a public library and look through the indexes of all relevant political biographies of the leaders of parties from 1900 onwards, making notes of references to Winston. What about Henry Morgenthau's book on the Dardanelles in the First World War?

Remember that Winston was a *politician*, who wanted to be a soldier. But he also wanted above all things Power for himself. Thus he also wanted to be a politician. The Army cast him out and he never forgave them. I speak of his early life. His immense unpopularity among his brother officers was not wholly due to their 'cast-iron' brains. As a boy and a young man he must have been quite an un-

45

pleasant specimen to those with whom he had to deal in the military sphere. Winston can never have been a self-controlled gentleman, thinking of the feelings of others and prepared to accept as his duty whatever state of life he seemed to have been called into.

But proper consideration must wait until I can think.

Meanwhile as always I salute the lady Aemilia, and particularly in the height to which she aims—according to you. If she is going to try to teach brats at Clare to read, understand and enjoy the works of the said Roman classic authors, she has undertaken a heavy task. I suppose that if she began on the more colloquial of the Latin plays, she would be requested rapidly to remove herself elsewhere. Even the remaining chronicles of the Senate to be found in the Scriptores Historias Augustae, and the short biographies of the said Augustas contain many useful words and expressions not to be found in the more solid works.*

Awaiting more and not in vain.

Yours ever rejoicing.

*P.S. Some of them useful in situations such as when someone walks one way in Harrods stores and looks another way, thus failing to put out my eye with an umbrella!

From R. W. Thompson 7th July, 1960
Your letter of the 1st as usual brought stimulation into the house. I don't like to call you a rudder, but without you to steer me through the shoals and shallows of the O'G's of this world I could easily be led astray. No. I prefer to call you a 'tall ship'—and a star to steer me by. But I do like the O'G. My correspondence is becoming formidable. He, the O'G, ferrets out references all over the shop, and Basil L.H. sends papers relevant to the period. Some of these I am having copied in case you may be interested.

My lady Aemilia is setting me a wonderful example, swotting up her Latin while I 'swot' up my Winston. Next week I shall put in some research reading at the R.U.S.I. on the political background of the early days . . . It's pleasant reading there, and if there is anything they haven't got they get it. Also I can pop in to the War Office or the Cabinet Office without difficulty. One of the things rather troubling me about my *The Price of Victory* is that I haven't given Paget half enough credit, and Morgan too much. The 'Skyscraper' documents are only just released, and as usual Monty did not give a glimmer that he owed anything to anybody. 'Skyscraper' seems the basic plan for 'Overlord' as it finally was. But there's always something new, and always will be.

I have just had an amusing letter from O'G, 'following up your thinking,' he writes, 'on the Second World War . . . it occurs to me that, from July 1942 onwards it was Ulysses Grant's war'. He then goes on to construct a fantasy equating the war henceforth with the U.S. Civil War. Having done that, he asks, 'Is this too fantastic?' And the answer, I feel is Yes, but probably an aspect of truth. Coming on top of Shaw[1] one wonders sometimes whether this last line is not near the mark. I wonder if we really know anything about anything. We only guess. We don't even know a great deal about ourselves and our motives. Nevertheless it is tremendous fun to try to sort it out, but then it occurs to me that one is often attempting to fit things into a 'reasonable' frame, whereas the frame in fact may well have been sublimely un-reasonable—even fantastic: 'All that follows is fiction and you can believe every word . . .'

Mel and I have a plan to visit the O'G's . . . partly holiday, partly talk and research . . . If I come back all Irished and full of strange thoughts I shall rely upon you to exorcise me.

P.S. Blackett has some rather diabolical 'notes' on the Prof. Was there, would you say, anything 'sinister' about the Prof.?

From Sir Desmond Morton   9th July, 1960
At last, after a frightful week, with another as bad looming ahead, I have an hour or two to reply properly to your letter and enclosures of 30th June, and your letter of 7th July.

Whence did W.S.C. get his more outrageous strategic ideas, very much including Trondheim, and many more later? The answer is strictly and absolutely from his own brain. I can certify that. It is very important to realise this. Perhaps—on occasions I know it to be so—he would try out a fatuous notion on such people as Beaverbrook, or one of his Ministers. Usually however, these notions, springing fully-armed from him were suddenly shot at the Chiefs of Staff or at the Joint Planners through them. He did not at all like individuals who attacked these ideas of his as soon as they heard of them, no matter how silly the ideas were, and only persons like Beaverbrook who would answer in effect 'Splendid, splendid!' without any sort of intelligent consideration, with the probable intention of spurring him on to action and no more, would be consulted. The Prof. could be included, by reason of the latter's blind hatred of Hitler, which if possible excelled that of Winston. But he and indeed the others were only used by Winston at such times as an audience, not expected to reply to the speech.

Winston's attachment to people like Wingate and Mountbatten, when the latter was Director of funny operations, or whatever it was called, was a different affair. Winston adored funny operations.

[1] The film *The Devil's Disciple*.

Unfortunately, he seemed unable to connect up funny operations with the great strategic plans, or to see the effect of one upon the other. He addressed his mind to them as the Managing Director of a vast railway might have, as a hobby, a miniature railway in his garden.

But, I repeat, the crack-pot major strategical notions were strictly born of his own brain.

The Prof.'s graphs delighted Winston, it is true, as also that they had a very limited application, which Winston was not ready to appreciate. I do not think that the Prof. ever seriously affected Winston's mind one way or another on direct strategical plans or any matter save the supply of arms, the availability of transport and such like.

As he liked what Paget calls 'buccaneers' and I call 'swashbucklers', so he loved funny stunts, side issues, conjurers' tricks and so on. Behind all this was his burning desire for ACTION. If the great regular forces and their commanders could do nothing—no matter what the reason—then let us try tricks. He was not a patient man. He also began by thinking that all the 'rules of war' adumbrated by his *official* advisers were out of date and fundamentally wrong. He learnt in time that however out of date they were, some of them were of permanent application.

I have already written to you about Bomber Harris. Winston did *not* like his all-embracing bombing ideas; though he began by being attracted, since it was something new to try. Curiously enough, I think he *never* cared for Harris as a person. I do not know why not, though I know why *I* did not.

Winston was always intensely sentimental. Never forget that. He was emotional as well. He could not get on with persons whom he disliked as such. He never liked Jack Dill. He *did* like Brookie. He began by liking Ironside, but 'never forgave him' when as C. in C. Home Forces, Ironside made the oddest speeches about politicians. As we now know, Ironside had temporarily lost control of his mental powers.

Winston never approved of 'unconditional surrender', as has surely now been made clear. It was sprung on him by the President at a Press conference. Winston was horrified, but for once so taken aback he could not think what to say or do. Only later did the arguments against this frightful pronouncement occur to him, when it was too late; and then as a result of the observations of others.

Winston's relations with Roosevelt were deeply affected by the fact that he, Winston, was half an American; but also from the undoubted fact that Power, in the sense of money, men and arms was in the hands of the Americans. I do not think Winston's hatred of the Nazis comes in there, nor did it affect his relations with Stalin, whom he regarded with a mixture of detestation and envy.

These brief comments are based on Paget's letter.

Turning to the O'G's letter.

On the Greek business; there is a lot more than he suggests. For example, the Chiefs of Staff were militarily dead against weakening North Africa for a diversion in Greece. But what were they to do, when they were told and not only by Winston but by Anthony and the F.O. that for political reasons, it was imperative, if possible, to assist the Greeks with troops? The military cons and the political pros were argued out repeatedly. Finally, the Chiefs said that they stuck to the military unwisdom, but, if the final direction of the war was in political hands, and if Wavell would agree that he could send troops to Greece without over-weakening his front, they would reluctantly agree too; but still only on political grounds which was not their affair. Hence the mission to Greece and Wavell.

But whereas Wavell had hitherto stuck out against losing any troops, no one was more surprised than the Chiefs, when, after he saw Anthony, after Anthony had been to Greece, he, Wavell, agreed to the sending of troops from his command. What happened to make him change his mind I do not know. That is probably the key to much. That, especially in the light of subsequent events, was a grave error of military strategy. There was talk at the time that Wavell became convinced that the addition of British troops could inflict such a serious further defeat upon the Italians, that even if the Germans sent over-whelming reinforcements, the British troops might be withdrawn safely, and even parts of the Greek Army. That a defence line might be set up which would have held against anything etc. etc. I do not know what is true in that respect. But it all sounds very odd.

It is probably true that if the Chiefs of Staff had been running the war, they would never have sent troops to Greece. But it is incorrect to say that in the end Winston sent the troops against their fully expressed will.

I don't like Eden as a man, and I have never liked his foreign policy. But recognising that he is a greater and cleverer man than I shall ever be, I must say it is dangerous to make hasty judgments on any event and especially one such as the intervention in Greece, without the very fullest information. Of course, it was a mistake. That cannot be denied in the light of after events. Many—including myself—thought it just short of lunacy at the time. I remember my own bewilderment at seeing the telegrams—there was more than one—from Archie Wavell giving his support to the idea.

One of the lessons of that business is that no sort of emotionalism must be allowed to cloud judgment in war (or peace). Byron, Missolonghi and even the First World War; 'the brave little Greeks', and other pure slogans, mostly incorrect, are fatal advisers.

Again, although he has a very valuable idea on page two about Winston without a Ministry of Defence creating one out of the Cabinet Offices and the Joint Planners, the working out of that idea by the O'G is too drastic. Of course, all his quotations are perfectly accurate. But the implications and meaning of them *at the time* they were issued, and how they were or were meant to be obeyed, is more important.

Again the O'G's phrase that Winston did push the Chiefs of Staff out on a limb, has something in it, but is not fully accurate. He did not push the Chiefs aside, not does the O'G say so. He continued to work *officially* through them always and with them (at unconscionable hours). But he gathered information from other sources behind them, e.g. the Joint Planners. The General Staff in the War Office was not entirely the 'poor relations' of this very doubtful system. The Joint Planners worked loyally and sent copies of everything they did to their Chiefs and to the G.S. at the W.O. But it is true that by these means Winston saw *their* first efforts before the G.S. or their Chiefs did, or at least at the same time.

Here and elsewhere is the very point of Paget's demands upon the O'G to consider and write about the highest direction of war under modern conditions and in the future. That must be considered too in the case of having no King Stork to conduct affairs, but a political King Log.

The O'G's point as to whether we should have *in war* (not only in peace) a Minister of Defence as a different person from the Prime Minister, is the centre of the problem. There is a case for having a triumvirate. I do not press it. A Minister of Defence, and a Minister of Civilian Affairs, with the P.M. to decide when one says the demands made by the other will be disastrous upon the country.

In trying to find out what really did happen and what ought to be the set up in theory and practice in any future war, from which all Gods defend us, psychological matters and the situation *at the time*, are of primary importance. It is easier to say what was right or wrong in retrospect. But it is impossible to say what *would* have happened, had some other course been pursued. That creates a hypothetical state of affairs.

I am not sure what the O'G refers to in his last sentence, especially by his use of the word 'blasphemies'. There is no shadow of doubt in fact, that at certain periods of the war—not at the very beginning and not at the end—and speaking in the Freudian vernacular only, Winston *was* the father figure of an overwhelming majority (some say over ninety per cent) of the British voters and their representatives in Parliament. Certain very important consequences flow from that, evil as well as good. But it is quotable only in the strict Freudian meaning.

For something like a year after he took office, Winston had no idea of his political strength among the voters, which is a mercy. It would have been a greater mercy had he realised that in 1945 he was no longer the 'father figure'. Yet curiously enough, he could have been, I believe. The number of voters who voted Labour, but felt sure that Winston would still be Prime Minister of a Labour Government, is incalculable.

All the psychological forces must be taken into account.

I could go on writing yards as the spirit might move me, and would be perfectly ready to correct my own impressions and views in the light of other evidence I do not possess; it is a fascinating matter.

A private person may correct his ideas as he goes along. A writer may do the same until his ideas are put into type. But a politician, and, indeed, a fighting man who has to give public utterances or orders, sometimes at short notice and with inadequate time for full reflection, and still more frequently with inadequate information as to relevant facts, has a difficult row to hoe.

From R. W. Thompson   17th July, 1960
It is a delight, as well as an enormous aid, to have this guidance. I have been working all week at the Editor's desk in the R.U.S.I., dredging through Amery with growing pleasure, doing a preliminary skirmish with Morgenthau, North[1] and the peculiar Ashmead Bartlett[2] on Gallipoli, and reading Winston's *My Early Life* on the train journeys homeward.

So it has been a very full week . . . I have been busy taking your advice on reading matter. Meanwhile Basil L.H. advises me to ask Dawyck Haig for a look at Haig's papers, wherein, he says, there is some interesting stuff relevant to Winston's military career. But you would probably know a good deal about that.

One of my first feelings on the whole matter is the perhaps rather obvious one that Winston is already past his 'prime' when he comes to power. This, I feel, while making perhaps very slight differences in his attitudes might have accounted for the 'timings' of his existence, which he imposed upon everybody else. A younger man might not have forced his entire staff to keep such fearful hours, and thus would have worn them out less, even causing them far fewer frustrations. But it is impossible not to be deeply impressed by the strategic conception of Gallipoli. O'Gowan remarked in one of his early letters that Winston never envisaged the work of a staff officer, and was incapable of the hard labour involved in real planning. He threw off ideas (and, of

---

[1] Major John North, military historian of distinction, author of Official and unofficial histories.

[2] Ashmead Bartlett, journalist, eccentric writer on the Gallipoli disaster, First World War.

course, you must be right—how odd it is that one always searches for the birth of ideas outside their creator!) I think Winston's record of schooldays and after tends to show that anything in the nature of real study—unless congenial—was alien to his nature. In that sense, and in a far larger sense, he is guilty of my own failing. You remember that you once diagnosed many of my own difficulties as arising out of a dislike of the basic toil? On the face of it Winston could answer—how absurd! 'Look at the extent of my production, books, paintings, political achievement'—even I might answer that I had (at the time) written some twenty books, travelled and reported over most of the world. Yet none of this was 'work' in the true sense of the word, the work that leads to scholarship.

At any rate, for the next few weeks I shall clearly be immersed in background, long before my own story begins. My purpose is the hope that it will enable me to write a lucid piece introducing my main characters on to the stage, setting the stage. By dint of this I hope to form a much better understanding of Winston in the 30s and 40s. Above all (for my purpose) his dealings with and attitude to, Roosevelt.

The O'G's reference to 'blasphemies', I think, meant daring to criticise what he calls 'The Myth'. I find Butler's[1] vol. ii of *Grand Strategy* most helpful, and also Playfair's[2] latest H.M.S.O. history, vol. ii *Middle East*. Kennedy and Chatfield are also helpful, but possibly you will feel that I shouldn't trust Kennedy? And what of Ismay? His book is due to appear very soon. Your private views on that could be of great service. You are my only sure guide through all these thickets.

From Sir Desmond Morton   20th July, 1960
When I find it clearer in my mind—and yours for that matter—what is to be the more precise shape of your book, I may be of some greater help. You are obviously not going to write a 'Life' of Winston in the normal biographical sense, though I see your need for much study of that life before you tackle precisely what you want to do.

By all means follow L.H.'s advice about asking to see D.H.'s papers. He may know better than I what you are really up to. I have no idea what will be in them of use to you. There must be references to Winston during the First World War; but I wonder if there is much about Winston's own military career prior to that. There will no doubt be unpublished references in the original Diaries about the time when Winston, having been slung out of the Government, over Gallipoli officially, but for other reasons too, got himself attached to a battalion

[1] Professor J. R. M. Butler, Official Historian, Second World War, editor, *Grand Strategy*.
[2] Major-General I. S. O. Playfair, Official Historian, Mediterranean and Middle East.

in France and was then given command of a battalion. Winston always thought he ought to have been made a Brigadier-General straight away. Then there will be references later to Winston as Minister of Munitions, coming frequently out to France.

Of course, D.H. loathed all politicians, particularly Lloyd George, but Winston was regarded by him as one too, which he was.

As to whether Winston had 'passed his prime' by May 1940, I cannot judge, but in the ordinary sense of that phrase, I doubt it. I find it difficult to agree that if he had been younger he would have acted differently in the ways you mention. In fact, I think he might well have been even more of a nuisance to his staff and colleagues, if that were possible.

When he was out of office in the 1930s, his energies were stupendous, but I cannot say that they had diminished in 1940. Presumably his body had grown older, but to make up for that, he had, in 1940 onwards, to expend less bodily energy on many things, which were then done for him.

I think it perfectly true that Winston 'never envisaged the work of a Staff Officer' *vide* O'G if that phrase means, as I think it does, that he never had the foggiest idea what appalling trouble and hard work he caused Staff Officers in looking up facts, compiling memoranda, etc. etc. That is completely inherent in his character and always has been. He was one of the most egotistical men I have ever met. That is *not* being *selfish*. Since I consider a man selfish only when he realises what trouble he is putting others to—perhaps quite unnecessarily—and does not care. Winston simply never had any idea of the trouble others took on his behalf.

As to whether he was 'incapable of the hard labour involved in real planning', I do not know, but doubt the accuracy of 'incapable'. He had never done it and that is that. He was *not* a trained Staff Officer.

Moreover, the boy is father of the man. Leo Amery often told me about Winston at Harrow, and hotly denied that he was classed as a stupid boy there. Far from it. Winston's trouble was that he would only work at Harrow at what interested him e.g. English history and language. When Amery was Head of the School and Winston quite a junior, the latter frequently wrote Leo's English essays for him, and Leo easily dashed off Winston's Latin prose for him. Latin and Greek, foreign languages, mathematics etc., bored Winston stiff. He just would not try to learn.

On the other hand, both then and later in life, my goodness! how he would look up references and talk and consider when it came to a historical point or an expression in English.

You have hit the point when you describe your own reactions to basic toil. That is also precisely Winston's. Winston could produce his mighty conceptions on political, or military strategic ideas. His rage when some horrible staff officer pointed out that the idea might be grand, but for some stupid reason, such as there was not enough transport to keep the divisions in shot and shell, was wonderful to behold.

Even then he was not done. He would set his brain to work out further suggestions (some of them sometimes brilliant) as to the general way (never in detail) how this might be overcome, and the staff officer would then have to work out a lot more facts and figures, in which W. was quite uninterested, being interested only in the conclusion. If this last was still hopelessly unfavourable to his plan, he might easily produce another, and yet another, set of ideas, to which no one could give an immediate answer. He would thus go on until some other 'plan' or idea struck his imagination.

Yet, it cannot be denied that out of a lot of this, though there was much chaff to be burnt or cast aside, genuine and feasible ideas were born.

As to Kennedy; do you mean the General (Jock[1]) who was for so long D.M.O. and Brookie's[2] chief help and standby? If so, his book, which harps a little too much on the Greek catastrophe—for catastrophe it was—is nevertheless quite reliable. I have not read Playfair's vol. on the Middle East, so cannot comment. I knew him very well once. He has a first-class brain and is an honest man.

As to Pug Ismay, I will comment when I have seen his book. I have heard *gossip* to the effect that more than one publisher has refused it on the grounds that it is as dull as ditch water, and where not dull, ridiculous. It might well be; but I would like to see it first. Pug has never had a first-class brain, in my opinion.

Dealings with Roosevelt. You have something there. But dealings of that kind are two-sided. I have a good idea of what Winston thought of R., but I would give a lot to *know* what R. thought of W. I think it doubtful if R. ever confided in anyone, even Eleanor. R. was in certain ways W.'s exact opposite. R. was a magnificent politician, with quite inadequate understanding of international affairs and none of military, naval or air matters. R. could never understand W.'s constitutional position, was greatly attracted to W.'s ebullience (and jealous of it) and never trusted W. a yard. I think it might be shown that R. never trusted anyone much.

On the R–W relationship, never, never forget that W. was by breeding half an American. Although he took a great and proper pride in his descent from John, Duke of Marlborough and all that entailed, the late Abbé Mendel would, I think, have had little difficulty in tracing many traits and characteristics from his Mother's father and his Father's mother.

[1] General Sir John Kennedy, D.M.O.
[2] General Sir Alan Brooke (later Field Marshal, Viscount), C.I.G.S.

History must eventually admit that by far the greatest contribution Winston made for England and the 'free' world in helping to win the war, was his public speeches. These were uniquely his own. His immense knowledge and powerful use of language, his 'dialectic', first of all made him—in the circumstances, which were none of his own making—something which 'the father figure' in the scientific psychological terminology of Freud clearly describes. His contribution to war strategy was very considerable, not in the making of plans, but in persuading other Allies, notably the U.S.A., to accept the British schemes. These schemes may well not have been initially his own. But this is all part of his persuasive oratorical power, akin to that of a Marshall Hall[1] *not* to that of an F. E. Smith.[2] Marshall Hall was the great oratorical defender of accused persons, whose knowledge of *law* left much to be desired. There have been other great Counsel like him. F.E. also had great oratorical power, but had behind him as great a knowledge of the law as any man has ever possessed, gained by immensely hard work.

So much for today. Having lunched with Jugo Slavs, whom I found most intelligent and with international views far closer to ours than to those of Mr. K who was referred to as 'that unspeakable crook', I go to try and reduce an architect's massive ideas to something a little more practical and so to save, I hope, about £250,000 to the Exchequer.

I propose to borrow a system, or device from Winston. The architects in mass assembled will tell of the wonders of the scheme they have devised. I shall say gently when they have done, 'That should cost £1½ million almost exactly . . .'

From R. W. Thompson   22nd July, 1960
I am hurrying to put this in the post, rather than to answer your grand letter of the 20th. I had this stuff copied so that I could file my own, and save you the bother of sending it back. The L.H. analysis might interest you, and evoke some comment, and the O'G. I find always stimulating. I had an hilarious letter from him last week. I had mentioned our visit to the cinema and *The Devil's Disciple*. I expect you can imagine well enough what he made of that. The chip on his shoulder is diminishing, he mellows, but he seldom leaves the ball, viz. Winston. Thus in a trice Winston is George Germain,[3] Burgoyne[4] is Auchinleck (or, in relation

[1] Sir Edward Marshall Hall, famous criminal lawyer of the first half of this century.

[2] F. E. Smith, later Earl of Birkenhead, brilliant lawyer, friend of Churchill.

[3] Lord George Germain (First Viscount Sackville), following the surrender of Burgoyne at Saratoga (1777) played a not very creditable part in the unwarranted disgrace of Burgoyne.

[4] General John Burgoyne, compelled to surrender at Saratoga, was made the scapegoat for the British defeat, for which he could not be blamed. He was finally reinstated.

to 'Battleaxe', Wavell) and so on. I find it not only amusing, but instructive. The Revolutionary war becomes almost a prototype for the campaign in the Western Desert and all clicks into place with a kind of sleight of hand.

I have seen some of the relevant stuff in the Haig Diaries, and don't think I need any more. All this is before my book (when it is gestated) will begin. It is simply that in attempting to unravel the Winston–Roosevelt relationship—which, I *believe*, will turn out to be the central problem—I must discover why, when, how and whether it *had* to be, that Britain should lose more or less 'all'. I feel that while we go on posturing as a first-class power we shall be unlikely to find our real place in the world—which might be a very good place. But first, I am trying to find out how we got here. I have a shocking fear that if I write such things, and you should read them at the wrong moment I shall make you snort so violently as to endanger your study windows—if nothing else. Forgive me, I am not, you know, half as confident as I may sound. It is, I know, a terribly tall order. However, it shall be my endeavour, and as soon as I know exactly what the shape and plan is, I will put it down. Your great knowledge is in those years of his 'stupendous energies' in the 30s and in those first years of war, the moment of realisation of power, his attitudes to Wavell and the Auk, and all those many things about which you have already given me many hints and tips.

Your paragraph about Winston's speeches hits the nail right on the head. The trouble with W. is—was—that there is so much of him in the same body! The super political Marshall Hall, as you suggest. As for those Jugo Slavs, I like them too, especially the Serbian variety. My liking, as you know, has an emotional base derived from childhood and my father's pro-Serb leanings, but it has since been fortified by meetings 'on the ground'. 'Brave little Greeks' is, as you pointed out, dangerous stuff. Brave little Serbs, a good deal less dangerous, I think, because more true.

Lastly to hope that your Winston tactics applied to architects come off a hundred per cent. Fortunately architects are unlikely to rush into print 'after your blood'—and why should they anyway! I agree with your point about selfishness and egotism. Judging by his writings, and especially *My Early Life*, Winston doesn't seem to have been aware of what or not anyone else might wish. Never did an oyster face such a sharp and dexterous blade.

From Sir Desmond Morton   26th July, 1960
My Winstonian approach to the architects came off precisely as planned. It only shows how easy it is, *if you have acquired* (no matter how) a position of accepted authority. This is a serious point, to which you can

give some thought. Winston did not realise for a number of months after becoming Prime Minister, that the English—whether they realise it or not—have an inborn veneration for the JOB, independent of their opinions of the holder. What the full processes of subconscious thought are, I do not know. But the fact remains and is of high importance in all English history. Winston the M.P., Winston the character, Winston even the First Lord, was one thing, but the PRIME MINISTER, is quite a different thing.

The phenomenon is abundantly manifest throughout the upper and middle classes, and not wholly absent by any means from the masses.

I have seen it with my own eyes ears and brain many a time—I felt it myself. The day before Clem Attlee became Prime Minister, he was 'Clem' to all and sundry with whom he came into daily contact. The very day he became Prime Minister, he was 'Prime Minister' and nothing else to all and sundry, save possibly in strict privacy.

The same with Winston.

It may by no means be the wish of the individual to undergo so rapid a sea change. But it is inevitable in England, and, in my view, a very good thing and one source of our strength, such as it is.

Briefly, the English have an outstanding respect for authority, as such. And that, incidentally is a Christian virtue.

What happens afterwards, when the personality of the man inevitably comes through the rank, is quite another matter. But it is of the greatest assistance to any office-holder in his early days.

The English are, in their corporate heart, a lot of bloody Tories, no matter how they vote.

All the rest of your letter, most interesting and amusing, but nothing there for me to comment on. Dr. Hugh l'Etang's studies sound deeply interesting.

Now for the enclosures.

1. *From the O'G to Liddell Hart.*

What does he mean by Churchill turning himself into a general-issimo *with an amateur staff*? It is the underlined portion, my own underlining, to which I refer the query.

I mention it because this idea has cropped up several times, not only from the O'G. That he 'turned himself into a generalissimo', I pass; but I cannot pass the 'amateur staff' idea until I know who is referred to. Failing that, I must strongly contend that there existed no such thing at any time, in any ordinary interpretation of those words.

Why the matter is important is in relation to Lloyd George's performances in that direction during the 1914 war. L.G. certainly set up in huts at No. 10 what could fairly be described as an unofficial and unauthorised personal (not necessarily amateur) staff. BUT, even here, his many times accursed private party were concerned far more with

57

matters of politics and foreign affairs than with the conduct of the war in the strategic sense. It has been much criticised, and in my view, had it not been for Maurice Bonham Carter, who died the other day, and was in some sort the chief of that staff, it would have led to disaster of a major kind. Maurice B–C eventually resigned most politely and quietly, because he could not stomach the intrigues which he had failed to be able to prevent. But I repeat that this party was more an unofficial Cabinet than a Military Staff, and dealt with politics. These had some repercussions on the conduct of the war, certainly; but not directly or intentionally on the strategic and tactical concepts.

Winston set up nothing like this whatever, either on the political or military side. What then does the O'G refer to?

So many people expected Winston to copy L.G. that they expected something of the sort, which did not occur. Winston's conduct of affairs was entirely different to L.G.'s. I could give you a lecture on both.

I could have told them that Winston would *not* act in that way, if they had asked me. Though I admit readily I was not at all sure how he *would* act, until it became clear.

Psychology is of the utmost importance in all history, and so few historians yet realise that. Why a man acts is far more important historically than how he acts.

If Jack Dill was 'pushed on to a limb' then he was pushed solely by Winston. Mind you, I personally agree that Winston did not behave well towards Dill. In sum, he had little respect for Dill. He had little respect for quiet, intelligent and well-behaved gentlemen. Anyway, the Winston–Dill combination would never have worked continuously— far too much difference in temperament and approach to problems.

'What a lot of mistakes that *vain* old man did make.' Now, that is a sentence in a private letter and could not be stated publicly; but there is a lot more truth in that remark of O'G's than in many others.

Equally true in background, but, as usual, because of *his* temperament, so over-bluntly stated as to suggest things which are probably not true, is the O'G's para about 'from then onwards Britain became a strategical satellite and subsequently a political satellite of the U.S.A.'

But, for example, it is not true that Marshall's brain was in un-fettered, unopposed and complete overall control of anything. I conceive it as one of the most important purposes of your book to sort these things out. Many a time it came about that what Marshall wanted was not done, to his considerable chagrin. Read and read again some of the factual stuff in Brookie's Diaries, forgetting even the heart-searchings of Brookie. Facts, facts and again facts.

Again, our lack of bargaining power at any time was certainly not due to military mistakes made by anyone, but bluntly and here truly, because we were financially broke.

So many people who write military history on the broadest lines (they can stick solely to military matters on the lesser lines of strategy and tactics) still seem to forget that stark undeniable economic factors are, in this very unpleasing world, at the back of most things. Among economic factors are imports, exports, manufactures, adequate provision of better arms than the enemy possesses, shipping, labour, and a thousand other non-military matters. Further there are 'political' matters, with which I include personalities and personal dislikes among the great, let alone ambitions, jealousies and all the clamjamfray of human nature.

When the O'G says that at Casablanca Brookie influenced *wrongly* for the invasion of Sicily against the invasion of Corsica and Sardinia, he gives a legitimate opinion, but one which must be worked out and reasoned out to be valid. There are enormous pros and cons involved and especially economic ones, which I would dare to take a bet that the O'G knows nothing about, and I doubt if Brookie did either!!

No. The O'G is too firmly wedded to opinions he has worked out for himself to make a sure guide to *you*. On the other hand, like Max Beaverbrook to Winston, he might well play the part of a useful wasp at times.

2. *L.H.'s paper.*

What a difference from the O'G! Here is a real and thoughtful historian writing with the very minimum of personal bias.

I am surprised that in view of his most just comment on page 18 that 'it was the combination of superior industrial power and superior material resources, with sea-power, that turned the tide and settled the issue etc. . . .' he does not mention this overwhelming point, in another connection and sense in the earliest, otherwise admirable and venerable appreciations of the 'crucial pre-war phase', and many of the earlier phases.

The German may only have been able to mobilise X Divisions to the Allied Y, but during the pre-war phase the Germans had fully understood *Wehrwirtschaft* and had prepared the industry and economy for the new demands of war. Neither the British, the American, and, were it possible, still less the French had any concept of this. They were all three told of this German foresight. But neither the politicians, soldiers, nor industrialists could understand it adequately. They also feared it.

The old maxim that a well-armed few can defeat a badly armed multitude was still not understood. The German Forces were, relatively speaking beautifully armed, whereas the British—and worse the French —were armed (save for the Spitfires and Hurricanes) with 1919 blunderbusses and the bullets therefor. AND industry had not received the jigs, tools or fixtures wherewith to manufacture more.

After Munich, Maurice Hankey produced a paper (still on the secret list) which showed how at the end of the 1914 war, some 30,000 factories in England were manufacturing *armament* stores,[1] and how that in 1937, only TEN factories in England were CAPABLE of such manufacture. (I will not swear to my figures, there may have been twelve instead of ten.)

The means of beginning to correct this appalling state of affairs was offered. It had been offered for several previous years. What did Neville Chamberlain and his friends do? NOTHING effective, because it would cost several million pounds. Several million pounds! God Almighty! If the Government and the Chiefs of Staff had understood the lesson and spent annually less than the cost of one day's war, as it turned out, from, say 1935 onwards, either there would have been no war ... doubtful ... or the war might have been concluded in a few months.

Mark you! I must qualify that last statement, I doubt if the French would have played anyway. They were practically mobilised on bows and arrows—I speak figuratively—and even if we could have built up an industry capable of arming both our own divisions and the French, it must be realised (a) that it takes some time to teach troops to use new weapons properly, both tactically and strategically, and (b) the best weapons in the world will not make up for a lack of desire to fight.

However, it will not be denied that the British were ready to go on fighting after the fall of France, which country deserved everything that she got. But it was the lack of weapons even more than the lack of trained officers and man-power which prevented us from really fighting during that phase, save in Africa, and even there we were similarly handicapped.

Any history of events, including a history of Winston's contribution, must take this matter into due account. Winston began to understand the general idea of this business too late. He learned it the hard way. Well do I remember when in one of my rare incursions into the military situation after the fall of France, I told him privately that if we could bomb and put out of action about a dozen smallish factories in Germany and certain other things, the German armies must die of malnutrition (in arms). He replied with agony, 'I am like a hungry man told to feed myself in the restaurant of Lucullus, who then finds he has but ten francs to spend.'

That was the time for bombing. Selective and careful bombing—not Harris's carpet laying. But we had not got the bombs, the bombers, or the sights for it. We did have the pilots.

Same story with armoured fighting vehicles. Our damned stuff was

[1] Armament stores and war stores are different things.

all inferior to the Germans and we had nothing new, either on the drawing boards or still less, factories tooled up for manufacture.

Same with the 88mm. German Krupp gun, a wonderful weapon, mountable for field work, for A.A. work or for submarines and anti-submarine. Full particulars of it were in the hands of H.M.G. as early as 1935 or 1936, when the Germans first began to manufacture. But what did we do to provide an equivalent, or better, an answer. Nothing. Because it would have cost so much! What would it have cost? Half a day's war.

We did not lose the war, though we nearly did. We have lost our position in the world for one reason only. Parsimony in defensive (and offensive) operations. Operations of industry and industrial planning and manufacture. Lack of imagination; though the same story has been written in every war in which we have taken part since Agincourt, Crimea, South Africa and the First World War. All the same story.

Everyone accepts that we were not 'properly prepared for war' on the scale and the sort which actually developed. But how many people have seen that this lack of preparation was actually twenty-five per cent as regards organisation and tactics, twenty-five per cent as regards the lack of trained military man-power, but fifty per cent as to lack of industrial ability to arm that man-power properly when the time came.

(I seem to have waxed eloquent. I apologise and take an iced drink and continue.)

The only part of L.H.'s most masterful survey with which I could not immediately agree is his comparison and rating of the various commanders. But that is obviously a matter of opinion. I am glad indeed, that he thinks Alexander would have been a 'greater' general, whatever that means, if he had been less of a gentleman.

I cannot imagine an epitaph I would desire more than that when I die, someone might say, really believing it, that Desmond Morton might have been a greater figure in the affairs of his country, had he been less of a gentleman.

If Bertie Alexander ever heard that anyone had so summed him up, I am confident that he would be humbly delighted with that encomium.

Arising from these and other matters, may I beg you, when you come to write your great book, you will observe two suggestions: (a) that you avoid like the plague saying didactically what *might* have happened if certain courses had been pursued which were not so pursued. After all, any such judgment must be hypothetical. Say, by all means what you think were mistakes. But to go further, and to claim what *would* have happened otherwise, is to be utterly condemned. One may say what *might* have happened, and with every caution and care; but no more: (b) avoid too direct judgment of any individual, unless it be to praise for what he *did do*. No man can know enough to judge of faults of commission or omission. No man can know why he did or did not do something which turned out wrong. One may point out indeed that the effects of the action or omission seemed to have brought unfortunate situations to pass. That is different.

One of the reasons that your *Cry Korea* should be a great book that will live, is that you recounted facts and largely left the reader to make up his own mind as to what otherwise might have occurred and, above all, who was to blame.

If I have to write many more letters like this, I shall start by addressing you as 'My long-suffering friend'.

P.S. to my letter just sent off, together with returning the two typescripts you recently sent me.

Letter from General Sir Arthur Wellesley to their Excellencies the Governors of the Honourable East India Co. at Madras written after his defeat of the Mahrattas.

Sirs,
I have the honour to inform you that the Army under my command has totally defeated the enemy.

I have further the honour to inform you that unless I am forthwith provided with the trains of supplies and ammunition, and with pay for my men, the Army will disintegrate.

I have to point out that these Trains were agreed before the outset of the campaign, but through *Your* inefficiency or obstruction have not yet been forthcoming. Without them it is impossible for the Army to fight or maintain the field.

> I have the honour to be,
> Sirs
> Your most humble and obedient servant
> (sd) Arthur Wellesley

P.P.S. The most satisfactory biography of Q. Victoria ever written: 'A great old lady, though not infrequently a nuisance.'
Every word tells.

From R. W. Thompson   29th July, 1960,
I take every word of your powerful advice and warnings with grave and earnest thought. As for the O'G, I am, I believe, well armed to be glad rather than afraid of his stimulating stuff. But you are so very right, and I feel sure that I have to thank some of your much earlier letters for being aware of the economic background and industrial potential for war. It astounds me, as it astounds you, that so many

generals appear to be unaware of the enormous pressures and priorities. It is this alone that gives me some confidence in my forthcoming book, for I think the spectre of shortage haunts nearly every page. I know a good deal more about it now than I did at the time. I wish I had known more about 'Skyscraper' for example, for I should have given Paget much more of his due for 'Overlord' and Freddie Morgan much less. But I am not in the book presuming to *know* the answers: I was trying to find out. If the book has virtue it must be in that anyone could have found out as much, for I had no special knowledge or inside information. But, perhaps I shall not have added a line or a word to the mountain of published material—I am not confident about it.

You mention Maurice Hankey's paper after Munich. What stories he must have had to tell—but no better than yours, I doubt. L.H. says that he was rumoured as deputy to Hankey from 1932 onwards, and was even congratulated on his 'appointment' . . . But nothing ever happened. That was the job (?) Ismay finally got, and no doubt he went down much better with Winston than L.H. would have done.

The O'G has just sent me some stuff, and I have some private papers of Blackett's in regard to the bombing policy. I met him the other day when he gave the Henry Tizard memorial lecture at the Royal Society. He and Tizard were, according to this paper, regarded as real niggers in the woodpile by the Air Ministry. It was said of anyone who added two and two together and made four, (Blackett writes), 'He is not to be trusted; he has been talking to Tizard and Blackett'. But Blackett has a bee in his bonnet about the 'Prof.'—a great many people seem to regard him as a most sinister influence. I am, therefore, doubly grateful to you, Sir, my magnificent guardian of bees—at least you do tremendous service to me in keeping my own bonnet reasonably unbuzzing.

From R. W. Thompson   3rd August, 1960,
Hugh l'Etang[1] has sent on to me a remarkable letter from an 'Ancient' well on in his nineties who writes: 'I have been reminded often in recent years of the fact that I have known of, and known personally, Winston longer than anyone who lives to-day.' The letter is meant for me, and his book *The Churchill Legend* is on its way to me with other stuff from the U.S. His name is Francis Neilson. He had won seats for the Liberals before the First World War at Kings Lynn, Holmfirth and Hanley, and appears to have been intimate with Churchill in 1914. He is clearly a very angry old man, but what an achievement—to remain angry and eloquent well into the nineties! What an achievement, too, for Winston, to inspire such emotions! We may live for ever if we feel strongly enough.

[1] Dr. Hugh l'Etang, student of the effects of disease on the world's leaders. Friend of General Fuller, Dr. Linnell and many others.

At any rate, I will have copies made of this stuff, for I am sure it will amuse you—if nothing more.

Meanwhile I am becoming so steeped in Churchill that I hope I don't begin to ferment like some potently charged vat! The magic, the wickedness, the brilliance of the man is so absorbing. Yet, I think, you were absolutely right when you wrote that perhaps his greatest contribution to victory (such as victory was) was his eloquence. I have now re-read with great pleasure his essays in *Great Contemporaries*, and pottered about in a first edition set of *The World Crisis* minus one volume (*The Eastern Front*) which I hope to pick up later. In any case, I know that volume best, having read it with great care when it was published, and written a long essay on it for a Sunday paper.

I have also found the two volume edition of his 'Marlborough' in first-class condition, and now possess more than twenty of his books while drawing upon the R.U.S.I. for all else, including some seventy-five various publications. Apart from the deadly dullness of political biographies and autobiographies I enjoy every moment of this vast exploratory journey. In any case I don't need to *read* the political biogs—take Cordell Hull,[1] for example. Or rather, don't take him, whatever you do. On the other hand I find Leo Amery irresistible, and valuable to me in many ways. I realised suddenly yesterday that I seldom really *think* of anything else but the book which (I hope) is steadily taking shape in my mind. I am not forcing its pattern. I think I know its outline. I do know its heart and core—the Roosevelt-Winston relationship, and the implications thereof. My plan now is to get down to work, night and day from September to March and come up with my book. By the end of September I hope to have digested a great deal . . .

Old man Neilson writes:

'Perhaps one of the most difficult parts of the record would be that of making plain the totally different conditions and plans of Winston and Roosevelt in the early stages of the war . . . Churchill had delivered himself into the hands of the American President . . .' He refers to Roosevelt's extreme unemployment problem; 'which amounted to 11,000,000', and its bearing on R.'s attitudes.

But no more for now . . . Eric O'G continues to chew the cud of 'the bombing policy'; Aemilia works well with her Livius, and sends her love.

From Sir Desmond Morton   5th August, 1960

Many thanks for two most interesting letters. Francis Neilson, b.1867—see *Who's Who* in a Club or Public Library. Was M.P. for Hyde Division of Cheshire 1914–1916. He seems *not* to have got in before or

[1] Cordell Hull, U.S. Secretary of State for Foreign Affairs, Second World War.

since, though he contested seats—apparently only Newport Salop in 1906 and 1908, but failed to make the grade. Was obviously mixed up in politics and would certainly have known Winston, especially 1914–1916. A most interesting life, Drama, Stage Director for Opera, librettist. Life member of all sorts of things to do with these last in U.S.A. and U.K.

I am sure his sayings and book will be a lot more amusing, though, if he is also a man with a chip on his shoulder about Winston, and a great many people of *his* generation had such chips, what he has to say will possibly be of great importance in general, but possibly overstressed in particular. His words which you quote at the end of your letter are very stimulating. I am sure he is quite right in mentioning the difficulty of expressing the 'totally different conditions and plans of Winston and Roosevelt in the early stages of the war', in which connection *you* must bear in mind that Winston was always quite unable to enter the mind of anyone else. The extreme egotist suffers nearly always from this disability, because he does not really want to enter into anyone else's mind, or else never thinks that any mind worth considering has reasonable differences of importance with his own.

Neilson is certainly right in drawing grave attention to the unemployment problem in the U.S.A. before she entered the war; in which connection it must certainly be recalled that Roosevelt was very much President of the U.S.A. at all times, and thought *for* the U.S.A. and not for the U.K. or France or anyone else. Sometimes what was best for the U.S.A. coincided with what was really good for British interests.

But I would like to know much more of Neilson's meaning, when he says, 'Churchill had *delivered himself* into the hands of the American President . . .' Reading those words in one sense, it is perfectly true, in others—possible, in others quite incorrect. But I will not write an essay on that very important issue, until I know what Neilson is referring to.

Of course, you are a 'mere infant', *sed non infans*. Even I am seventy next year. But remember *Multa reverentia pueris debetur, eis etiam mundi futuram detulerunt Parcae*.

To take your mind off Winston, so that you do not blow up, I recount the following tale, which has nothing to do with him.

During the last war, Admiral Stephenson,[1] known as a wag, was commanding destroyers at Rosyth from a cruiser, where he flew his flag. There arrived a lone Netherlands destroyer to join the Allies, commanded by a Dutch officer who had been Dutch Naval Attaché in London before the war, well known to Steve. The Dutch destroyer was painted in camouflage, Dutch fashion, which they claimed was a darned sight better than ours, and probably was, since we adopted it generally.

[1] Admiral Stephenson, British Admiral, friend of Desmond Morton.

On arrival the Dutch destroyer came to anchor some three cables away from the cruiser and made the following signal to the Admiral, on a bright sunny day.

'1. Reporting arrival.

2. C. in C. invites personal comments our camouflage.'

To this Steve replied at once.

'1. Arrival recorded. Welcome.

2. Where are you?'

Another one. Same actors. But Steve did not come off best.

Admiral Stephenson inspected the Dutch destroyer and asked that they should be put through gun drill. Thereafter he commented, 'Commander, I am honoured to command you and your men. You know your drill; but I must in honesty say you are slow, too slow, much too slow, in fact, damn slow. You remind me of a lot of tombstones in a churchyard. For goodness sake get moving.'

About three weeks later, Admiral Stephenson was being rowed in his barge in the firth on the way to somewhere. An order was given to the Dutch destroyer to cast off and put to sea as quickly as possible, as a German submarine was reported outside the firth. They did so in about a minute flat, and proceeded at a full thirty-five knots to sea, their natural course taking them not far from the Admiral's barge. The Admiral's flag-officer on the cruiser made a signal, 'Look out. Don't swamp the Admiral.' To which the destroyer replied by signal, simply, 'Tombstones moving.'

Steve told me both these excellent tales at the Club yesterday.

From R. W. Thompson   9th August, 1960

The Netherlands delegation left for home yesterday, having enjoyed your Admiral Stephenson stories with their breakfast. It now behoves me to gather myself together, and especially to collect my thoughts. Inevitably, although I 'live' with Winston's many ghosts infesting even my dreams, there have been many things to drag the 'top' of my mind away from my business.

Basil L.H. was delighted with some of your remarks (which I passed on to him), and has asked me to send you a copy of a 'Military Competence' piece he wrote about a year ago. I thought it was very good on Churchill, and I hope it may lead you to make some illuminating comments. As for Ancient Neilson, L.H. also warns me to absorb his sayings with care. His letter appears to have some differences of opinion with the account he (presumably) gave to *Who's Who*. However, to meet and talk with a ninety-three year old in full possession of his faculties, is an experience I have enjoyed only once before—with Winston's 'saint, clown, sage' of vivid memory. I would have written poet on the end—or the beginning of that—'Bread has no sorrow for me, and water no affliction. But to shut me from the light of the sky and the sight of the fields and flowers . . .'[1]

Your potent reminder of Winston's egotism comes at a fruitful moment. I was considering whether I had read a collection of essays on people, at once so shallow and so entertaining as his *Great Contemporaries*. Doubtless (I feel) he admires the qualities he imagines Lord Rosebery to have possessed. I doubt whether he knew anything about the inner man of such a one as Asquith. Nevertheless, in every essay he is giving insights to *himself*, patronising Lawrence, perhaps knowing his match in Lloyd George (not included), admiring Boris Savinkov, yet only rising to his full powers in his violent emotional tirade against Trotsky—'alias Bronstein'! One cannot help suspecting that, Communism apart, Trotsky may be nearer in most ways than the Balfours and Morleys. I wonder what he would have made of George Monck, 1st Duke of Albemarle?

Thus I look forward with intense pleasure to a careful reading of his 'Marlborough', for in this I feel assured I shall find many of the questions I am asking about Churchill. Here, if I am not mistaken, he will defend himself in defending his ancestor, and reveal himself.

But it is, for my book, perhaps the very crux that I come as near as possible to understanding the Churchill–Roosevelt relationship. The war is my study, and its aftermath, the world I live in, the world—or cinder—it will be the lot of my children to inhabit, or not. So, although as you remarked a few letters back, there is Winston the soldier, the writer, the family man, the politician, the *Prime Minister*, it is Winston with Roosevelt and Winston in relation to the British Empire and Britain's place in the aftermath world, that excites me. I cannot know too much about him, but whatever omissions there may be in a month or six weeks I must focus my mind on the main target. I shall keep all possible ammunition and 'stores' ready to my hand. I shall draw courage from your proximity, and the knowledge that I can depend upon your frank and sober judgment. But the battle will be mine.

I will now, using your notes, repair to the nursery for a brief spell in order to instruct my children in regard to the common or garden hedgehog or 'Urchin'. There are some urchins in these parts, not of the sea, nor of the mild spiny variety on land, but of the new age of 'The Tele'.

The O'G has just sent me Max Beloff's letter in the D.T. re Presidents and Prime Ministers. Ha! Winston, of course, began it.

From Sir Desmond Morton   11th August, 1960
Chiefly to acknowledge with very grateful thanks L.H.'s really wonderful appreciation of Winston in certain of his kaleidoscopic

[1] *St. Joan*, G. B. Shaw.

aspects. I agree so wholeheartedly with it, that all I can do is to admire with reverence the skill to observe and set down what is observed.

The essay does not cover everything. How could it, in eight pages? Perhaps also, it does not express certain changes in W.S.C.'s attitude and methods of thought towards the later part of the war. But to criticise what is said, would merely be to quibble.

The chief omission is the effect of W.'s realisation, about after Yalta, that England and he had dropped to second place. It is important that he realised it, as it is important to know how *he* proposed to rectify this later. The chief foundation of his belief that he could restore England to first, or equal first, place in the world with the U.S.A. was his own complete certainty that he would be re-elected Prime Minister after the war, and that his own direction of armistice and peace affairs would be such as would inevitably occasion what was necessary (whatever IT was). Neither then nor at any other time was he susceptible to economic arguments, especially if they tended to disturb his fixed ideas on fact or policy.

As he was *not* Prime Minister after 1945 election, he now has the satisfying—self-satisfying—argument that all we now suffer from cannot in any way be laid at his door! Had he been P.M. from 1945 onwards (how far onwards is not a question he would consider) none of these dreadful things would have happened.

I will browse on L.H.'s masterful prose and see if it brings me any additional comments likely to be of any use. They can only be in the way of addenda.

I like your comment on *Great Contemporaries*. As regards Marlborough, remember that he wrote all that before he himself was P.M. and (in imagination) Commander in Chief. Hence he would not be defending himself so much in the defence of his ancestor, as he would have been, had he written it after the war.

There is one curious thing about the Marlborough book, the attempt to prove that John Duke never took bribes. Ridiculous. Of course he did and everyone knew it. But it was the custom of the day. If Winston had been content with trying to shew (which I think he could have done successfully) that Marlborough never betrayed anyone from whom he took a bribe or 'present', but only took such presents when his own mind had already been made up to act exactly as the donor desired, he could not only get away with it, but would have cast a considerably more noble light on the Duke, than a futile attempt to prove that he never took 'presents' at all.

Winston was meticulous about never taking any sort of improper present himself. I have much evidence on that, which does Winston very considerable honour. Therefore it was not Winston himself, whom Winston was defending through the Marlborough acceptance of presents. No. I have a strong idea that it was more subtle and more in the subconscious.

Winston has a personal horror of accepting presents for which he would feel bound to do something in exchange. The real reason for this—probably unknown to W.S.C.'s conscious mind—was that to do so, put him under an obligation. This Winston's egotism would never submit to. He rationalised this by ferociously asserting that no gentleman could take a bribe; it was the abomination of desolation.

He was terribly anxious to show John Duke as the *Chevalier sans tâche*. Why? First, because *his* famous ancestor *must* be such. (I know of several other matters in John Spencer Churchill's life, which Winston knew of—and the world does not—which Winston suppressed, because they showed the great John in the role of anything but the modern idea of a gentleman).

Secondly—and here is the nasty, sticky part, so odd is the working of the subconscious minds of all of us—because he, Winston, was not quite sure that he, Winston, was a gentleman.

I dare even go further and suggest why he doubted subconsciously that he was what he would wish to be or to think himself, in the role of great English gentleman.

I suggest that it was his mother, whom he rightly adored, being an American (and look at *her* ancestors!) and also because in early life, that which he regarded as the beau ideal of a gentleman, namely the pre-First World War English Commissioned Officer of the Army—the younger ones too, contemporaries, let alone the older fogies, rejected him. They rejected him firmly and reasonably politely, because they did not consider his behaviour that of a gentleman according to their standards. Nothing to do with sex or money, and certainly nothing whatever to do with birth. To them, a gentleman was not self-centred and not a go-getter in a vulgar way.

That is why Winston in later life continued to dislike gentlemen of the type of Lord Alexander.

However, much of this is by the way, and obviously unprintable. Nevertheless, as a background thought it might have some value.

From R. W. Thompson   15th August, 1960
L.H. will be delighted with your verdict on his Churchill appreciation. I had thought it first-class, but with my limited knowledge had looked forward to your views. I was surprised that Winston did not realise until 'about after Yalta' that England and he had dropped to second place. It would have seemed inescapable that such awareness should have come sooner. But the whole relationship of Winston with R.

and the U.S.A. is complex and peculiar in the extreme. I find Sherwood's[1] *Hopkins* an invaluable source, the more as one's knowledge grows. But I do look forward to the next chance to talk to you about this relationship. It will be, in a sense, the nub of my book (it is, in fact, too early to say what will or will not be the nub) but that is 'one of my feelings' at this moment.

Your lights on Winston's nature, especially in regard to accepting presents and putting himself under obligations are particularly illuminating. It is, of course, one of the manifestations of egotism, but not (I hope) a very grave fault. It usually rebounds against the egotist. Winston's doubts of his own innate ability to play the part of the gentleman, great or not, are of great importance. In my view he is not a gentleman, as the term was understood in his youth and early manhood. One need go no further, I think, than the dislike for him of his contemporaries, especially in military circles. Marlborough '*sans tâche*', bizarre as it sounds, is more credible. I find Marlborough's statesmanship even more impressive than his military achievements. Assuredly he bore all the outward trappings and manners of a gentleman, the more so in the tradition of his time.

But Winston—in my eyes at any rate—does not begin to match up to the stature of his great ancestor. It may be that because his male ancestry is beyond his 'nature' he turns to his mother and gives her his father's kingdom?

One thing I must not forget: L.H. asked me to draw your attention to the last two chapters of vol. i and the first chapter of vol. ii of his *The Tanks*, in which he deals in detail with the armoured situation at the beginning of the war. Perhaps, if you have not these books available, you would glance through them some time, whenever possible. But I think L.H.'s point is simply to establish with you that he had not underestimated the weapons and supply positions. In short pieces, up to even 5,000 or 10,000 words, it is impossible to include everything, for as you remark about his Churchill appreciation—'How could it, in eight pages'.

My one really exciting piece of news is that I am lunching with the formidable Boney Fuller on Thursday. He does me the great honour of coming to London for the purpose, having heard from l'Etang of my immense interest, not only in his own works, but in Winston. You know how bad I am at asking questions—nevertheless I will try to ask some, and report to you the upshot. The following month I may be having a similar meeting with old Neilson. I think I observed before that the effect may be to make me feel almost in the cradle.

[1] Robert Sherwood, author of *The White House Papers of Harry L. Hopkins*. Specia adviser and confidant of President Roosevelt.

... Meanwhile I have been reading L.H.'s essay again ...

Here are my very few addenda, with the paras that stirred my mind to them.

1. Bottom of page 1, W.S.C. certainly 'inspires affection despite his intense egocentricity'; but it is interesting how that affection wanes without continuous contact. Though lacking any sort of 'hypnotic' power such as has been ascribed to Hitler; there is no doubt that the magnetism of his intensely vivid personality and his rapid thought movements, not to mention his laughable tergiversations [sic], were largely the source and cause of the affection; and such require the stimulus of sight and sound to remain effective.

It is not without interest that his *junior* personal staff with few, if any, exceptions, disliked him to the point of detestation. He treated them all like 'flunkeys', without any apparent interest in them or humanity. Several were ranked as 'Colonels' or 'Brigadiers' and the most senior as a 'Major General', (actually Principals and Assistant Secretaries with one Under-Secretary in the Civil Service). Typists all abominated him. Of course, with one or possibly two exceptions, none of them felt themselves to be in a position to treat him as man to man and to argue with him. The one or possibly two who were of good birth and higher calibre, and who told him what they thought of him at intervals, got off much better, but even so they did not really care for him.

W. was quite different with those whom he regarded as being on a higher plane, e.g. Chiefs of Staff, politicians and even my humble self, and others such as Bridges, Alec Cadogan and most Foreign Office officials, together with any officer in uniform, whom he saw.

He loathed 'Civil Servants' (I have some sympathy with that view). Really because the senior ones had always acted as some sort of brake upon his more excitable proposals within their purview. The F. O. he did not regard as Civil Servants (he had something there too).

I remember one day remonstrating with him at a peculiarly bitter outburst against Civil Servants, and mentioning a couple of very senior such who had recently been of great help to him. His retort was 'Nonsense! You will be describing yourself, Edward (Bridges) and Alec (Cadogan) as Civil Servants next!' He could not see why I roared with laughter.

2. Although L.H. does refer to it, more might be made of W.'s factual knowledge, which was astonishingly superficial and sketchy, even on matters in which he really thought himself something of an expert. He carried this off by a remarkable capacity for acquiring almost instantaneously the technical terms of the 'science' concerned, together with an ability to memorise effective phrases in papers or conversations

with real experts. All this was part of his dialectic, beneath which real knowledge was too frequently a mere skin on the surface. The things on which only a supreme expert could challenge him, and even might be rash to do so, were the English language, English and American history and, less so, the history of Western Europe.

3. Page 2. It is undoubtedly true that W. did great damage to the Army and Air Force when in Office in the 1920s. In that connection however, it might be usefully recalled that the Chiefs of Staff during that period regularly prophesied formally and officially that the U.K. would not be engaged in any sort of major war for ten years from that date. They got honours (but no honour) for so doing. The last to do so was, I think, George Milne, who made the usual prophecy in the spring of 1929 and so acquired a peerage. He was right (gulp!) by a short head, but he ought not to have been so.

You will realise the effect of this on any current politician, who wanted to use every penny of taxation that he could on other political objects, such as pianos for the poor, free of charge.

In 1934 Winston was out of office, looking for sticks with which to beat the Government, and began to have access to true facts, known to H.M.G., but not to the public; in which connection see Page 63 of Vol 1 of his *Second World War*, but keep me out of it personally, please.

4. Page 3. W.'s idea that the French Army was 'the most perfectly trained and faithful mobile force in Europe'. This was an obsession with the man. I recall how before the war I gave him, with permission, full information about the utterly rotten state of the equipment (which admittedly he does not mention) of the French Army and Air Force, and pointed out the certain consequences of this, he just would have none of it. We had many an argument. My prophecy in the winter of 1938/39 supported by facts and calculations, which was a Cabinet paper, that if attacked by the weight of German arms as then they stood, France would be over-run in less than a month, nearly made him froth with rage. And yet he accepted the conclusions drawn through similar facts and calculations, based on industry, economics and world trade, in regard to every other country in the world. 'The unshakeable glory of France' was an obsession. Even Neville Chamberlain's Government accepted my appallingly alarming conclusions, but . . . did nothing about it.

5. Pages 3 and 4. The Norwegian flop. In a sense I was up to the neck in that. With the joint planners, we put up a paper *before* the outbreak of war, showing the effects on Germany of the destruction of the very vulnerable railway joining the iron mines of Sweden with the West Norwegian ports. When war broke out, we referred to this, but adding reasons why it must be carried out in September or October 1939 *or not at all*. W. was entranced by the idea, but the Cabinet, rightly

or wrongly—I do not blame them—voted against it. But, later, *against the advice* given above, reversed this decision through the constant pressure brought by W. to do so. It was much too late and fatal.

Rather a typical example of W.'s actions whereby, getting an idea into his head, it was difficult to remove it, since he paid little attention to alterations in circumstances by the passage of time, especially when he did not comprehend the overriding motive of any action.

6. Bottom of page 4 and on. It was heartbreaking and maddening to see how both politicians of all kinds and high ranking soldiers, sailors, and airmen, completely forgot the lessons drummed into them from 1934 to 1939, at least, in regard to what the Americans later got us to call 'logistics', i.e. the supply of armament and war stores (and the interference in the supply of our enemies with armaments and war-stores) from the raw materials, through the factories to the fighting line, and the similar supply of food and goods for the population, who manufactured the war stores.

They had all been memorialised and lectured at all high levels on this matter for six years at a minimum, but as soon as war broke out, the spirit seemed to be, 'Now we are really at war, all this mysterious economic, civilian stuff can be forgotten. We are fighting men etc. etc.'

7. Page 5. I cannot quite reconcile with my memory what L.H. describes as W.'s delusion about winning the war with a bombing offensive. Not at least in the early days, to which this paragraph refers. I recall many conversations with W. at this time who was frequently deploring in no uncertain terms our lack of adequate aircraft of all types, but chiefly with the background view of destroying an invading force, or giving adequate support to our troops in Africa, or to our Merchant Navy. I should have placed this bombing offensive notion at a much later date. I agree wholeheartedly however with the following paragraph that he 'impaired the effect' of his strategy of indirect approach and constant pressure 'by pursuing too many divers aims, with limited resources'.

8. Page 6. The lamentable Greek affair. I have already written you about that and need not repeat. It was always pressed and defended by W. as a political necessity, in that did we not rush to the assistance of the 'gallant little Greeks', we would never be able to hold up our heads in Greece when the war was over. Sheer emotional lunacy. Any suggestion that the 'gallant little Greeks' were a set of self-centred and unreliable sods, like most nations regarded separately, and that there was no such thing as national gratitude in politics, merely brought forth a burst of memorable eloquence, based on nothing.

He was the same at other times about the 'brave, steadfast, religious hard-living Arabs', of whom he really knew absolutely nothing.

9. On pages 8 and 9 my only comment is that, in my opinion, W. did play in certain ways, not mentioned, a very important part even after America's entry into the war. What is said by L.H. is true enough as far as it goes, but you will see from Vol. 11 of Alanbrooke's Diaries, how and how frequently W. managed to change the official American attitude towards certain major strategic plans and to modify these more in accordance with British views.

The American Chiefs of Staff were on the whole anti-British, (a phrase which wants careful analysis) and frequently held views diametrically opposed to British plans. They were well aware, too, of their own preponderance in men and arms and fighting potential. But their constitution made the President their Commander in Chief in war, and the final arbiter of everything. They obeyed this rule like angels obeying God. They were highly suspicious of the British Chiefs. Frequently at their level (with the British, any arguments on strategy between the British Chiefs and Winston had been ironed out *before* the British Chiefs started to argue with the American Chiefs; with the Americans, the rule was for the American Chiefs to obtain a final decision on their own views from the President, until they had squared matters or arrived at a deadlock with the British) they got stuck with the British Chiefs. The latter would then go to Churchill, who, see above, had already agreed the broad line, and get him to go direct to the President, whom he saw alone. Almost always, when this happened, W. would persuade the President to *his*, Winston's, views. Thus, when the full Session took place between the joint Chiefs and the President and the P.M., the American Chiefs found to their discomfort that their own C. in C. had already agreed to the British view. The occasions on which this happened want looking up, (key: Alanbrooke's Diary). They were all very important.

10. One thing you will have to study very carefully is that appalling Yalta conference. I have told you or written to you about that already. That is the key to much of our difficulty during and after the war. But W., who hated the decisions more or less imposed by the President, who was a dying man, always claimed that he would have set things right in this regard, had he been re-elected to power in 1945. And he was firmly convinced at the Yalta conference and right up to the fatal day of the poll, that he *would* be re-elected.

To omit this nodal point in what I understand you are hoping to write, would be to omit the Prince of Denmark from Hamlet.

Have just got your last letter, which indicated the great value of the point made above.

I have not got a copy of L.H.'s book *The Tanks*. But can probably see a copy at the Club. However, since I have no papers whatever, I fear it would not be possible for me to comment on the accuracy or otherwise of the figures he gives. The man who almost certainly has papers and could do so, is Boney Fuller.

From R. W. Thompson   19th August, 1960
Yesterday was triply memorable: by a miracle the postman delivered your letter before I left the cottage, and I had all the pleasure of it in the train. It sharpened my wits for the redoubtable Boney Fuller, with whom I lunched. At least, I imagine we must have eaten something, but we talked and talked from twelve-thirty to three non stop. Even with our gin and tonics he remarked in his remarkable mellow voice: 'Trouble with this country is that we don't assassinate chaps like Winston!' He then recounted an anecdote of an evening with Duff Cooper, Winston and another after his (Boney's) return from the Abyssinian War. Winston suddenly said: 'I wish you'd stop talking.' To which Boney replied: 'I'll stop when I've finished.' Whereupon this ancient, but vividly alive piece of humanity, slumped back in his chair (all seven stone of him), pouted, and looked like the spoiled child Winston looked like on that night. 'Sulked like a baby!' Boney observed drily. The whole performance was wonderful. And so it went on.

In the course of these hours, Ike, Marshall and many others were consigned, metaphorically, to the 'ash can'. The idea of Winston as an historian made him snort with scorn. Yet all the time gems of strategic wisdom were pouring out. I shall have to marshal the facts. From experience I know that they are forming into place in my mind, and will present themselves in due course. Meanwhile, Hugh l'Etang assures me that there is no danger of triplets! We briefly discussed Yalta and Roosevelt at death's door. Describing his appearance at the last Cabinet meeting before his inauguration in 1945, Frances Perkins[1] wrote: 'When he came in I thought he looked bad . . . His clothes looked much too big for him. His face looked thin, his colour was grey, and his eyes were dull.' By the end of the meeting, two hours later, 'The change in his appearance was marked. I had a sense of his enormous fatigue. He had the pallor, the deep grey colour of a man who has been long ill. He supported his head with his hand as though it were too much to hold it up. His lips were blue. His hand shook.'

There can be little doubt that the effects of disease on the minds and energies of many of those who have almost literally held the fate of the world in their hands is profound. The shocking physical condition of Woodrow Wilson had altered the course of history, for following 'the left-sided hemiplegia' which developed on 2nd October, 1919, his 'actions destroyed any hope of the American Senate ratifying the Peace Treaty and agreeing to enter the League of Nations.' (I quote l'Etang).

[1] Frances Perkins, U.S. Secretary for Labour, Second World War.

What a lot of angles there are. But when I reached home there was old Neilson's *The Churchill Legend* confronting me. Even a rapid glance through is enough to convince me that here is a mine of information, and written, it seems, with a cool and steady gaze. He quotes the Dowager Duchess of Marlborough's remark to Consuela, D. of M.: 'Your first duty is to have a child, and it must be a son because it would be intolerable to have that little upstart Winston become a Duke.' But the book is a work of scholarship, a whole life time of study. He remarks somewhere that Winston is really a job for a novelist, a Dumas. I think that, too, is revealing of great understanding. In a way Winston and Dumas *père* were of the same kidney. At the end of a very long book Neilson reprints his long reviews of Winston's *History of the Second World War*. These are brilliant. His last words: 'What an end! What a triumph! Stalin on the Elbe and a Socialist Government in Great Britain!' He might have added, the Empire lost and Britain a satellite state. But on first 'skimping' he never goes too far.

Meanwhile I have also two quite good sources in Trumbull Higgins'[1] *Winston Churchill and the Second Front*, and Feis's[2] *Churchill, Roosevelt and Stalin*. In my view these American historians draw fundamentally wrong conclusions arising out of false premises. Nevertheless their research is exhaustive and their facts, I think, sound. They should be, since these chaps have the backing of Universities, Rockefeller Foundations and the like and whole teams of research workers.

As Boney Fuller said: 'We chaps who work alone must not attempt to do that kind of think.' It is important. We are writing lone impressions, much more of what we think and feel than the 'Official' Historian could permit himself. In a big way (Boney), in a small way (me) try to translate.

I brood upon Yalta. If that is my 'Hamlet' I must know him well— Alas, poor Yorick . . . But I cannot find anybody who *liked* or *likes* Winston. I cannot find anybody who really *thinks* he was a great man, or wherein lies his greatness. You, I feel sure, did not really like him. His egotism appears to be supreme, inasmuch as it comes second to nothing. The world is his oyster. The purpose of his life is to consume it, and this he has done, to come at the end of his days to a chair on the yacht of Onassis. Surely there must be a bright shaft of light shining through this tragedy! Where is it? My purpose is to find it, to know it, not to dream it. It is not in his prose, which too often defeats his own intention and obscures even the outline of the River Nile and the bleak arid desert. De Gaulle is ten times his master in this alone. His romantic dreams impair his true visions of past and present times without number.

[1] Trumbull Higgins, professor and distinguished American historian.
[2] Herbert Feis, professor and distinguished American historian.

Even in his 'history', 'Alfred the Great' and 'William the Conqueror' are merely Winston. (I owe that to Boney!)

But in all this comparative excitement of books and meetings your letter shines out. Every word rings true, and through you more than any other I sense the good in Winston, perhaps merely the small boy, the chap 'who wants to be a soldier', who wants, perhaps above all, to be a decent chap, but doesn't know how, the chap who could never be Marlborough, or even a Duke, and in his heart knows it, the chap who won't really get down to work, and yet must prove himself as good or better than anyone else, the chap who knows the lack of depth in his own thoughts, and has not the true conviction to stand up against those who stand steadfast against him—the Chiefs of Staff many times, for example.

Yet, where is Winston Churchill. Perhaps—indeed, probably, I shall never know—but there is always a chance that in feeding all this into my imagination, subjecting it all to those mysterious processes of the human mind, ninety-nine hundredths subconscious, Winston Spencer Churchill will emerge.

Some time ago I wandered more or less alone about Blenheim, contemplating that small room and brass-bound bedstead on the ground floor wherein he was born; and across the park to the little church where Randolph was buried, and where, I know, Winston wishes to lie with his family. The church was heady with new bright pine, simple; its age whittled away, not even beautiful—except for its yard. And it seemed to me that there was some pathos in all this, neither a Marlborough, nor an American, the vices of both sides, but somewhere also the virtues. The inheritor of little more than a name—and what to do with it. Well, it is enigma. How could any man have done more with it—or less . . .

Forgive my ramblings. I do not curb them to you, for, if you will put up with it, it is very important that I let myself 'talk to you', as if I had partaken of this new L.S.D. (Diethylamide?) they speak of.

To the grindstone!

From Sir Desmond Morton   20th August, 1960
I think your letter of 19th is the best you have written, by far, on the subject you have in hand, and it probably ranks as one of the best you have ever written me in your life—so far.

It is now clear that the sleuthhound is on the job and has got the true scent of the quarry.

As a hunter of experience, may I now remind you that you are hunting a stag and not a fox. Your object is to bring the great beast to bay and not to let the hounds kill and eat it.

In less allegorical language; when you come to write the book, do not forget that you have so much information from sources who either had a chip on their shoulder, or *knew* they *dis*liked Winston. I think you have that in mind. It is essential—absolutely essential, that you acquire this information and then ponder upon it. Avoid like the plague anything which appears to be tending to be one-sided, and do not dip your pen in vitriol.

There has been a spate and a fashion for writers, good ones too—to write what is, after all, little else but denigration. How right you are that there must have been some good in Winston and that you must search for that; not only for the sake of truth, but because a book will only live if it does contain an effect of truth, though a purely denigrating book may cause a temporary sensation.

After all, we cannot get away from it that Winston was un-questionably a Great Man, as the world counts greatness and, however much later historians than any now alive discover and disclose his terrific weaknesses or worse, they will still be bound to write his name in Valhalla, even though it may be more difficult to find it in Heaven. He will always be a great Memory for two principal reasons, by reason of his speeches and by reason of the genuine (if somewhat unbalanced and ill-informed) adulation accorded him by many millions of human beings.

Undoubtedly *through* and *by reason of him* great things in a very short period of the world's history were done. His name and *alleged* deeds will live as long as anything like reasonable history of certain years is written.

After all, Stalin was a Great Man as the world counts greatness, though he was or became something indescribable for beastliness.

You add at the side, 'But Winston has something bogus in his male-ness!' That is a very interesting remark. I have never thought that way before, and the only immediate comment which comes to me is, that if you are right, I do quite see what you mean. I can affirm that he was magnificently courageous, both physically and psychologically. The latter is obvious, but I have direct evidence of the former. We have discussed together (W. and I) the question of courage and he readily asserted, and I believe it to be true, that he adored physical danger, which gave him a thrill almost of a sexual nature. This is NOT for publication. He was psychologically completely male and a textbook example of Freudian maleness in his relations with his parents, children, wife and friends.

On the other hand, you may not have realised that to a certain extent one might rightly say that many of his actions and activities partook of the bogus, because he was a consummate actor, whether he knew it or not. (He knew he acted, but perhaps that was one part of his genius of which he did not realise the magnitude.) Had his life been conducive to one on the boards of a theatre (not the opera; he did not know one note from another) he could easily have been as great an actor as has ever walked the stage.

How do I assimilate that with his utter inability to enter the mind of another living person?

Easy! It would have been *his* interpretation of how Hamlet, Macbeth, Lear ought to have thought and reacted. And, as I have written before, there were so many Winston moods that one of them would have suited the part portrayed.

You ask, at least by implication, whether I like Winston and whether anyone ever liked him.

I can say with certitude that that very great lady, Clementine Hosier, Lady Churchill, adored Winston and loved him to the exclusion of almost everyone else, even her own children by him. And he adored her. I have known one or two other women, one of whom was next door to a saint, who have had the profoundest and most real affection for Winston. But as regards women, I should judge that, apart from his own mother, whom I never knew, and Clemmy, whereas Winston liked having them around and in a sense liked them, I doubt whether he had much which you could call affection for other women.

Winston *loved his* children, and there was some sort of mutual affection reaction. But the mutual father-child relationships would require an essay, especially in regard to Randolph.

Winston had a deep admiration for his father, coupled with a beautiful Freudian 'jealousy', and a determination to do better than his father had done; and at the same time to jolly well show his mother what a fine fellow he was. There was a time when he was a boy that he thought (with what reason I do not know) that his mother liked his brother Jack better than she liked him. There were some staggering exhibitionist consequences.

As regards other friends, outside the family, I find it hard to be sure of anything. It has been said that he has only had three real friends, Brendan Bracken, Beaverbrook and Barney Baruch. I know nothing sufficient about Baruch or the latter's contra-reactions. Of the three, I would say that Brendan really did feel genuine affection for Winston. I knew Brendan very well. In certain ways of importance he was a good chap. He was genuinely kind, without an eye to future recompense. I should guess that Brendan's affection for Winston was greater than Winston's affection for Brendan. But Winston knew of Brendan's devotion and that he could trust him with any sort of secret of his own. Nor would Winston say unkind things about Brendan behind Brendan's back. I think he would not have done that either in regard to Beaverbrook and Baruch. But I do not think he trusted either in the same way that he trusted Brendan, who, probably, psychologically, much represented what he would like to have seen in his own son.

Of course, it is quite untrue that Brendan was any sort of blood relation to Winston whatever.

I can recall one other person who not only liked Winston and more, but who sacrificed his whole career for him, that was Eddie Marsh (Sir Edward Marsh, K.C.V.O.) but even before he was dead, Winston used to say that Eddie had 'never been any use to him at all' (sic).

Eddie was fascinated by Winston.

I have always said that Winston is the most fascinating personality that I have made close contact with. Nearly everyone if not everyone who has had really close contact with him in his later years (I have known him since 1917) has felt that fascination in greater or lesser degree.

Quite unusual things were always happening in Winston's surroundings, which was part of the fascination, as were his reactions to these things, of which his own personality was largely the cause as well.

Speaking of myself. I am quite sure that had I been a rich man in 1945, when Winston lost the election I would have retired from Government Service; and, equally sure, that Winston would have welcomed me as a part of his continued *famille militaire* in the Tory party, which I probably would not have liked for other reasons, and then I would probably also have accepted a peerage. What for? God alone knows.

I am just as sure that the fact that I did not retire and devote myself to Winston in some capacity in 1945 has in effect caused me to be blotted out from his serious memory. This, despite the fact that I have lunched with him and dined with him at intervals thereafter at his invitation.

I do not think that as in the case of Eddie Marsh, Winston would say that I had 'never been of any use to him'. My point is that when anyone *is* of use to Winston, that person, if he gets by certain standards of behaviour i.e. is broadly a gentleman, is Winston's friend for so long as he continues to be of use to Winston. Thereafter, in varying degrees, he does not re-enter Winston's conscious mind.

To answer truthfully the blunt question, 'Do you like Winston?' I find quite impossible. I can say that he fascinated me quite easily, that he always treated me with great kindness when in power, as much as when he was out of power at Chartwell. In power, he treated me as a friend, when he felt the need, and always as if I was a Minister of the Crown and not even as a Civil Servant. I am grateful for all that.

I think I can say that during the period of close association, roughly 1924 to 1940 (I *knew* him on a social basis from 1917, as I have said) I *did* like Winston, but whether that liking diminished when I saw the Winston which emerged when he realised his power in about 1941, it would be hard to say. I know that when he did fall from power and circumstances made it impossible for me to resign and follow him, I was relieved that the circumstances were what they were. I am now very glad indeed that matters so arranged themselves.

One thing is quite certain, Winston owes me no debt, and I have no chip on my shoulder about him. I wish him well to his life's end and beyond; but I do not care if I never see him again and certainly would not wish to attend his funeral, though I would pray most heartily for his soul.

I think I am one of the lucky few who have been Winston's friends. Several others I know would give you, as they have given me, some very dusty answers to the query. One whom I will not name, and with whom, as with others, I have discussed the very point you raise, said, after a long talk, 'I suppose I liked Winston once, and I believe I even loved him; but to be frank, I think I hate him now!'

But this person had not been in so long and close a daily relationship with Winston as had I, in peace and war.

I most certainly do not hate him and can say this naturally and without any background of moral theology. But do I now *like* him? I cannot answer. I do not *dislike* him. But together with the fact that the Winston of today is now a pitiable old man, there is with me the feeling that Winston is something past and done with in so far as I am concerned and almost as though he had never been.

Odd, is it not? But that is the best I can do.

But as far as you are concerned, I think you have a wonderful mental line of enquiry to follow up and go on following up, in your query, which I suggest you phrase to yourself in less downright terms than in your letter, namely, 'Who really liked Winston and why?' Also, 'Did they stop liking Winston and why?'

Your question as to whether anyone *now* really thinks he *was* a great man, will not do at all. Of course he was a great man, *as the world counts greatness.* So was Henry VIII and Ivan the Terrible.

On the other hand, there is no doubt that he was not nearly so great a man as many people have thought him to be at some specific time, or as many people still think of him.

But if you write a book tending to try to show that he was not a great man at all at any time, then you will be as ludicrous as was Winston himself when he tried to write a book proving that his ancestor John Duke never took bribes.

Hoping that all this drivel will give you some part of the interest that your most invigorating letter of 19th gave to me.

From R. W. Thompson   25th August 1960,
Your most generous letter of the 20th will be of immense help to me. I have a great complexity of 'material' to pan—as a miner in a water course panning for gold. It is here, especially, that your hand on the

tiller forces me to patience, to accept nothing until and unless it rings true. There is much I want to say in reply, but first I must tell you that Neilson's book is a great disappointment. My first impression was almost wholly false, and I doubt whether I ever read a more wrong-headed book. Nevertheless, it can be of considerable value. It points to innumerable valuable sources, notably Esher's letters, Fisher's Memories, Asquith's, and pin-points various phrases which I must check. For the rest, the old man has become—or possibly has been for many years, probably since the First World War—a man without a faith, political or otherwise.

I think he is one of those, like my father (who would also be ninety-three were he alive), who failed to cross the barrier between the world before the First World War and the world after. In a sense this must have been one of the most sudden, sweeping, and startling changes in history. The roots of old Neilson's nagging dislike of Winston are deep in those years between 1906–10. It was then that Winston, an opportunist before all else, seeking political power for his own sake, first evoked great hopes in the liberals with his brilliant speeches on Land Values, and then, without a qualm or backward look, chucked all that overboard. I can imagine my father—in fact I do not have to imagine, for he shared some of Neilson's friendships with leading radicals of those days—feeling the same about Winston. I remember his disgust with W.'s behaviour at Sydney Street . . . He felt much the same about Percy Fender's[1] behaviour on the cricket field! Winston's brash behaviour, seeking the limelight, was extraordinarily offensive to these old strait-laced liberals, 'free-thinkers', the 'Humanists' of their time . . .

So I think I have a certain insight into that. Of course, Neilson dredges up all sorts of evidence to prove the obvious—we all know W. is an opportunist. We all know W. wanted power above all things. He wasn't the man L.G. was—at least, I don't think so, but is vastly more fascinating. L.G. had some principles, I would say, and strong ones. W. I doubt.

That phrase of mine 'Bogus maleness'. I agree it is one of those phrases, clear in the mind of the user, but needing careful thought and explanation. I think it is evident in the story told by Captain Haldane in regard to W.'s escape from Pretoria. (Not that old General Sir Aylmer Haldane would have said a bad word against W.) But W. lacked loyalty. He lacked patience. I do not mean to suggest for a moment anything to do with 'sex', as such. But W. seems to me to lack those male qualities of steadfastness, even of the right kind of ruthless-ness, of moral courage, which mark, say, a man like Auchinleck. Comparisons may or may not be odious, but they are rather impossible

[1] Percy Fender, Surrey and England cricketer, eccentric, often brilliant.

to avoid. Nevertheless Auchinleck is one example of my conception of a man, a man into whose hands thousands of ordinary men would put their lives, who would sleep happily in the gravest danger, never for a moment doubting that it would be over the Auk's dead body that harm would come. With W.—it would be astonishing if he were still there by morning! His aim was survival, at any cost. Not so a man. This does not suggest that he would ever be afraid, physically, but that his values, in my view, would not be consistent with honour in the extreme.

I think your strictly confidential information that physical danger gave him a 'thrill almost of a sexual nature', is a clue. It should not. In a sense that is a very feminine streak. Mel reads a very strong feminine streak into his nature, and she *likes* him. It is easy to understand that, whatever his faults—in this particular way I think I should say 'flaws' in character—Clementine Hosier should love him. Such men are adored, loyally, and forever by women. Furthermore, it is characteristic, in my understanding of W., that he would be absolutely loyal to his love. Perhaps the only true and absolute loyalty he would acknowledge. This would be his strength. It could be (but isn't) his weakness.

Another strange thing occurs to me: he was brought up—at least from adolescence, more by his mother than anyone else. But she does not seem to have been a stabilising influence, as was Auk's mother, for example. She does not seem to have impressed upon him the virtues of courtesy, of good manners, of loyalty. In short, two more different products of mother upbringing it would be hard to find . . . But I think W. always wanted to be a kind of d'Artagnan—if you ever go into the R.U.S.I. there is a large portrait in oils in the second floor hall of a bold and dashing Captain of Dragoons. It is the very 'image' of maleness—a certain Captain Innes. Such a man W. (in my reading of him) could never be. W. is always going to live to fight another day— at whatever cost to anybody—except himself. Not so, the Innes's, or the Captain Haldane's.

Churchill should have been surrounded by mastiffs to keep him— the terrier—from yapping too much. A terrier is not without virtue. You are a bit of a mastiff. The Auk was a mastiff (but not present), but Alan Brooke was not—he was too sensitive, too enclosed. A courageous man withal, yet not the man to keep W. at bay. Admittedly he did great service in keeping him at bay, at least partially, but at great cost to himself. The terrier nagged incessantly at his nerves, and he (Alan Brooke) lacked that inner calm of the spirit. And perhaps, it is that above all, that marks the complete man.

But what a task it is to try to discover the nature of W.'s greatness. I do not seek to prove anything, except to discover him, and thereby perhaps to bring some new light to bear on the tangle of these times, so much of which, I believe, derives from the legends and myths of the war years. Doubtless, the myths—or some of them—were necessary at the time, even if only for W.'s personal 'fortunes'—a soldier of fortune, if ever there was one! But now they stand between us and our proper place in the world—whatever that may be.

I thank you deeply for answering my questions on your own personal liking for W., and that of others. Clearly the man had a remarkable fascination, but far short of 'hypnotic', even in the manner of Hitler. Possibly one might call it an 'elusive' charm—such men are dangerous.

*   *   *

Meanwhile L.H. has sent me a mass of stuff on W. most of which he noted from time to time in the war years. It is astonishing how often it confirms much that you tell me. L.H. has a very fine mind, I think, and is as objective as a man might be. So with you both I am well armed against the Neilsons of this world. The old man appears to have turned into some sort of 'screwball' fascist, so pro-Boer and then anti-war as to turn himself inside out in the First and Second World Wars—of course it was all Britain's fault! Practically all Winston's! Fearful, but sad, rubbish. It is very difficult to stop the conveyor belt of history, and say, here at this point, but for this, thus—if that makes any sense.

L.H. (not to mention the O'G) still nags away a bit about W. and Bomber Harris. L.H. would also greatly appreciate knowing something more about your own distaste for Bomber Harris?

You were also going to tell me, I think, why W. feared Alexander?

A further point, which also interests me is expressed by L.H. as follows:

It seems astonishing that Winston did not realise until after Yalta that 'England and he had dropped to second place'. He had been extraordinarily slow in waking up to the consequences of all out victory over Germany, and the complete destruction of her defensive power, in clearing the way for Russian domination of Europe. I pointed that out very early in the war and so did L.G., I know. But Winston appeared impervious to such arguments, and the way he talked from the start was on the all out victory line regardless of the ultimate consequences.

That is why I am puzzled by M.'s remark that Winston never approved of 'Unconditional Surrender'.

But I have gone on and on. It is a great relief to me to write freely, but please only answer as the fancy takes you. Now, like Hamlet, I am alone. I think I shall go in search of some wild sanctuary and rest awhile.

I quite see about Neilson and am sure you are right. In this connection, you need to be a bit careful about Winston's crossing the floor in the early years of the century. As you know, he defends this himself in one of his own books—and he always so defended it orally—by pointing out that (a) it was not he who deserted one group of political thinkers for another, but they who in developing their theories moved away from him: also (b) an honest politician cannot bind himself to serve a group or party, if his own views change! (I don't know how (a) and (b) can be assimilated!) There is something in this, though one may wonder how much political honesty and opportunism were intermingled.

I did not know Winston in those days, but have heard him talk about them. It would be worse than dangerous to reject completely his point of view. Everyone's motives for doing anything are mixed, though one is naturally disinclined to stress the less creditable to oneself!!

In Winston's case, the matter was more embittered since I think it is probably true that neither the Tories nor Liberals had any *affection* for Winston in those days.

Your simile of Percy Fender is very apt. He brought 'professionalism' further into what was then considered to be a gentleman's game. But in the same way as W. his compeers did not think he acted like a gentleman. That is what keeps on cropping up in the case of W. His equals and competitors at all stages of his career wrinkled their noses at W. because he did not play the game according to the accepted, but unwritten, laws of the day.

It is not easy to compare W. and L.G. I myself would make W. the greater man. You would not. I did not know L.G. as I knew W., but I did know Guillam L.G. He *is* a gent and is therefore very reticent about his father whom he did not like at all. Not a question of politics either.

Of course L.G. was faced by a quite different situation in the 1914 war. His friends in politics and among the nation were few. His power correspondingly less. W. came to power with over ninety per cent of the people and nearly the same proportion of the elected politicians feeling 'here is the only man who may be able to save us'.

I knew Aylmer Haldane very well indeed and was even his A.D.C. for a while and afterwards a Staff Captain Artillery in his Division, the 3rd Div. in France. I can assure you that old Aylmer Haldane said all sorts of bad words about W. and the escape from Pretoria, when in his own circle.

I am still not very happy about your phrase 'bogus maleness', though I know such a phrase would not appear in your book. If you had written 'a bit of a bogus *gentleman*', I could have understood it better.

It would be quite wrong to write W. down without principles. In his private life he had and held firmly to the strongest principles in certain ways—courtesy, to his 'peers', but not to servants, manners, magnificence without showing off and all sorts of things. No swearing allowed! etc. To sum up, he 'performed' in the manner of a disciplined English gentleman of means of the early eighteenth century. His public life, on the other hand was in many ways different!!! In conducting himself as he did without variation in his *private* life, he must frequently have done violence to his own inclinations. The American half of him must have often wanted to rebel. Now, free of the necessity for restraint, the American half is enjoying itself with customary American vulgarity—Onassis and film stars.

This may be nonsense, but I think there is something in it.

One important thing in both private and public life is that he was never vindictive. He fought an enemy tooth and nail, when the enemy collapsed or surrendered, he *never* pursued him. And that was *not* from any base reason.

Winston had plenty of faults, but it would be worse than stupid to forget any good points, of which there were not a few.

With respect, I say that at the moment you are looking for the bad points. Necessary indeed, but do not get wholly carried away by them.

Speaking of L.H., you say he has a fine mind. I agree, and add: with great powers of expressing it.

My own distaste for Bomber Harris was—I think—(it is hard to be sure of one's own likes and dislikes) based on a personal distaste for what I thought, rightly or wrongly, of his personality. He seemed to me to be a bit of a boor (not bore) with little of any sort of fine thoughts or signs of anything distinguished in his mind or person. I am always attracted by anyone who seems to be, or to be trying to be, and behave like a gentleman in any way. I found nothing of this sort in Harris.

The idea of 'a gentleman' is as hard for me to define as it has been found hard by others, but I can say that I do not care whether a man is the son of a Duke or dustman, whether he was educated at Eton or Borstal. An Etonian Marquis may be a cad; the opposite sort may in my eyes be and behave like a great gentleman . . . It is a question of general conduct and behaviour. What one does and does *not* do, and how one does certain things. What one says, how one says it and what one does *not* say.

I am not condemning Harris absolutely. He did many great things doubtless. It is not easy (if possible) to become a Marshal of the Royal Air Force without doing many notable things well. But in my opinion, many of the things he did and said and did well, were done and said in a manner lacking refinement.

I agree heartily with L.H.'s para quoted by you, expressing astonishment at Winston's lack of recognition of the drop in England's power etc. It is abundantly true that he talked 'from the start' on the all out victory line regardless of consequences.

That is Winston's way, All or Nothing. Black or White. In anything he would always start that way, and often carry it through that way too; refusing to listen to caution or modifications. To a large extent he could only think of one great objective at a time. But when his objective was really in sight, and only then, he might begin to think of consequences less pleasant than the gaining of the end he had in view. In his experience that method of action paid dividends, because he was always supremely confident that after his object had been gained, he would be able to mend the eggs he had broken in cooking the omelette. That is of course opportunism, but rather an unusual and 'magnificent' variety. 'Magnificent' in the medieval sense of that word, derived from moral theology in Latin, and conveying a sense which the word has now lost and for which there is no single substitute in English of which I know.

As a side issue, magnificent—*magnalia faciendum*—means the doing of great things, independent of whether the things done are good or bad. 'She is a magnificent liar', would be immediately comprehensible in those terms, and not merely a modern colloquialism.

Despite all that many people—including myself—said to Winston about Russia and Communism, he would brush all that aside as being matters to attend to after the war was over. Russia was on our side in the war, therefore Russia must be regarded as White for the time being; nevertheless agreeing that Communism was Black as Hell.

His really great disturbance at the unexpected statement in public by the President about Unconditional Surrender, which I can guarantee was genuine, and not the result of later comment and thought, arose from a quality that I have mentioned above—namely his personal refusal to pursue a beaten enemy. At least that is my opinion. Also, I think he dimly saw at the time vague and troublesome visions of who was going to do what with Germany if there was no sort of Government left after the Surrender.

I can guarantee his main feelings against the declaration, since he told me of his dislike of it on the very evening of his return to England, when the Press and most of the public were excited and jubilant at the notion.

At the famous Press conference, he was completely taken aback when the President came out with the phrase in answer to a question by a pressman. True, that phrase had been used at dinner the night before, but in very free conversation and without thought. Nor had he then cavilled at it, never supposing it to have been said with all seriousness. Was it?

I think too, that even at the dinner he had mentally translated 'Unconditional Surrender' as 'Surrender on the Allied terms', which is of course quite a different thing in reality.

Up to that time he had refused to think about the terms which would be 'offered to' or 'imposed upon' Germany. He had refused in public and private to make any statement about this, save that his object was the defeat of the Nazis (Narsees) or of Germany. That was true in character. The defeat of the enemy and the following 'terms' of surrender were, to him, two different things. There would be time enough to think of the latter when the defeat was actually in sight.

Even if you are now 'Hamlet' for a while, I refuse to think of your wife as 'Ophelia'. It just does not fit.

From R. W. Thompson   5th September, 1960
I had a sudden last minute demand to review an important book. It is, in fact, one of the best to come out of the Second World War, *The Desert Generals* by Correlli Barnett.[1] I say this because Barnett is one of the new generation of historians, a mere twelve year old when these deeds were wrought. His insight into the minds and natures of his 'generals' is remarkable. He sets the desert record straight unequivocally, and I would say unanswerably. I had read carefully the papers of the divisional commanders, plus L.H.'s analyses a year or two back, and there was nothing new to me. But it was startling in treatment.

In an appendix Barnett sets down clearly the O'G story. It is absolutely ghastly. I do hope you see the book, for I am sure O'G can be forgiven almost anything.

You do me great service in compelling me to think about my 'rash' phrases. Bogus maleness, apart from a certain brashness and vulgarity—a feature of many Americans, whose words may live up to their deeds, but would be better without so many words, is, I think the survival of the *'puber'* in the adult. The desire to be a 'glittering hero'. This does not imply that the subject cannot be a 'glittering hero'. I should have said that strong elements of the adolescent have survived in Winston. He lacks steadfastness, I believe. He is, again I believe, predominantly for himself, and Devil take the hindmost.

I begin to feel very clearly that I understand the pattern of Winston's life: he was a soldier-adventurer-journalist from start to finish. The record from the Malakand Field Force onwards is exactly that of a 'freelance' correspondent-adventurer. Soldiering comes second to the 'story'. His forcing himself into Kitchener's entourage is pure foreign-

[1] Correlli Barnett, military historian.

correspondent stuff, also the Boer War. For the sake of the story he will put up with any insults.

Imagine yourself when young brazenly sitting at table with (or joining while riding) a very senior officer, three times your age, to whom you are fully aware you are anathema! I doubt whether any normal person can imagine themselves in such a position, yet Winston —and almost any American top-line reporter—did it without turning a hair. Lord Roberts would 'come round', so would Kitchener etc.

But the theme carries through. Antwerp, with W. leaving the Admiralty 'empty' while he dashes off to run the show, Zeebrugge, Gallipoli, and the final tremendous 'copy' of *The World Crisis*. Then in the doldrums between wars, the Marlborough job, early recollections, and finally the 'crown' of the reporter's dream: to make his own stories! If there isn't a battle make one, if there isn't news, make it, and so on. Hence from this angle, Norway, Greece, Singapore—never a dull moment, and the 'copy' piling up for the tremendous piece of journalism, serialised world wide, coming off the 'presses' from Timbuktu to Tokyo, and the 'Old Man' with a finger in every moment of it, cabling cuts, changes, subbing it even to the ultimate moment. I don't want to over-play it (and I won't). Winston has been many things—he's a many-sided man—but the theme of the super-journalist is constant and he runs true to form.

I am sure that your view of Winston's acceptance of Unconditional Surrender must be correct. He couldn't have thought it meant what it said. How should he? How should anyone? For it would make non-sense of war—as it did—and wash out all chance of peace—as it did. But why couldn't he have done something about it later? Even many Americans had become worried—even Ike. And if the Japanese had known they would keep their Emperor there would have been peace, no atom bombs.

I don't feel a bit like Hamlet any more, and I'm sure Aemilia is not Ophelia!

From Sir Desmond Morton   6th September, 1960
I feel quite sure that your summation of Winston's life and spirit as that of a 'freelance newspaper correspondent-adventurer' hits things off magnificently. I have never heard that said before by anyone, and I think you have really got something and somewhere. How you put that into print and descriptive ideas, I do not know. But I do feel that with that at the back of your mind you are as near understanding what made him tick as anyone has ever got. What is more, I think that some-how this can be got across without giving grave offence and without leaving any bad taste in the mouth. I think it is just a splendid founda-tion.

I certainly intend to read Correlli Barnett's book, of which I have only so far seen a number of reviews. Which and where is yours?

I will not prejudge the book, but my temporary summary of the reviews is that, on balance, the book will be a best-seller, but it is nevertheless an unfortunate product, in that the author, having hit on certain great truths, which greatly wanted putting into the light, has spoiled the whole effect through immaturity. How immensely right to aim at putting Auchinleck—and others—on to their own proper pedestals and doing something to right the great wrong that has been done them; how right and just too, to lower the absurd pillar of Simon Stilites upon which Monty has been placed, not without his own encouragement in the building. And, finally, not to have suspected that he had not got sufficient of the whole story, particularly the political end. Probably no one will ever get this last. By the time that the whole of the necessary documents are put into the public domain, years from the event, no one will be alive who has even heard a smattering of the truth from those who saw it happen.

Nevertheless, a more mature and experienced writer would have smelt the lacunae in his facts, even now. But I must read the book before I can be sure my criticism is justified.

If I am right, or indeed, whether I am right or not, I do pray you will not commit any similar errors. There is a world of difference between doing justice to those who had had injustice, and brutally denigrating others who have had more than justice. One can gently lower the pedestal of Monty, which is a fair thing to do, and one can even lower it very considerably, but one must not write so as to seem to be trying to blow up Monty's pedestal altogether. That is merely silly, and allows dirt to be thrown at the whole book.

Your own phrase, 'strong elements of the adolescent survived in Winston', is admirable, being not only perfectly true, but words, and an idea, to which no exception can be made. I would not call it in the least insulting, yet it accounts for much. Your ensemble in the story of Winston riding or talking with the very senior officer, is priceless, as is also the implication thereof.

Winston the super-journalist! Beautiful! Regard his *History of the English Speaking Peoples*. History—Pah! Journalism at its highest level.

Your idea in 1947 that the Soviet and the U.S.A. might link up, was not, to my mind, ridiculous. Look at the reception Winston's very reasonable and moderate speech received at Fulton. Actually however, I never did think they would link up even at the time, but I did think that the crass ignorance of the great American people and their politicians about international affairs, might lead to their taking up some queer and disastrous line, such as, 'This Communism business is only a Russian twirk, which need worry no one else, and after all, they (more than the British, whom we don't like any more than we used to), did a lot to help us win the war. And look how they have suffered more than anyone else and pa-ta-ti, pa-ta-ta.' Backing this would be all sorts of things not said, such as, 'What a chance for making huge profits selling this and that to rehabilitate that vast country' whereby their thoughts betrayed their utter ignorance of the economic nature of Communism as of its other shortcomings.

As regards why Winston did not take any later steps to 'do something about' the Unconditional Surrender nonsense. He did try. See what he said in the House.

From R. W. Thompson 7th September, 1960
All kinds of thoughts about Winston surge constantly in my head, as you would imagine, and I would like to write some of them down at random. Otherwise I am likely to overlook them when I come to answer your letters.

Before getting on to W. 'proper', I want to try to express a thought that was with me when I awoke this morning. You know that I have given a great deal of thought to the whole business of W.'s behaviour to the Auk, and his (as it seems) incredible attitude to the victory of 1st Alamein. This has puzzled many of us for years. L.H. analysed the whole thing from the private papers of all concerned, and I have seen nearly all the papers myself over the last two years. Nevertheless, it is outside my special sphere of military interest—or study—except as it concerns W. Besides, I knew about Correlli Barnett's book, and had discussed it fully with the principal characters involved. It is, in a real sense, tragic that Montgomery should have been built up, and have been himself such a willing party to the process, and to such ridiculous heights. Especially at the genuine expense of far greater and nobler men. However, I could never accept the usual explanation of W.'s behaviour, to wit: the unrest manifest in the Maldon By-election, the vote of censure and so on. My mind must have been chewing this over for a long time as 'second-class matter', and suddenly it seemed to me that the explanation of what is dastardly—even utterly irresponsible behaviour—lies in a far more serious matter at that time on W.'s mind. He was terribly anxious to get the U.S. Forces committed in the Atlantic Theatre. In the first year practically every man was going to the Pacific (not to mention landing craft!). The pressure to move to the Pacific as No. 1 priority was always strong, and often touch and go. At the same time there was the pressure from U.S. and Russia for a second front in Northern France in 1942, 1943. Since 1942 was (in my view) utterly impossible, and 1943 only marginally (again in my view) less so, what could Winston do? He must, I submit, get U.S. committed—and the only possible place is North or North-West Africa.

Here, at any rate, is a legitimate U.S. security sphere—Monroe Doctrine extension[1]—But if the victory is won in June–July 1942, and there is no future for Rommel, then what hope has Winston to persuade Marshall and Roosevelt to mount 'Gymnast' (Torch). On this basis, even his ambivalent—and disastrous—attitude to Tobruk makes sense. In short, he sacked the Auk, swept a great victory under the carpet of history (that it was a far greater victory than Montgomery's 2nd Alamein, is now proven), and laid on a victorious battle perfectly timed thirteen days before Torch, church bells 'n all.

Montgomery nearly mucked it—indeed he did muck it, for the Gatehouse papers,[2] plus, left no doubt of that.

But W. *did* get U.S. committed in the Atlantic theatre, and but for doing it then the Pacific might easily have won top priority. Does that make sense?

En route for Washington in the week after Pearl Harbour it is clear that Winston was worried in this sense, although his victories in the desert were still a year ahead or more. He expressed his anxiety and relief in the House later in the year. Higgins records: 'He (Winston) suffered keen anxiety lest his hopes and dreams of winning American support for his defensive type of operations in Europe and Africa be thwarted by an over enthusiastic American response to Hitler's Japanese diversion.'

With regard to W.'s influence, I believe it waned greatly, and by Autumn 1943 had become slight. (This is all argued in my book—but unhappily I did not know so much about it then as I do now.) The C.C.S., according to U.S. sources, 'was developed, under the acknowledged leadership of General Marshall, into an instrument, through which . . . Mr. Churchill was progressively removed from the direct and personal control of Anglo–American strategy in the West . . .'

I do not altogether agree with that statement. First, because I have a poor view of Marshall's ability as a 'grand' strategist, and secondly because I think it an over-statement to credit W. with being a virtual 'generalissimo'. You have given me a good deal of guidance on that point—I do think his bludgeoning and wearing down of anything less than dedicated opposition made him *almost* so—at times. Nevertheless, as you have said, he never actually went against the Chiefs of Staff.

Incidentally, I was shocked to read in the *Observer* review of

[1] Monroe Doctrine, introduced by the U.S. President Monroe in 1832. It arose out of the American fear of European intrusion into any part of the American continent, north and south, following the collapse of the Spanish Colonial power. In effect, it threw an American 'Cordon Sanitaire' around the entire American continent.

[2] The private papers of Major-General Gatehouse, prominent British Commander of Armour in the Western Desert, Second World War.

Barnett's book that Dill and Eden should take the blame for Greece. Eden, of course, but not Dill. And Winston, I believe, *must* take a lion's share of blame for that. It infuriated even the Greeks, one of whom in command was almost as broken-hearted as O'Connor that his great victory in the desert was thereby scotched.

Other points at random. It occurred to me how often W. was at the mercy of a phrase . . . as a writer might find certain phrases irresistible, and to be used even if the facts had to be fitted to them. Thus I wonder, whether Jackie Fisher's words—'Alexandria is the key to Islam, and Islam is the key to the British Empire'—would be the kind of 'music' to reverberate in W.'s head through the years. Especially as he was much younger and impressionable in his time with Fisher. Thus he would clothe the Middle East in a false garment of glamour.

Earlier, of course, there was Clemenceau's 'We shall fight before Paris, we shall fight in the streets etc. etc.'

And do you remember the piece re. Gallipoli where Enver Pasha says to Morgenthau that he is sure that the Gallipoli job (1915) is a personal answer to him? He had discussed Britain's role in regard to sea and land power with W. a year or two earlier. Winston is the kind of chap who would not be above fighting a private war in the midst of a public one.

But extraordinary how many people seem to have captured aspects of Winston in phrases. Harold Begbie, for example: 'Churchill carries great guns, but his navigation is uncertain.' or D.L.G. (many times): 'Winston has half a dozen solutions to it and one of them is right, but the trouble is he does not know which it is.'

And F. S. Oliver in a more general way: 'The defect of brilliant brains is not necessarily want of courage—daring there usually has been in plenty—but they are apt to lack fortitude. They are apt to abandon the assault upon positions which are not really invulnerable, and go off, chasing after attractive butterflies, until they fall into quagmires.'

Points on which, if you have time, I would greatly like a word, are:

1. Winston's attempts at 'collusion' with Vichy behind de Gaulle's back, mainly in regard to French North Africa.
2. His attitude to Spain in the Civil War and after. (I would have been on that Grand Canary job if it had happened!)
3. Americans say that W. became P.M. in place of Chamberlain largely because of his hoped for influence with the U.S. Is this true—or partly true? And if so, who were leading figures in that attitude? And, of course, above all I should like to try to get clear in my head what actually happened, the actual assumption of power, when he first knew and how.

I hope all this doesn't bother you too much.

From R. W. Thompson   8th September, 1960

Your reaction to my growing ideas about Winston delights me. An important factor is that once one begins to regard Winston in that light much that he did becomes, not only understandable, but even 'endearing' (that is not quite the word I wanted).

You know, the more I read the more I wonder whether the actions of great men can be attributed to the wise—or even reasonable—motives for which historians (naturally) seek. Immense ability allied with great power and position does not basically change the natures of men. They remain children of their emotions, their conditioning, their particular milieu—which may have standards totally different from those of the seeking historian. Besides, when one is in the midst of the turmoil of affairs a number of factors, obvious later, may be quite obscure, even unknown at the time. One can—and must—forgive almost any course of action which is honest, and not stupid. One cannot —or should not forgive (I mean as an historian)—dishonesty and malice.

I am about to begin with that (as I see it) 'Crucial Year' of 1894. Winston is twenty. Willy is writing his naive, even pitiful (at this distance) letters to Nicky.[1] The wolves are tearing at the great amorphous carcase of China. Nicky is getting his trans-Arctic railway. Japan, Korea; Germany, Kiachow; Russia, Port Arthur; and Britain (not to be outdone!) grabs Wei Hai Wei.

Winston is concerned almost wholly with polo, the beginnings of his 'education' (at Bangalore), his journalism. He appears to be totally unaware of the powder keg the world has suddenly become. As for Hitler, he is five, a desperate unhappy child, Roosevelt a twelve-year-old schoolboy with a background of ease and certainty, more of an aristocrat in his setting, I would say, than Winston in his. I always have a sense of the 'poor relation' about Winston, and aware of it. Lord Randolph not really being of a fibre to match W. or his mother, these two, mother and son, a couple (almost) of 'outsiders'—the old Duchess thinks so. These two against the world: 'we'll show 'em!'

(But I digress!) Stalin, that dark Georgian, even then at fifteen probably knowing more about the 'dark side of the world' than the others—even Adolf—would ever dream on.

At any rate, that's where I set my stage. In twenty years all that world is gone. There is no room in the ruins and what emerges from the Morley's, Rosebery's—even Kitchener's, Fisher's—this is a new world, and Winston is on 'Tom Tiddler's ground'. I remember a phrase of his I read years ago—I can't think where—on Merchant adventurers,

[1] Willy-Nicky; Kaiser Wilhelm the Second, German Emperor, and Nicholas, Czar of Russia. Their 'secret' correspondence before the First World War was known as the 'Willy-Nicky' letters.

circa 1906: 'This money gathering, credit producing animal can not only walk—he can run. And when frightened he can fly. If his wings are clipped he can dive or crawl.'

And so can Winston! So did he, magnificently (for, as you pointed out, magnificent may be so applied).

. . . I hope and believe that you will emend your views on Barnett . . .

From Sir Desmond Morton   11th September, 1960
Have been in Oxford for two days . . . Two letters from you. That dated 7th, which crossed mine; and that dated 8th which showed you had received my last. The first produced a raft of questions.

. . . Your long and brilliantly subtle analysis of W.'s behaviour to the Auch etc. etc. suggesting that W. did what he did, and more, consciously to get America committed to the West, rather than to the Pacific—won't do for me at all, I fear. No living human being, before the events, could have possibly thought out such a Machiavellian arrangement. Moreover W.'s mind did not work in the least in that immensely tortuous way.

You must simplify your ideas of W. You produce that most admirable statement in your letter of 8th when you wonder if great men were moved by the wise or even reasonable motives which historians seek; and that immense ability allied with great positional power do not basically change the character of a man. That whole paragraph is not only eternal truth but great writing. For goodness sake preserve it and use it.

Then apply it to W.

Of course not only W. but any informed observer on the inside could see after Dunkirk that the only hope of a satisfactory outcome of the war would be the practical intervention of America, and all obvious things were done to that end. But one idea at a time. The idea that America when she did eventually come in, after Pearl Harbour, would want—again for the most obvious reasons—to concentrate her energies on the Far East, was equally obvious and stated openly in secret conversations. The business of weaning America from that idea to the exclusion of all others then came to the front, but was dealt with without any sort of Machiavellian subtleties. Ambassadors, Chiefs of Staff and others all played their allotted part in this, not only W.

Bottom of page. Higgins' '. . . anxiety lest his hopes of winning American support for his *defensive* type of operations in Europe . . .' is entirely vitiated by the insertion of the adjective 'defensive'. I cannot imagine any moment when Winston had any notion of promoting a defensive idea. His whole idea everywhere and at all times was 'Attack, attack, attack', combined with a cloudy idea, which became clear in the event, that any general who *did* attack and not win a smashing victory was no use and must go.

I agree very much with your second point. Most certainly you will be wrong to credit W. with being a virtual generalissimo. You are right in saying that he may superficially appear to have acted as such at times. But he knew too well that his whole position was at stake, if he went dead against the clear and united opposition of his own Chiefs of Staff. There were occasions when he tried very hard to do so; but though his fury at being unable to do so was that of a lion baulked of his prey, he was equally magnificent in that the said fury, which might last for two days, would suddenly disappear overnight, and he would then back the Chiefs to the limit, even though it was dead against what he had wanted originally to do. Mind you! He *never* admitted he was *wrong* in the first place.

Schoolboy! Head of the School and Captain of the First Eleven. That is your clue all along.

Again how good to say that Winston was at the mercy of a phrase. But, mark you, the phrase must always be his own. If it was not his own, and it attracted him he would make it his own, to an unbelievable and laughable extent. The *sort* of phrase which fired him was *not* Jackie Fisher's as quoted by you, and anyway anything Jackie Fisher had said, would be unlikely to appeal as he had written J. Fisher off. But Clemenceau's phrase which you quote also, about fighting before Paris, fighting in the *faubourgs*, etc. THAT would appeal, and would become his own, as it did.

I disagree with Enver. Winston was never capable of fighting a private war in the midst of a public one, *in which he was a major actor*. He would certainly fight a private war if he was *not* a major actor. But he was a man of quite simple ideas, one of which would move him to the exclusion of all others; one at a time. Sometimes, however, quite a different idea would suddenly become the ruling force.

David L.G.'s remark *was* brilliantly true at one time and always carries much force.

F. S. Oliver's (what a brilliant man!) remark does *not* apply to Winston, save when he was frustrated in the 'Great Idea' of the moment. His trouble was more often that he would *not* abandon a genuinely invulnerable position.

Your points 1., 2., and 3.:

1. Vichy (a) He never liked de Gaulle. Those two wildly differing personalities were never likely to see eye to eye.

(b) The President disliked de Gaulle, partly because he was written down as a 'British Discovery'. W. never liked to go dead against the President. But he *did* get an agreement with R. to the effect that Britain would look after de G. while the President looked after Vichy.

This could not be a hundred per cent arrangement. This is all a very long story, which cannot be stated without an essay.

(c) It was wise to have a foot in both camps, in case Vichy was to be the French accepted post-war Government. The same applies vice versa to R.

2. Spain. In the civil war he backed Franco, because (a) W. is a Tory in regard to methods of forming a Government, though not a Tory in regard to what the formed Government then proceeds to do!! (b) He thought Franco was going to win. (Quite simple ideas, you note). After the Civil War (I am not sure to which period you refer but anyhow W. was not going to see Spain become a second Hitler's country) and during *our* war, his one idea was to win *our* war.

3. W.'s replacement of Chamberlain had absolutely nothing to do with any sort of possible influence he might have on the U.S.A. It is fantastic nonsense. No one from the King through both Houses of Parliament and down to the most ignorant voter or even the daily Press, which I regard as lower than the last, ever dreamed of such an element in the matter of Chamberlain's successor, after his moral defeat in the House.

Briefly, most of the Tories would not willingly serve under anyone but W. The Labour Party refused to form a coalition with anyone but W. There were only two conceivable choices, Lord Halifax and W. Some Tories would have preferred Halifax but gave way—as they had to—when the facts emerged, as above, as they did within a hectic thirty-six hours.

Sometime I can expand all this to you orally; but I do not fully understand what you want to know, as all that matters has already been published.

Many thanks for letting me see L.H.'s notes, herewith returned. Look at the admirably restrained and simple phraseology that fine writer uses even in his notes . . .

From R. W. Thompson   14th September, 1960

My gratitude for standing up to such a bombardment . . .

I will 'simplify' my ideas of W. Indeed, I do so more and more. One searched (as I wrote before) for subtle, profound, important reasons for this or that event only to feel drawn to some quirk of someone. Do you remember the disaster of the leading brigade at Gallipoli pausing 500 yards from the summit of the hill for tea? By the time tea was over the 'summit bristled with Turkish rifles'. But for the 'tea' Gallipoli might—indeed, some very balanced historians say 'would'—have succeeded. The Russian revolution averted; world history changed. All for a cup of tea!

As to the U.S. Higgins' statements about Winston's 'defensive' desires, I agree absolutely with you. Even now the Americans are arguing that only Winston stood between them and their second front in North-West Europe in 1942/43. They never produce any (to me) even remotely convincing arguments. But there is no need for me to write a letter about this, since I have already written a book[1] about it which, I hope, will be in your hands in a day or two. I understand it is being referred to as 'extremely provocative'. This I do not understand. It is simply the thinking of one person, in Belchamp Walter, applied to the problems of the second front.

Of course, Enver Pasha was quite wrong. Gallipoli was an obvious must, and it is wrong that Winston should be blamed, whatever Australian historians may say. You can't blame a man for having the right ideas simply because others fail completely to do the 'staff' work necessary to carrying them out. But this is where I begin to come to grips with the whole fearful problem of 'Power'—how it is that the Winstons of this world can bend men so to their will as to impose ideas upon them against all judgment. Power—the magnetism, the astounding confidence, of these beings (as you have pointed out)—is at the heart of the matter.

Many thanks for your remarks about Vichy. I have just read with my scalp tingling (the hair refuses to stand on end at anything any more) Irwin's[2] account of Dakar in this quarter's R.U.S.I. (There is also a review of the H.M.S.O. Middle East book of Playfair's worth reading.)

Finally, as to Chamberlain's replacement, I imagine Leo Amery is as good a guide as one could hope for. It all reads and sounds completely true.

I now approach warily the first of 1,000 blank pages, all of which must be filled this winter. A sculptor facing a chunk of stone must wonder whether the figure of fact and fancy will ever emerge. But his stone is somehow more tangible than my blank paper: not too hard to imagine the figure in the stone—but the paper—the pencil. It will all depend on whether or not I am blessed with imaginative insight. I pray for it.

Meanwhile, I hope you will tell me if my *The Price of Victory* is all wrong, or simply silly. It cost a great deal of labour.

And now, surrounded by some seventy works of reference, and pages of notes, I confront my task. I will cling firmly to my conception of Winston and pray for guidance. Your letters, more than any other factor, will help to keep me on the rails.

[1] *The Price of Victory.*
[2] Anthony Irwin, author of article 'Defeat before Dakar', R.U.S.I. Journal, August 1960. Major-General N. M. S. Irwin commanded military force.

So far I have seen of Pug Ismay's book only those extracts which have been and are being published in the *Daily Telegraph*. I am sure, however, you should read that book. Pug adores Winston and in Pug's eyes Winston can do no wrong. Nevertheless any little stories told by Pug about Winston are absolutely true, and deserve the deepest consideration by anyone writing about Winston's character. You will probably get from Pug a picture of the very best side of Winston's character. Having heard and observed, from others matters relating to not so pleasant a side, you may be disinclined to accept the former. You would be wrong. *That* is the enormous difficulty in assessing Winston. But, if you disregard that side, do not refer to it, or fail to assimilate in one picture his many-sided personality, you will be lost.

Agreed, that there cannot be any over-simplification here! What you have to do is to simplify as far as you can, the most complicated thing there ever was. That may be an exaggerated statement; but I myself have never known nor conceived such a mass of contradictions as Winston.

I am greatly looking forward to reading your book [which is] about to appear. I will certainly tell you quite honestly what I think of *The Price of Victory*. If it is 'provocative', provocative of what? Thought, Rage, Sleep? Mr. K. announces as provocative any statement other than, 'Great is Marxism-Leninism and the U.S.S.R., so ably represented by Comrade Krushchev!'

Your reference to the Press, in answer to mine, and your admirable story of the 'Cup of tea which changed history', which I had of course heard about, allows me to preach another little Caudle lecture.

Were one writing really great history on Gallipoli, one would certainly move heaven and earth to find out the real truth of that 'tea' story. The tale can be told in two entirely different ways. Accepting the rough outline as sufficiently correct, one could write a blazing and blasting journalistic article (high class too) under the title given above, 'The Cup of Tea which changed History', but if one were aiming at being a historian and telling the truth as far as possible, one would search and search for it here. Why? Because it is in truth utterly inconceivable that a battalion or brigade in action should stop for any sort of meal within 500 yards on the wrong side of a crest in hostile territory. It is as ridiculous a suggestion as that a bricklayer should begin building a wall and forget to insert mortar between the bricks. That is, if you accept a *simple* version of the tale. Obviously there must be other factors, neglected in the telling of the 'Good Story'; factors which do away with the good story as such, but which probably explain the otherwise inexplicable. Some appalling error there almost certainly was, but not a simple lunacy.

The Press (in the abstract) would be delighted with the simple and erroneous (or incomplete) story, but a historian must not be like that.

There is probably truth in what you now suggest may have been a cause of the American coldness toward your book.

Your remarks about how certain very powerful personalities can bend men so to their will as to impose ideas upon them against all judgment—are very pertinent, and 'provocative' *of thought*. It has struck me that a relevant thought is that no real issue seems, at the time a decision has to be made, a simple alternative; an either—or. By 'real' issue, I mean any highly important matter; while please note carefully, my insertion, 'at the time a decision has to be made'. Of proverbs, 'It is easy to be wise after the event', is truer than most; though it is not *always* easy to be wise even then. Often it is quite *im*possible to trace out why someone proposed, others agreed and so it was decided to take certain action or refrain from it. Yet the historian has to do nothing less than that.

Incidentally in this matter and as regards Winston, you must be most careful to justify any suggestion that Winston '*imposed his will on anyone against all judgment*', taking these words literally; recalling that the judgment must apply to what was known and believed by all concerned *at the time* of the allegation. The words mean that everyone concerned agreed with Winston *at the time*. I might make you a bet that if you give me an instance where you allege that Winston *imposed* his will (by implication therefore the others were of a different opinion) 'against all reason' (by implication therefore some of the others originally had a reasonable view, which they either abandoned or suppressed in favour of what appeared to them *at the time* to be a wholly *un*reasonable view) I would guarantee to shoot your instance full of holes.

Of course a historian writing later than the event described may demonstrate how much better it can *now* be seen that some other course would have succeeded in all probability than that chosen at the time. But in no circumstances can he criticise the actors for reaching the conclusions they did *at the time*, unless he can demonstrate that they disregarded facts known to them, acted with duplicity or malice or were demonstrably unfit for the positions they held.

However, down now to the pile-driving for a secure foundation of the structure.

P.S. Democracy judges *solely* by results. Historians must *never* do so.
P.P.S. Don't bother to answer this for the sake of answering only!

From R. W. Thompson   19th September, 1960
Your understanding P.P.S. notwithstanding, your letter underlines certain points of great value. I agree with you about Ismay's book. It

is clearly the work of an honest man whose boyish 'hero worship' of Winston has never waned nor faltered. I regard this as a lovable trait in a man's character. I shall certainly read Ismay with care (for anyone who imagines research is all excitement and joy is a fool). Besides, the last thing I would want would be to produce a 'boss-eyed' picture of Winston. He sparkles on all sides like an elaborately cut diamond, but the real flaws—whosoever is without sin . . .

As to powerful personalities imposing their wills—or *seeming* to impose their wills—I think one has to bear in mind that one man, the powerful man, has the initiative; he is running the show, and naturally ideas and decisions must stem from him, or they might not stem at all from anyone. Thus he, the powerful one, is not only many times more liable to error than his subordinates, but also, inevitably, the apparent architect of many wrong decisions. All this, not least due to your guidance, I seek to keep constantly in mind. It is not my purpose to plug a line for this Winston or that image in the public mind, but inasmuch as I am blessed with imaginative insight, to attempt to create a portrait of the real man. I shall only know what I have done when I have done it!

From Sir Desmond Morton   1st October, 1960
There is a most arresting statement by Bill Slim, who is a wise old bird and who always presents himself as a simple soldier, the adjective being wrong, in a commentary on Pug Ismay's book. It is that in all the exchanges and debates between the Americans, the British and the Russians on the strategy to be pursued in the last war, it is clear that the Americans never gained *all* they wanted, the British *usually* got a *part* of what they wanted and the Russians *always* got *exactly* what they wanted.

This is a very great text for thought, and I commend it to you in its application on any further books you may write either on the war itself or how Winston ticked.

Hidden in that is the greatest mistake that Winston made *during* the last war. Hidden in this last is probably all the important facets of Winston's character. No very brief statement can contain the precise description of his mistake, which was not a single act, but an attitude. The cause of the attitude would contain or, better, be derived from, some of the chief components of his character.

You have probably seen something of this already in your thoughts. To give this due weight in exactly the right wording is anything but easy.

Meanwhile, I recall your writing to me once of your correct and deep interest in the *real* Churchill–Roosevelt relations. I suggest that you should never forget that these cannot be isolated from Churchill–

Stalin and the Roosevelt–Stalin relations. There is therefore not only a triple thought here, but a sextuple thought, of which the only absolutely *post facto* conclusion (which to anyone who understands what Stalinism means need not be *post facto*) is the aims and objects of Stalin. Until the war was over and Winston was out of power, he never would grasp the truth about Stalinism and about its inventor. By the time of the Fulton speech he had begun to do so. Why was this? As for Roosevelt *he* never began to understand the business up to the day of his death. Why was this?

In my view the easiest way to unravel all this is to begin with Stalin, not with Winston nor Roosevelt. This means explaining Stalinism, the heir of which is Krushchev, no matter that certain facts, important in themselves, have caused superficial changes in the interpretation and practice. The ideology, the basic facts of the 'Faith' have not changed one iota. The world is only beginning to see this.

Papers my party wrote in 1920 are as valid today as they were then, when no one really believed them.

What anyone does about it all depends on time and circumstance. But no one will do anything effective until they first understand and believe what Communism *is*, based on Lenin (Marx is really unnecessary), later on Stalin and now on Krushchev.

It almost requires something like religious meditation in order to comprehend the mind of any person with or without power—(the acquisition of power allowing that person's mind to find expression in acts comes later)—who really and truly has not only put aside, but has actually lost the ability to view *anything* with a background of what *we call* truth.

At first people like you and I, both of whom have some sort of imagination, find it impossible to accept that the individual we are considering, who, in the hearing of hundreds of persons and as reported in the Press which he controls, says, 'The moon is now proved to be made of green cheese', and a week later, in similar circumstances says, 'It is now proved that the moon is *not* made of green cheese', really believes that he was telling the truth (as he defines truth) on both occasions.

He does not, of course, believe that both statements are true in any sense of that word, at one and the same time; but he *does* really so interpret truth that he can say and believe truly that both statements were true when he made them, and that the only one which is *now* true, is the last one he has made.

Actually it is a perfectly logical system of thought, if you cast aside any idea that there can be an absolute truth. In fact, I go so far as to say that it is the only logical system of thought, if you do cast aside the idea of there being any possibility of absolute truth existing.

Surely it is clear that with anyone who thinks and acts like this, no sort of promise is binding. The only controlling motive is expediency; and expediency for the furthering of his own aims and objects. If his aims and objects can be ascertained, and they are quite easy to ascertain, you know what he will do next.

The aims and objectives of Soviet Communism . . . are simply that, as soon as possible, by all and any means, which will not *ipso facto* risk the military or economic defeat of the U.S.S.R., to destroy all Government and all Authority in the world which is not based on Soviet Communism, and to substitute centralised control from Moscow for whatever form of Government or Authority exists at the moment.

No sort of accident or circumstance can change this single aim and object.

In the attainment of this aim, anything is permissible, with the one qualification mentioned above, that is, that the physical integrity of the U.S.S.R. shall not be seriously risked.

Start from there and think of the effect on the mind of a non-Communist statesman or politician, who is accustomed to bow frequently to expediency, but in greater or lesser degree retains some moral standards based on absolute truth. To begin with, whatever you say to him, he really cannot believe in the existence of a system completely without *any* basis of absolute truth. At best, he assumed that 'these people', the Communist Government à la Moscow, are really only newcomers to the game, who will sooner or later find that you cannot, for instance, deceive all the people all the time. 'We shall sooner or later find out what are the basic standards of behaviour to which he might adhere, if his people are not to rise in their wrath and throw him out.' THAT is their dreadful mistake. They cannot understand that for the first time in the known history of the world, there has arisen a philosophy or way of thought, which permits the hitherto impossible to become possible; and we now know it has become actual. It has only become possible because, were it not possible, Soviet Communism could not continue to exist.

Our non-Communist politician meets the Communist politician and finds the latter using language (perhaps in a different tongue) apparently conveying political ideas which seem to be basically his own. He may not wholly agree with those ideas, but they are couched in a political langauge he readily understands. He says to himself, 'All these people who tell me that Communism is something different, are wrong. It is only, at worst, an exaggeration of my own attitude' (though not necessarily my point of view on detail).

The non-Communist politician agrees with the Communist politician over something, admitting that the something suits the Communist as well as (or better than) it suits him. Later he finds the

Communist declaring that he never agreed on this point, and is puzzled and rather angry, but starts all over again.

And so it goes on and will go on, until the non-Communist politicians really understand the nature, the aims and objectives of Communism.

Most of them, I am afraid all of them, still fail to comprehend the very foundations of the Thing with which they are negotiating.

From R. W. Thompson 4th October, 1960

But this kind of thing won't do! I have read very carefully your remarks upon the nature of the Soviet Beast. But for small points of emphasis they accord with my own conclusions (thus far: for I am not at the end of my concluding!). I am studying, from the slender resources available, the Churchill–Roosevelt–Stalin relationships. Like you, I find it difficult to grasp that Roosevelt's ignorance on these things appears to have been total. As for Winston, I am in a sense even more astonished, not because he failed (until Fulton, as you point out) to add up the score, imagining, I assume that the Russian Revolution had been a kind of Cavalier–Roundhead show, which would suit his imagination; but that he should have failed to realise fully the natural strategic aims of *Russia*—not U.S.S.R., but 'Mother Russia', that old Russia. As Toynbee[1] has pointed out, she was bound to go for as wide a buffer holding as she could get against '400 years of Western aggression'. Communism, of course, must lap up the same territory for those reasons, *plus*—an enormous plus.

It seems to me that until Western politicians appreciate the aims and objects of U.S.S.R., add up the factors for and against like soldiers, and agree on exactly what are their own aims, and how to carry them out, we shall remain on the brink until the moment when we go into it. Disarmament, and all that kind of thing will follow—not *precede*—a clear pursuit of 'Objects'—or if it doesn't, the answer is simply that there is no co-existence in this world between the two sides. For my part, I believe that if Winston had lacked his overpowering obsession with 'the English speaking peoples', we might well have had three worlds instead of two. I am, as I have said in my book, a European. I believe we could have provided the cement, the drive, the purpose from which a coherent Europe might have arisen. With its diverse peoples, its acute ranges of intelligence and culture, its resources, its innumerable peoples, it could have compelled—by virtue of its being—the two sides to back away from each other. The centre of gravity is in the middle. Now there is no middle.

And all this tragedy, as I see it, stemmed from Teheran—as much as any such scale of tragedy can stem from a clear source.

[1] Arnold Toynbee, historian.

Reading 'Gallipoli' (several versions) these last weeks I jotted down some personal thoughts relevant to my conception of Winston as a 'super-journalist'. As a war correspondent myself I had realised the unbridgeable gulf between the 'observer' and the truly 'involved' or committed: between the men on the shores of Gallipoli; the men in the ships; the men at home—and Churchill. The journalist does not and cannot share in the pangs of life and death he observes and writes about. His escape route is open. He is like a bee buzzing from flower to flower. And so it is with Churchill. His involvement is never with anything but himself; the Play's the thing! And he is both audience and recorder—even instigator.

Europe was Winston's continent. There lay his role. Without his American obsessions, which were in the blood, he might have been one of the greatest Europeans of all time. His blood split him, and it was too much. It enlarged his horizons beyond the reasonable bounds of his intellect and of his imagination. Yet, without the blood of the Jeromes, he might well have been simply an 'ordinary' man, leaving not even a faint pencilling upon his times.

From Sir Desmond Morton   4th October, 1960
I am so glad that your connecting Jack Dill with 'dead wood' was an unfortunate accident. There was nothing wrong with his health which was not the effect of trying to deal with Winston, though it is true that, later, his health did give way and he died.

It is deeply interesting to learn that what you said about Freddie Morgan was from subconscious deduction and not through direct connection with him. You must have been *en rapport* with him, I think.

★   ★   ★

Communism, Russia, Winston etc. Nor can I believe that he had forgotten the 'Czarist' expansionist policies. But I think—I certainly do not know—first that his entire concentration on winning the war, 'I would make an ally of the Devil, if he was fighting against Hitler', blinded him to post-war consequences. That fits in too with his 'I know that so and so is all wrong, but remember I shall be Prime Minister after the war, and I shall then set it right.'

Secondly, I do not think he realised until after his fall from power that Stalin was in effect a reincarnation of all the worst Czars (and the cunningest) rolled into one, or that the U.S.S.R. would so rapidly achieve such economic pre-eminence. Steel, iron, coal, science, oil etc. as well as skill and atom bombs. At that date was it not thought 'We the Allies have the atom bomb, Russia has not. That gives us plenty of time.'

Of course, none of the great Western politicians—or other, saw the great *attraction* of Communism, if the subject is not greatly attracted to any other rule of life.

How greatly I agree with your view that until Western politicians determine clearly what are their own aims, we are like an unorganised, but fairly good-willed mob milling about and wondering what to do next when rumours are circulated of an impending descent onto the Earth of inhabitants from Mars.' No one tells the mob what the Martians are like or may be expected to do, only newspapers imply all sorts of things, while no one (by which I mean no one in accepted Authority) tells us either what to do or WHY we should do it. The last is as important as anything else.

I appreciate your comments arising out of Gallipoli and Europe etc. about Winston and the comparison with a journalist.

From R. W. Thompson   6th October, 1960
Thanks for your additional comments on Winston and Russia. Winston seems to have seen everything and everybody from early childhood solely in relationship to himself—including the world—and never his relationship to anybody or thing, including the world. When, for example, as a young man he is clearly intolerable to Kitchener, Roberts, Rosebery and others, it only occurs to him that 'they' will come round in time. After all, *he* is Winston! Well, it must be a happy position in some ways. His son Randolph has it, but without the great talents of his father.

From R. W. Thompson   23rd October, 1960
Winston has never ceased to hubble-bubble in my thoughts, and on a dozen occasions I have rushed to my desk to fill odd sheets, even the backs of envelopes, with 'thoughts which must be imprisoned'. But incoherent, fitting as yet into no pattern. I perceived, suddenly, (it must seem to you that a man might as well write that he perceived—suddenly —the shining sun) the Industrial Revolution. Why a Revolution? Because, of course, it was no less. This must have been the great upsurge, against the facts of which even the thinkers and philosophers turned their minds (save Marx and Engels who saw and did not see, and added it up so cleverly and wrongly and dangerously). But what did Rosebery, Morley, Lord Randolph—and finally Winston—really understand about such a Revolution, seething beneath the surface of the world they knew? That is the question. It seems to me that Winston continued to think in terms of the 18th century until the end. But it was a *Revolution*. On this I ponder as 'Willy-Nicky' and all the rest thrash about in the last days of their power. The new power is arising, not only Industrial power which Lloyd George (and you) understood so well, but a new social power which would engulf Russia, finally China,

and prove remarkably indigestible elsewhere. There are many factors I must attempt to 'see' and to add up.

Tomorrow I swear to hammer the first 10,000 words of Winston into lucidity—not the whole 10,000! Thenceforth day after day until the end.

Do you remember telling us about Jerome, and the book Winston chuckled over? There was a book on the market here—Leonard Jerome, but this, I think, is not the one to which you referred. A sight of the one you mentioned would be invaluable to me, if that is possible. I begin to see the climax of my book as the Autumn of 1942. That is the moment, in my view, when Nazi Germany has lost the war. It was up to us then to plan for the 'kind' of victory essential for the future, for a world, based not on eighteenth or nineteenth century realities, not least the still very much with us 'Industrial Revolution', only 'stirring' in China, a colossal driving force in Soviet Russia, soon to be again in Germany, a new world, but a world to 'live in' as well as to die in. Instead 'Unconditional Surrender'! That, as I see it, is the crucial moment, the end of 'foreign policy' of 'defence policy'—of all that has made sense, and must make sense again—or else!

From Sir Desmond Morton   30th October, 1960
Our last letters crossed and I hope that our 'rapport' is not so strong that it happens regularly since it breeds confusion.

Yours dated 23rd arrived on Monday last, but I have not had a moment to write since then, having been on the go from seven a.m. until dinner time or later every day since.

Your letter tells me much that I wanted to know, but I am still more than hazy as to what sort of shape it (the Winston book) will take or even what is the general idea. Hazy, not wholly without some sort of vague notion. But I am puzzled by your two relevant queries in your present letter. The Industrial Revolution and the history of Winston's mother's father. As regards the latter, I have searched everywhere for the book of which I made some mention to you, but cannot find it. But, beyond the obvious generalisations which are known, I do not see how this affects seriously anything you propose to write about Winston.

It is the same with the Industrial Revolution, only more so. What are you after? Your query as it stands—'What did Rosebery, Morley, Lord Randolph—and finally Winston—really understand about such a Revolution seething beneath the surface of the world they knew?'

The answer is undoubtedly, a very great deal, each in his own way and time. But none of them were prophets; while all of them were politicians having to deal first with the *world they knew*, as it was at the moment and likely to be, by reason and deduction, in the near future.

I suggest you are somehow mixing up in your mind, the Industrial Revolution and the consequences of the way it was handled. Per se, the Industrial Revolution need have had nothing to do with Communism or the growth thereof.

First, 'the Industrial Revolution', as I have always understood that term, did not take place in a few weeks, but over a period of years. It is the name given to the change in the economy of England (first) and later to other countries, from the more or less agricultural economy to an almost complete (in England) industrialisation, in the sense of manufacture, particularly in iron, steel, metals and machines.

The cause was the discovery of the industrial power of steam, the British possession of coal, the Bessemer process of producing steel, whence railways, machines, and an industry of manufacture succeeding an Industry based on sheep and other farming, with light industries, such as woollen and cotton (imported) cloths of all kinds etc. based on hand labour and largely wooden machinery. It started at the end of the eighteenth century, was in full blast by say the beginning of Victoria's reign and had 'boiled over' before the end.

To understand it, you have to consider foreign trade too. The victory over Napoleon and the Battles of Trafalgar and Waterloo, presented England with practically unlimited (at that date and for long after) foreign trade, exporting machinery and machine made goods for war materials and luxuries.

With all this Socialism had nothing to do *directly*. It was the selfishness of the new aristocratic class—the millionaires and rich men made by the Revolution, which included many real aristocrats as well as the new rich middle class—their selfishness towards their workers in the factories and mines etc, which produced Socialism.

To suggest that Rosebery, Morley and others knew nothing about this, or even to suggest that they and their colleagues did not try to do anything about it, is out of sense.

Another factor producing Socialism was education of the masses. Yet another failure of industrialists and politicians to listen to advice from thinking men; but politicians have been like that since the world of politics started.

As you are presumably not going to write an Economic or Social History of England, I will desist. But I do not see what all this has got to do *particularly* with Winston.

In the *Observer* today there is a very interesting 'Profile' of the present Randolph Churchill. If you read that and first consider that the character depicted—that of Randolph—is precisely the natural character of his father Winston, you will start well. If you then discover why how and why Winston succeeded, when Randolph has failed, you will have something.

Every point made about Randolph's charm, self confidence, and general natural gifts are true and have always been true of Winston. So also are the bad points mentioned (with restraint and hinted at; while others are not mentioned e.g. drink and women, which were never true of Winston.)

P.S. I do hope you have sketched out some sort of plan for your Winston book before starting to write it. Of course, you can modify the plan as you go on. But if you start without a map of the territory, no matter how inaccurate it may be found in proceeding, you will run into difficulties.

From R. W. Thompson   3rd November, 1960

My correspondence has multiplied to such an extent in these last months that I suddenly find I am out of note-paper. When my ship comes home I shall have to place a bulk order. Meanwhile, please forgive this stuff. I was very pleased to have your first letter, but refrained from answering since my own had crossed. *En rapport* is good, but it can go too far, as you observe!

One of the greatest shocks in my young life was when I first met those in very high positions, and found them—inasmuch as I was able to judge—far from my idea of great. Certain others, yourself and Claude Auchinleck for example, have more than filled the picture in my mind —and I'll bet Auchinleck doesn't think of himself as in any way 'great'.

But now all that must be forgotten . . . Can Winston, honourably, fill something of the role of 'Bread and Circuses' and provide enough bread for me to carry on with my 'Historian' type plans? There must be a good chance. First, as you know, I am fascinated by Winston. I believe I can write about him in a way that is different, entertaining, slightly shocking to those with a certain image, but sound and valuable in its way. At any rate, a contribution to a better understanding, not only of the man, but of his impact on our affairs.

You are right about a 'Plan'. Without a plan it is at best difficult beyond bounds, at worst impossible to write such a book—coherently. I have wads of notes, and wads of 'writing', much of which will go into the book in the right places, I hope. I am working hard on the plan and, as you remark, it need not be hard and fast. In the writing, as the work progresses, deviations may come and go. But the Plan is of the essence—as indeed it is with most things, not least 'battles'. As soon as I have this clear to my satisfaction I will send a copy.

My interest in the Industrial Revolution in this context is because I try to imagine just what this meant to men like Winston—and not only Winston, but Rosebery and others. Of course, they knew 'all about it', but could they 'know it in the bone', as new men, spawned by it, knew it? That is what I doubt. To them—and I think especially Winston: he reveals his thinking in the prefaces to Marlborough—it was clear that the Industrial Revolution had put immense power into war, for example. It had upset the balances of power in new ways. But did they see and fully understand that war was not simply a question of more powerful weapons, more devastation, but different *in kind*. The search was for a new kind of power. War by the time Hitler and Stalin were on the scene was revolution and counter revolution—with Britain in the middle, even the U.S.A. not knowing which 'side it was really on'. Or no side at all! *It knows now.*

In a sense, as I see it, all war has become a form of 'Civil War'—like civil war one side or the other must go out of business. Co-existence may be impossible in the nature of things. In this context 'unconditional surrender' makes sense. But this is the 'Dilemma'. I think men, even in the late nineteenth century, were able to foresee such developments. But not Winston's ruling class. To them, the game had become infinitely more dangerous, but fundamentally the same game they knew so well; that *was* in their bone.

But, as you observe, so very wisely—I am not embarking upon an Economic and Social History. I have the kind of mind which likes to grasp underlying factors from which the stuff on the surface springs. It leads me to 'waste' much time I can ill afford, but it is in my nature.

Again in regard to the impact of the I[ndustrial] R[evolution] and the awareness of its portents in the minds of the 'Winstons' of the world, I wonder whether even the most long-sighted politician could do much about it; whether it is not essential, in the nature of politics, to live from day to day, compromising endlessly, coping with 'tomorrow' when it comes. It is, after all, the Art of the Possible.

Finally, I enjoyed the profile of Randolph in the *Observer*. I thought it excellent, and am glad you confirm its value in relation to the father. I do not know Randolph well—frankly I don't wish to. He is quite impossible except in small doses in my family setting. But he behaves always extremely well when he does call in—quite differently, I understand, from his 'wildness' elsewhere. He is well worth observing and considering most carefully.

Later I will try to focus on certain aspects of Winston's deeds, especially in the Second World War. The more I think about it, the greater appears the Greek catastrophe. I begin to think that it wrecked our 'strategy' in the Med., and that our thinking thereafter became woolly. We could not sell the Med. to the Yanks because we did not know what we wished to sell. If only we had plugged subversion in Hitler's Germany, and walked Rankin C. So much—or more—for hate and arrogance in the affairs of men. Alexander the Great's performance may have been too far away in time for Winston to remember, but Mao was here and now, moving on his 'Alexander' course through China. Eden saw that. Pity his 'eyesight' became so bad.

From Sir Desmond Morton   4th November, 1960
Your letter of 3rd November is of great interest, although the Auk is most certainly a Great Man, while I equally certainly am nothing of the kind.

What you say has given me furiously to think. I think your thoughts are gradually shaping themselves and you may develop a general idea of great importance.

What you have written has produced an induced current in my brain and a general idea, which, if it can be worked out, may be quite different in many ways from anything I have seen written before.

This induced current, which I give you free of charge, if it is of the slightest use even indirectly, is as follows:

1. How did war arise in the history of mankind?
2. War created the 'gentleman' and the 'gentleman' then made war.
3. This lasted until a new element, gradually introduced, altered the old order.
4. What urge makes war nowadays?
5. How does Winston fit into this frame?

Explanation and Expansion.

1. How did war arise? Primitive man fought beasts for survival. The father of the family was the war leader, by nature. The family becomes a family tribe. The war leader is then not necessarily (and probably not) the oldest man, but the strongest man; the other men following him, and his orders in war. The family tribe becomes a Tribe, through the joining up of several family tribes, after there had been 'civil war' between family tribes over women? food? grounds?; anyway one or another necessity for survival. The war leader of the Tribe being the strongest and most skilled man of the combined Tribe —all other men following him. (The older men acted as counsellors, but we are not at once concerned with that.) Thereafter the juncture of several tribes became a Nation. The war leader of the Nation was as before, the strongest and cunningest man in war. But the strongest man in each tribe forming the Nation, became deputy leaders to the war leader, whence the idea of King and Nobles was born.

Carry this idea forward to more organised and civilised Nations and the idea of the 'gentleman' emerges.

Naturally, for a book on this subject alone, which could be well written (but that is not your book) one must introduce other ideas regarding the arrival in the world of private property and riches, that the war leader, the nobles and gentlemen, automatically acquire personal wealth. Also with this, is the idea of Religion, Priesthood and so on.

2. The 'gentleman' makes war. After the development of human organisation reaches the stage at the end of 1, it is in the interest of the 'gentleman', the king, nobles etc. to make war. They are the war leaders. In times of peace, others are more important and may increase their importance and riches at the expense of the war leaders. Also, the idea that *Si vis pacem, para bellum*, arises—long, long, before the Roman said this. Being true, the idea could not be combatted successfully. Hence the position of the leader and leaders became established, both in war and peace, BUT could only remain established so long as war was a real danger. Also, however, the pleasures of ruling were by now very clear; also material gains from making war—gains to the whole Nation, if the war was successful. Hence the gentleman, so created by war, became the war leader *and* the peace leader and it was to his interest (and to the interest of the Nation) that he should make war.

3. The new element. All wars between man and man are civil wars in one sense only. By strict definition, however, a civil war is not between different and clearly defined 'cities' or 'nations', but only between contending parties in the one city or the one nation or state.

It is *bellum inter cives*, not *bellum inter civitates*. How did civil war start? Surely politics. A religious war or war of different religions has no real existence. A difference of religion has always been a trumped excuse for war, invented by the politician, whether the war is international or civil. This is not the real new element. Wars of conquest continued; wars of survival continued; but there did enter in (when exactly is hard to say) the idea that peace was a greater benefit to the Ruler and Nobles and gentlemen than was war—as well as to the ordinary man. In the West, the Romans got this idea first. The position of the 'gentleman' as Ruler in war and peace was firmly established. The intervention of Christianity furthered this idea. Later Christianity also produced the idea that a leader must be a good man and conduct himself in war and peace by certain well-defined rules. Hence the period of 'knightly' behaviour in war, and the idea that the knightly leaders must be braver, more courteous, more merciful etc. etc. and see to it that their followers acted accordingly. There were Rules of War. War was still the 'gentleman's' sport and proper profession. What was the new element, which caused the history of war not to develop along the reasoned path outlined above, but to drop all idea of Rules of War, fighting without hatred for your enemy, not fighting purely for material gain etc. etc.

Here I am going to break off—at the most provocative point. I have plenty of ideas; but they can for the moment rest. My query 5. How does Winston fit in to all this framework? Obviously depends upon the answer given to queries 4 and the selected answer to 3.

Frankly I do not think that the proper answer to 3 or 4, had anything to do with the Industrial Revolution, the coming of the steel and manufacturing age or anything of that sort. The I.R. merely increased the horrors of war and the power of certain nations, as they got industrialised, to make 'modern' war. British world power arose through the fact that she was the first country to become industrialised and her war potential thereby increased above that of other nations. It began to fall, as soon as other nations also became industrialised. The fact that the U.S.A. and U.S.S.R. have become greater industrial powers, makes them *prima facie*, the most powerful potential warmakers in the world.

As a first thought, I would say that today, two things make wars—Discontent and Fear.

That Fear does so, is easy to understand. Fear that a 'way of life' really dear to *a nation*, is threatened from outside. Discontent is more complicated. Fear may be artificially engendered. Discontent cannot be, though it can be artificially fermented and increased. To cause a war, Discontent must be discontent with the existing 'way of life'. Your Industrial Revolution caused discontent through the genuine oppression of the poorer by the richest; but that was internal and might have provoked civil war. If a situation arises where there is widespread discontent in a nation and the leaders of the nation can do nothing peaceably to remove that cause, they may, given certain conditions, make an international war, not only to take people's minds off their discontents at home but to remove certain causes of discontent by enriching the people. Up to quite recent times, that was possible. It is so no longer.

Again, how does Winston fit into this. We must remember that Winston did not himself *cause* the last war, or the war of 1914. He, in a sense, *fought* both wars, one in a subordinate position, and the latter in the Supreme position. He fought them because it was in his blood and in his training and ancestry. He was (as to fifty per cent) a scion of a great war-making family, a 'gentleman', whose trade was still subconsciously war. Has it struck you that no war leader has ever yet arisen who was not (at least by some sort of definition) a 'gentleman'. Men have risen from the ranks to become great war leaders, but by rising from the ranks they have either adopted the outlook or the trade of a 'gentleman' in the process.

God forbid, for other reasons, that we should have to define a politician as a 'gentleman'; but it is the politician who is now the maker of wars and the war leader. Truly soldiers have become heads of states and have themselves made wars. But that is not because they were imprimis 'soldiers', but because they made themselves into politicians.

I am running dry at the moment and am the slave of time. But I must add that if your book is to 'focus on certain aspects of Winston's deeds, especially in the Second World War', (your own words) I fear it will become just another book about Winston and a sort of life of Winston. I cannot see how that will work. They can already be counted by the dozen.

Of course you are right that the Greek catastrophe was a catastrophe and probably altered the whole course of strategy in the Middle East and indeed the whole war. It was also possibly (but it is too hypothetical to be sure) that it even was the cause of American predominance, with which you have, in my mind, so ably dealt with in the main theme of *The Price of Victory*.

But a number of people from Jock Kennedy[1] upwards and downwards have said all that. You have got to deal with something *new*.

Again, had we (untrammelled by American lack of knowledge and thought) stuck to the War Aim, 'We fight against the idea of Hitlerism and Fascism and not against Germans and Italians', with which we began the war and stated publicly until 'Unconditional Surrender', there is in my mind, no doubt that the war would have ended sooner, through a revolution in Germany. But that has been said too, *ad nauseam*. It is perfectly true; as true as that if even Hitler had announced (and acted accordingly) that he fought *not* the Russian people but Communism, there is no doubt that he would have won in Russia. This was true at that date, but may well be no longer true, should a new war arise, which God forfend.

Finally, in re. the Industrial Revolution, have you ever read the great Papal Encyclicals, *De Rerum Novarum* and, forty years later, *Quadragesimo Anno*? I have an idea that the dates were about 1860 and 1900, or even earlier. How many people or nations ever paid any attention to their excellent foresight and advice?

From R. W. Thompson   10th November, 1960
Wrestling with the structure—or framework—of this book keeps reminding me of an idiotic performance on the music halls of some forty plus years ago. The character is explaining the difficulties of building a chicken house. It is not like building a church, he says. Oh no—there's all that wire netting, all that corrugated iron, all that boarding . . .

Forgive me. It must read like the first breakdown of the brain. Your letter of the 4th has given me much food for thought. A great deal of it will be valuable for my personal book, *War was my Peace*, to follow this one. I shall store it against the day. It is also good stuff in regard to Winston and war generally. Your No. 3 . . . the new element.

It is my contention that the new element, which the old Order was unable fully to comprehend in its power implications, was the new element. It put revolutionary and terrible weapons into the hands of

[1] Major-General Sir John Kennedy, D.M.O., Second World War.

new and terrible men. The 'Old' men—that is the gentlemen, strove to use them as gentlemanly weapons, even pretending they were when they demonstrably were not—the Zulu War, and so on.

(I see I've typed the new element as the new element! I mean, of course, my pet Industrial Rev.)

The Gentlemen could not really understand that the new people—Hitler, Stalin, Musso etc. were the power boys. They failed to realise that Britain's power in the nineteenth century sense was doomed as the Ind. Rev. spread to countries with 100 millions. Fifty millions was roughly our limit. In no time the 100 million countries *could* be great powers. And here we are. Had all this been understood Britain could have remained a Great Power in different terms, and not simply Communist target number one.[1]

No. 4. Fear makes war nowadays. *Only* fear. It's worth breaking this down, and setting it out, but I won't attempt it now. I'm sure, in any case, you could do it much better.

On top of that is the awful truth that there is no war. Man must find something else. There is no possibility of disarmament until the fear is dispelled. It confounds me that this cart is always put before the horse. Begin to get rid of the fear and armaments will take care of themselves.

No. 5. Winston. That is the 64,000 dollars question!

Winston is the cross between a gentleman and a nineteenth-century tycoon, Yankee model, trying to live in two worlds at once. War remains Marlborough's wars, whatever happens. The Second World War is merely the First World War all over again, repeat performance.

The O'Gowan debated this with me some time back, most intriguing. The Kaiser becomes Hitler, Dreadnoughts–Bombers, Antwerp is Norway, Dardanelles, the Balkans and so on.

But Churchill's 'fertile imagination' is not an imagination tuned to modern war (Second World War I mean). It is all too reminiscent of Omdurman and all that. He is a furious tactician, trying to jump about men on a world board, not grasping the long-term strategies which alone can save us—and perhaps the world. His performance in the Second World War was Jerome, Jerome all the way. I can't imagine anyone more removed from Marlborough, with his patience—with his Allies, with the development of strategy. No one would jump him into anything, nor would he attempt to jump anyone else. His camp seems to have been devoid of nerves. But Winston! Poor Dill—poor Alan Brooke—poor you! And John Kennedy and his boys compelled to work themselves silly on multitudes of cracker-brained plans, night and day. Of course, as you so rightly reiterate, it had its wonderful good side. But, above all that was the VOICE—the right words to the proletariat perfectly timed, catching an heroic mood, the timing sheer

[1] We were in the 'forward foxholes' if nuclear attack came, as Winston pointed out.

genius, a collection of sustained dramatic performances perhaps without equal.

It would be a bold man who would be prepared to state exactly where we might have been without that service. And yet, and yet, Winston is the permanent adolescent, the baby, bottle, cigars, bottle again, first childhood to second childhood, middle childhood of the baby Giant. What could be more terrifying than a baby Giant?

Yet all that you say is true. These are simply thoughts, all of which, as you can imagine, teem in my hot head. But I swear that my book, whatever it is, will not be just another book about Winston. It will be my book about Winston, probably outrageous. But with perhaps a new lead for future writers, a lead to an image that may be nearer the real man. Something poles apart from Lewis Broad's, and even Guedalla's, something combining your insight, Amery's insight, Asquith's, Esher's—and, of course, mine. Not so much insight as imaginative insight.

The Legend propagated by Winston himself in his great body of written work. As Asquith remarked of his *World Crisis*: 'I'm reading Winston's brilliant autobiography disguised as a History of the Universe!'

I think—I pray—I hope, in all humility, but not without faith and courage, that I can put down something new. If it fails, it will be a bold failure. His mistakes were inherent in him. He could not alter that, not one word or deed of it. But he was always a 'Baby' man—with a Giant's strength. I think he was unbelievably lucky to have found you and kept you with him. I believe you have a special quality—many special qualities—but one of 'grown-up-ness' Churchill needed most desperately, apart from your integrity, which again in a special sense arises out of and has its great strength in your religion.

I hope and believe you will forgive me if this letter is rather wild and rash. I am so pressed in my thoughts. I simply am going to be myself with you.

From Sir Desmond Morton   19th November, 1960
On consideration, I think my last letter to you merely indicated that in my belief politicians and no one else make wars. That is fairly obvious but has got more so in the last 2,500 years.

I agree with you that the inventions of material science have been responsible for putting into the hands of politicians more and more horrible and devastating weapons. This is, however, not due to the Industrial Revolution, as you call it, but as I regard it—the development of modern industries. These two last things, material science, the inventor and industry which combines therewith to manufacture the inventions and apply them to warlike use, assist the politician. Mind you, they always did this; there is nothing new in that; only as with other things, the curve of progress has become steeper in geometric progression. Chariots, Greek Fire, the screw, catapults, gunpowder, modern explosive up to the atom bomb; with the discoveries of the internal combustion engine, aeroplanes and electronics for good measure.

The Captain of a Greek Trireme would be as appalled at gun-firing battleships of Nelson's day, as would Wellington at armoured fighting vehicles, or Douglas Haig at the atom bomb. The only difference is the speed of invention and development. 2,000 years the first, 200 years the second and little more than twenty years the third.

Your point of the rise of a different class of person to power in these matters, is pertinent, I think. But I also think it wants very careful handling. Not in order to avoid offending anyone—that does not arise —but in order to arrive at the exact balance of truth and the true causes of the said rise. To my mind the 'Industrial Revolution' is inadequate.

Enough of that, however, for the moment.

I am in great agreement that Fear is the great cause of war, and greatly intrigued with your thought that if war be abolished, Man must find something to take its place. I would add, 'or else radically change his nature', with vague thoughts of that being impossible, or alternatively, what would be the effect on Man if whatever it be in his psyche which causes him to desire (even against his conscious thought) war, were to disappear.

I find what you say about Winston intensely interesting and I am sure there is a lot in it, save in any part which I played *during the war*, towards braking his less exuberant cerebrations or actions. Leave me out of it, even out of your mind in that connection.

I will give your boiling brain another thought about W. What was his attitude towards Authority, and why?

You would be wrong to think that he had no respect for any Authority, save his own, at any time.

He was not a Christian, but believed in a single God—a sort of Theism, prevalent in the eighteenth century, where this God was looked upon as so far off, so omnipotent, that he only dealt in the immense world movements and had no respect to individual human beings, who were His tools.

In my view, such a belief may result in a sort of wondering awe at a Being which one could in no way understand, but would result in the very opposite of respect for this God's Authority.

Winston clearly held no mundane Authority, such as teachers, masters, pastors and superiors by place and position. In fact it is probable he was always inclined to think such accidental Authorities were always wrong unless they agreed with him.

I do not really know what his view was about his father, Lord Randolph, or his mother in respect of their authority over him. Did they have or exercise any? I do not know. I do know that he adored his mother and was jealous of his father in the accepted Freudian sense. That is all.

But I also know that ever since I have known him, he did literally worship the Authority of Parliament, and of the British Monarch, even if the latter had really ceased to exercise much authority.

Parliament and the Monarchy were to him sacred things. Above all Parliament, since the idea had control over the Monarch, in theory. He would never hear a word of criticism against either, though his worship of Monarchy and his worship of Parliament were slightly different mental reactions.

He had fear for the authority of Parliament—real fear, and not only from what Parliament might do to him, or how it could affect his fortunes. It was a real mystical fear, not wholly susceptible to reason, and going far beyond respect. He had no fear of the British Monarch, but a respect which also was somewhat mystical, transcending the person who wore the crown. Yet he had little or no respect for foreign monarchs, above ordinary politeness. Presidents and other Prime Ministers he treated as equals with himself, only he was rather more equal than others. The 'others' were respected according to the degree of power they actually wielded.

This last can be demonstrated by his changing attitude throughout the war to the President of the U.S.A.

Nevertheless, in short, he had a measure of respect for Prime Ministers and Presidents, immense mystical respect for the British Monarch, and for the *British* Monarch alone, but he had a mystical fear and worship of the British Parliament, whose authority was the very guiding star of his life. Why?

There is no easy explanation of this. To suggest that it was Parliament which gave him his own authority and through which he then exercised that measure of authority which they gave him, is quite inadequate. If he really worshipped anything in his life, he worshipped Parliament in a way approaching what an ordinary man gives to God.

The comparison between W. and an 'ordinary man', by which I mean one who would call himself a Christian and be greatly offended at doubt of this, who had some sense of religion, without being deeply religious, or well informed about his religion, is good. Just like the ordinary man, W. would not hesitate to break the little laws of Parliament, so long as he thought Parliament would not notice it, but would generally avoid breaking the major laws; also, he would get into a real and almost hysterical tizzy if he thought Parliament might object to something he wanted to do. He would regard defeating a vote of censure with no less relief and joy than would a Christian at news of absolution for his sins. Like my ordinary Christian man, he would show the utmost respect for the formalities and service of Parliament and, at considerable difficulty to himself, would either obtain Parliament's permission for absenting himself when expected to attend, or, apologise humbly and give a good reason afterwards for non-attendance—and the reason had to be a good one too, or he was in a tizzy again.

To say that he did all these and many other things, right out of his general character, merely to 'keep Parliament sweet', would be quite a wrong interpretation; though it might well be a rationalisation of his real motives.

No! His 'God' may have been complex, but forming a very large part of his 'God' was Parliament, and in a manner far above logical explanation of an easy kind.

From Sir Desmond Morton 21st November, 1960
In Compton Mackenzie's latest, and probably last, book, there occurs the passage:

'In his (Hitler's) own words, Greece was the catastrophe which destroyed him.'

An enquiry from a historian of my acquaintance brought the reply, 'Yes, indeed, I am sure Hitler said, or is reported on good authority to have said that, but I cannot recall the source of the information.'

If this is correct, it is important for you to know it, identify the matter and deal with it.

The argument is that against the wishes of Hitler, Mussolini attacked Greece. That is true. Hitler did not wish further embroilment in South-East Europe, while he was bent on reaching Moscow before winter.

When the Greeks (Metaxas) on 28th October, 1940, refused the Italian ultimatum presented by the Italian Ambassador, war came and the Italians were not only resisted but thrust back and it looked as though Greece might do something like defeat Italy locally. We recall all that and that Hitler had to send troops to help the Italians overcome the Greeks and to turn the British out of Crete. Etc.

It has been claimed by those who support Winston's decision to send British forces taken from North Africa to the support of the Greeks that all this business so delayed the advance in Russia that the German defeat there followed and that led to the defeat of Germany, etc., etc.

Now, if it be true that Hitler himself thought that and gave that view voice somewhere, you will readily see the importance of acknowledging this and of dealing with it accordingly.

My own view is that even if this is all true, the sending of the

British forces taken from Africa to Greece did not help the Greeks, and did temporarily destroy the African campaign. But that requires to be demonstrated, i.e. that the arrival (and departure of the British forces in Greece and subsequently in Crete) while certainly causing the trouble it did in Africa, owing to the dispersal of just the force required for Wavell to press his advantage to a conclusion, did not help the Greeks in the least and did nothing more than the Greeks had already done to hold up Hitler's plans.

I take it, however, you are abreast of all this and can show that Winston's decision, certainly strategically unsound, was based on emotionalism, 'These grand little Greeks, who have not lost the spirit of the Persian war . . .' or something of that kind. Of course this emotionalism would be disguised even to himself, as great *political* strategy, since the Greeks 'would never forget our action when the war was over, and would never have forgiven us, had we not gone to their aid', etc., etc. Actually more emotionalism, but what psychologists call a 'rationalisation'.

Does any country show gratitude in politics or world affairs? And as for the Greeks! Santa Maria! or perhaps I ought to say, 'Panhagion'!

Apart from the above, there is nothing in Compton Mackenzie's book for you. He is a strong supporter of Winston's action in regard to Greece, but is a cracked Philhellene, being quite unable to see that the 'Glory that was Greece', was caused by a race of men totally different from those inhabiting Greece today.

From R. W. Thompson   23rd November, 1960
Yours of 19th and 21st brought great pleasure and instruction. Winston's attitude to Parliament and to a lesser degree to the British Monarchy fills an important missing piece of the puzzle. I am grappling with my 'great subject', as you have so rightly called it, letting my mind work itself out and leaving cutting until later. The irrepressible Boney, whose new book is eagerly awaited by the knowing, refers to Winston as 'The super Cad of the Cadocracy'. But do not fear that the vituperations of the survivors of his generation against 'Our Hero' will lead me astray. Frankly, cad or not, I have sympathy with Winston. I have the audacity to believe that I have certain traits in common—he would, for example, have liked to have been a kind of d'Artagnan—do you remember how he drags d'Artagnan into his life of Marlborough, when that Gascon (as free as rain) goes sword in hand into the breach at Maestricht with John Churchill and Monmouth 'deathless in Dumas's prose'.

Your second letter about Compton M. and Greece reminds me to get his book when I can. If Hitler's words are true, I should say that he was a poor judge of the causes of his own catastrophe, although it may be that Greece was more of a headache than it seemed. Compton M. is, as you say, a cracked Philhellene, but he has given such pleasure with his writing of adolescence that he may be forgiven all kinds of nonsense. My own course of Byron at school makes me understand how easy it is to harbour such illusions. We need some 'glory' somewhere, and if there isn't any, we have to make it up.

As to fear and war: what are we to have not only in place of war, but in place of fear? There have been lately some semi-learned enquiries into the primitive survival patterns within us, adrenalin surging (apparently) at the dropping of the strangest hats. Civilisation has deprived us of most of (our) natural emotional outlets, and perhaps we shall have to institute some sort of Red Indian tribal ceremonies of ordeal to 'blood' the males, and send them forth hunting for this and that. I think I may have been on the right lines in my desire to think out 'positive peace'. Why shouldn't it be exciting—and dangerous?

I am fully committed to Winston, and since my whole conception is broadly in the *The Yankee Marlborough* idea it promises to land me in difficult water. I think we can be sure not to sell it in the U.S.A., and any suggestion that Britain is a second-class power or in any way 'a satellite' is absolutely out.

There was an upsetting paragraph in *The Times* this morning. Norman Mailer who wrote *The Naked and the Dead* about the war in the Pacific is being put in a mental home while protesting his sanity. And he sounds sane. In China, U.S.S.R. and their satellites brain washing is commonplace. Actually the wide spread 'telly' probably makes it unnecessary here, and the 'limitation of news' is very carefully controlled. Thus people who may still want to think are not given the facts upon which to arrive at valid conclusions.

But for these rather shocking shadows haunting the background of our lives, I should be cheered about my grapple with Winston. I really begin to believe I may be putting something down worth putting down.

From Sir Desmond Morton   28th November, 1960
... Did you happen to notice President-to-be Kennedy's reply to W.'s telegram of congratulations? The end read '. . . May your unconquerable spirit be . . .'

I quote only the important words. The idea behind 'your unconquerable spirit' is of the utmost importance. It contains much truth as meant, and it is *that idea*, which renders it so difficult to assail or question his alleged and real deeds until much water has flowed over the dams. Partly because the idea has much truth in it and because, whether they can put it into words or clear thoughts or not, it is how he is regarded by the mass of the peoples of the world.

If you can analyse what went to make up that part of Winston so referred to—and you cannot dismiss it as merely obstinacy, self-assurance or conceit, and by no means can it be denigrated, whatever other idiocies or even wickednesses he did, you *may* write a grand book.

From R. W. Thompson   7th December, 1960
In general your remarks are true beyond a doubt, but with Winston one cannot be sure. He is undoubtedly one of the most fascinating figures of the century. A book about him that was 'different' could sell. All pork is pork but my 'mincer' is my own. What will come out? The stuff begins to write itself as though I were a kind of ouija board— Planchette—or spirit writing. Mel likes it. Certainly it is not like anything else anyone has ever written about him. At least, not to my knowledge. The odd thing is that it doesn't denigrate him, in spite of his warts. After all, we are only men, not Gods, and the public cannot bear to have good men for their idols. Indeed a public idol must have feet of clay, else the people become uneasy, knowing that demands will be made which they cannot meet. They insist upon bad men. Hence Acton's dictum is normally correct in regard to men and power. But if a 'Good' man was at the top it might not be correct.

I know I am rambling in the most wild manner, but you will forgive me, I know, in this state of trance. But I do believe I can write something worth reading about Winston 'alive or dead'. I don't want the 'Old Man' to die. After all you told me how he roared about Jerome. (I wish I had that book.) If he can still read—or listen—he might roar about himself through the Thompson 'mincer'. He's a mixture of eighteenth-century blood and nineteenth-century tycoon—plus. A heady mixture to rush with into the twentieth century. What could anyone *expect* to happen! A terrific One Man Band.

I know it's difficult. I think it's exciting, and I think it could win, and it *might* be good . . .

From Sir Desmond Morton   9th December, 1960
Two letters from you. Delighted. Am first replying to yours about the review and returning the copy.[1]

The review itself.

I have not read Higgins' book, so cannot say whether I think your review of *it* is beyond criticism. As a brief essay, it is a masterpiece. My chief point, though, is that it hardly tells me enough about the book, unless the points you make are direct riders on what Higgins says, and upon any main conclusions he reaches.

If you have used his book purely as a foundation for developing

[1] *Winston Churchill and the Second Front*, Professor Trumball Higgins, Oxford University Press. Review in R.U.S.I. Journal.

your own theme, it is not so good *a review* as it might be. Only you who have read the book can say.

I am assuming that Higgins actually says in his book much about the lack of an 'Object', and if he does, your literary masterpiece is also a first-class review of the book.

My other comment, whether on the book or your review of it, I do not know, is where you say that both Winston and McA. 'pursued unlimited aims with limited means'. Perhaps that is what Higgins says. Anyway, I am inclined to challenge that as regards Winston. I would say that *he* pursued a very limited aim—too limited an aim—his only aim was to win the war (nothing to do with 'Unconditional Surrender') and he gave no reasoned thought to anything else whatsoever. He refused to think of the ensuing peace, of Communism, of the future of world economics or anything else. He never even gave thought to international (or national) politics, save in their immediate connection of winning the war.

I will not expatiate on this point here, though I consider it one of the biggest potential criticisms of Winston's conduct of the war. It is both highly arguable and intensely interesting, but anyway, I would find it hard to agree ec dum that he pursued *un*limited ends. Just the opposite. This also was his permanent character. He always concentrated on the immediate object—though that object might not be what it appeared to be on the surface. As a golfing simile, his shots onto and on the green were magnificent, when he could physically see the hole; but his drives and approach game lacked foresight.

From R. W. Thompson   1st February, 1961

. . . I have an excellent life of Baruch, but find some of the most perceptive stuff about Churchill in the writings of Sir James Grigg. My task as an 'Outsider' is to attempt a creative outsider's view of Churchill. There will be, and there have been, insiders galore, led by Randolph, but none of them can, in his nature, see Churchill in the terms of anyone like myself. Liddell Hart must know a great deal about him from his angle. You must know a great deal more from yours. But I, in a sense, knowing nothing, may regard the whole tapestry of his life and times in a different fashion. Admittedly it may be useless: it may fail totally. On that I must take a chance—like swimming when you don't know that you can swim.

Meanwhile I await whatever remarks you have the time and inclination to send me. I had a morning with my agent . . . In the afternoon I wandered in second-hand departments, coming upon a first edition of Lady Randolph's memoirs for five bob; a good volume ii of Fisher and an equally good Asquith's *Moments of Memory*. I now have quite a good shelf of Churchilliana, and another of relevant political biography and memoirs all ready to my hands. But whatever I may yet read, and of all the considerable body of work I have read, it is, however unhappy you may feel about it—and it must be needless to say how greatly I hope you don't—that your correspondence has given me a touchstone—almost one might say 'a crib'. If I do not use all this well it will not be for want of trying.

From Sir Desmond Morton   3rd February, 1961

You say that your 'task is to attempt a creative outsider's view of Churchill'. You explain this further by pointing out that various people who knew Churchill more or less intimately, have acquired a point of view about him, and that these points of view must and do differ. That is certainly true. You then say that you as an 'outsider' (that is, someone who never knew Churchill privately, or intimately, 'in a sense knowing nothing') may 'regard the whole tapestry of *his life and times*' in a fashion differing from any of the others' points of view.

This is most reasonable. It is in fact the very essence of the Preface to your book. That book will thus be an attempt to summarise and analyse all that has been written about Churchill by those who had much contact with him and distil from these sources, which include his own writings, what *you feel* to be a more complete picture.

Admirable idea.

But you also use the phrase, which I have underlined, his 'life and times', which I quite agree is correct and essential. You cannot suggest an explanation of a man's actions unless you also discuss his 'times'.

From R. W. Thompson   19th February, 1961

You may be surprised to learn that I have emerged from my studies enchanted with the Jeromes, especially Leonard. I can echo Winston's, What a Man! In my view, considering the background of the Wall Street jungle in the 1850s Leonard was a better man than the old Commodore Vanderbilt, and streets ahead of the Fisks and Tammany Hall mob, morally and in every way. In fact he more than anybody broke the power of Tammany Hall in those days.

But I expect you know the whole story. Doubtless I shall come upon more sources (oh, how I wish you had that Jerome book! Or it was obtainable somewhere.)

Baruch I do not like. I have delved into him pretty deeply, and I don't like his influence on W. one little bit. I think he appealed to the worst side of W.'s character, but I also think that W. owes a tremendous lot to his Jerome blood—without it, it is difficult to imagine the Churchills producing much. Randolph was about the best in 200 years and I wonder how he would have got on against genuine competition.

In any case he lacked stamina, and stamina was a Jerome product in tremendous quantity.

I have also read Hassall's book on Marsh, which I like very much. What a curious chap Marsh was! Did you know him at all well? Likeable, but insipid, at least for me, and hero-worshipping Winston. I don't think it did W. good to be H-W'd, and to treat people like 'little boys'.

. . . Money or no money I shall go ahead with my book very soon, not questioning my right or lack of right to write it, but simply write it. W. is a good test. If a man can't write a highly readable book about such a man then one is no writer, and should take to some other activity. I was, by the way, very distressed to read of the death of Bernard Paget. He had written asking me to lunch with him, but I knew he had been very much below par for some weeks. There is another man who did not have half his due. And now Alexander. Forgive me if I feel rather surprised—and shocked.

I had to review Monty's Leadership nonsense the other day. It really is the most pitiful rubbish—and yet, in many ways he seems a good chap—even a nice chap. Obviously he should avoid putting pen to paper at all costs. But you could say the same for me.

Our love to you, and hopes that this horrible winter has failed in its assaults upon you.

From Sir Desmond Morton   20th February, 1961

I go straight to Alexander. I too am alarmed and regretful in some ways that he has burst into print; but have not seen him for some time and do not know what has made him change his mind. I cannot pass judgment on the whole, until I have read the whole; but on the first article which I read yesterday, I am fairly well satisfied that he maintains gentlemanly standards. I do not know what advice he took on the writing, if any,[1] but it reads like Alex in person, as I would have expected. Knowing him pretty well, rather better than even I have known Brookie, I can see that he has written with his usual extreme care, tending always to see what he can say in favour of any person mentioned by name or specifically commented upon, and yet—for those who can read, and not merely scan a newspaper—not refraining from adverse criticism, when he feels to do so would distort the truth or give a false impression. I would say that the statements he makes in the first article about men or events, are the absolute truth as he sees it. That is the most important thing of all. The second thing is that he is a better judge of truth than many other persons and, fortunately for him, has no personal axe to grind.

[1] I have found out later today that he did employ a 'ghost', but like Winston, took the 'ghost's' facts and essays, and wrote every word of what is published himself.

At the same time, do not fall into the error of supposing that he is without subtleties of intention. For example, I am quite sure that he told that silly little story of Winston and his cigars for a very definite purpose. Some of his apparently innocuous phrases are a delight.

Pending the appearance of the later articles, I would say that the first is a model of how such things should be done.[1] There is not a hint of 'journalism' anywhere. Yet there is fine, clear writing, easily understandable, apart from a sly allusion or two, quite unequivocal; and an avoidance of all rhetoric in what must be, by the nature of the statement, a simple, direct account.

Of course, he is telling *his own* story. He is not writing history as such. He is not trying to do so, and might be quite incapable of it. He would certainly say he was. Also, of course, the value of the statement largely lies in the fact that it *is* the plain unvarnished tale of the man who himself did the things, or was in supreme charge of doing the things, described.

When we see the rest I will write more.

*　　　*　　　*

I know nothing whatever about the Jerome end of affairs, save what I have read, or of Barney Baruch either, save what I have heard. Eddie Marsh, on the other hand I knew extremely well. You have, I think, got hold of a reasonable idea of a large part of Eddie. Withal he was an absolute expert on water-colour paintings. Lucky for him, for when he was dropped out of sight, he could at least sell at immense profits the collection he had acquired and so live. In some ways, too, he was a very intelligent man capable of the most witty sayings. He had elected to be, and to be regarded as, a sort of 'Auguste', not a Clown. He ought of course to have been a don at a University, which he could perfectly well have been; but he chose otherwise.

For years I have had a great friend who is a psychologist (genuine; I don't mean psychiatrist like even Freud, Adler and Jung, though Adler was a bit of a psychologist too). Psychologists aim, unlike psychiatrists, most of whom do not know the first thing about psychology, at trying to understand the working of the human mind, first in health and later, if necessary, in sickness.

*　　　*　　　*

So do not get worried if you feel in any difficulty about examining the 'psyche' of Winston; or anyone else.

I personally find no value in assuming that we are all more or less cracked. The truth is that we are all more or less sane, but each of us in a different way.

[1] If they are done at all!

My love to you and Mel and everyone except the 'flu virus. I find it hard to love Mr. K., newspapers and politicians, save in a somewhat involved fashion.

From R. W. Thompson   1st March, 1961
I am still giving my celebrated imitation of a man running up the down escalator, and the ordered life is no more than a microscopic vision afar off through the wrong end of a giant telescope . . .

So I am weary and not very well, and longing to be able at long last to give my mind to the Winston book . . .

And thus to Alexander, and much brewing. I didn't see the stuff until mid week owing to having left off the *S. T.* and confining myself to the *Observer* . . .

But the odd thing about Alexander was that I didn't know at once that John North had written the stuff. But I was very much up to date on the North–Connel, Monty–Auk feud conducted by these two admirable (usually) citizens. Alexander's notes and papers must have seemed to North the Heaven-sent chance to hit back, a chance rather absent these many weeks, and not helped by Monty's nonsense on 'leadership'. I was meant to lunch with North last Thursday, but could not, rather fortunately, for at that stage I was innocent as a new born lamb, not having read Piece 1 nor aware of North's part. Had message from N.'s secretary that N. tied up in feverish argument with Thomson (newspapers)—this meaningless until I arrived home to find article 1, plus long letter from Eric O'G. I hasten, therefore, to put you abreast of developments, although you may be a good length ahead of me. First I was a bit shocked by North's stuff. (a) Because I have studied all the breakdowns of the Alamein 2 battle, and the background from the spring of 1942 onwards, from the statements of Army and Divisional Commanders concerned right through, and with the aid not only of Basil L.H., but of official opinion. I know, therefore, that it is an historical fact that Alamein 1 (not 2) was the real turning point, and is regarded by historians as a defensive victory, and that the Nile Delta was thereby saved, not for a day, nor for an hour. But saved.

Furthermore, I don't believe it can be argued that Monty fought Alamein 2 well. The figures speak for themselves. In my view, having given some years to an analysis of Monty's battles from October 1942 to the end, he could not win a battle because he could not lose one: that is by building up great strength and taking no chances whatever, not only at Alamein 2 but from Normandy on, he certainly ensured against defeat; but by the same token made real victory impossible. He would never go in and win. Furthermore, from Alamein 2 onwards the enemy was going backwards anyway, not forwards, immensely powerful, of course, capable of inflicting terrible injury on an opponent, but—in spite of the Ardennes—not being able truly to advance again into any kind of future.

But I grow tedious. The crux of article 1 is that North omitted the following vital piece from Alexander's Despatch: I quote whole passage, piece left out in Caps:

> The plan was to hold as strongly as possible the area between the sea and Ruweisat Ridge and to threaten from the flank any enemy advance south of the ridge from a strongly defended prepared position on the Alam Halfa ridge. GENERAL MONTGOMERY, NOW IN COMMAND OF EIGHTH ARMY, ACCEPTED THIS PLAN IN PRINCIPLE, TO WHICH I AGREE, AND HOPED THAT IF THE ENEMY SHOULD GIVE US ENOUGH TIME WE WOULD BE ABLE TO IMPROVE OUR POSITIONS BY STRENGTHENING THE LEFT OR SOUTHERN FLANK.

This plan, which Monty found in existence, was O'G's plan-appreciation of 27th July, and whatever North (or Alexander) may say this is an historical fact. But North (or Alexander—which it would be hard to credit) then goes on to sneer at O'G by implication: 'The author (of the plan) must count himself lucky not to have prepared it for the new commander of the Eighth Army'.

And this of admittedly the finest Staff brain the Second World War produced, *vide* Wavell on many occasions, and the Auk—and Boney Fuller . . .

Of course the O'G hopes that Auk will do something about it, but I hope not, for I should then become unshockable. In my hero-worshipping mind (not unsupported by history) Wavell and the Auk remain outstandingly the greatest generals on the British side in the Second World War. As an Army Commander the Auk was second to no man on any side. What a pity he could not have been an army commander. But I do hope that the *S.T.* will let the O'G—or preferably L.H. or someone of that calibre outside the squabble, set the record straight. Playfair perhaps? A good name for it, anyway.

Beyond that I agree that the stuff is very well done, but then North is a fine writer, a scholar and no mean historian. A stick-in-the-mud, but a good chap, merely slightly demented on Monty (tried to make him head of Military Circle: we all had to act fast, and get Slessor[1] into the breach).

*   *   *

I have cherished a secret ambition for years, and one day, if I have a chance—or take a chance—I shall try it out. And a-propos of that, have you ever read Ambler? I dote on Ambler, as Durrell might say. I think he is an astonishing man, thrillers which no one can put aside for

[1] Sir J. C. Slessor, Marshal of the Royal Air Force.

five seconds, and not one word of sadism or sex . . . But the forecasts of what is going to happen—and does, are startling. Picked up *Justice on Deltchev* in a Pan paper back on my way back from Town. Did me good. I was there then (Bulgaria—Petkov time). Fascinating. Why don't I do it! And *The Nightcomers*.

If you read Ambler in your bath (Heaven forbid!) forgive me. But if you don't read him at all, please try just one—*The Schirmer Inheritance*, for example. Very odd.

And as to sanity, I should like to write quite a piece on that; there is a good woman near by, farming excellently and profitably, and believing and practising natural compost fertilising and so on. Neither wild birds, foxes, or anything else dies on her acres. So she is mad. Everyone else uses all the latest killer dopes provided by monopoly chemists. Same goes for wild oats. Chap invented means of eradicating *sans* chemicals. Hushed up. Regarded as 'insane'. And, of course, I have the honour of being insane also, and hope very much that you are too. Otherwise it's a lonely life.

From Sir Desmond Morton   7th March, 1961
The Alexander articles—I did not know that John North was the co-adjutor, but I wish I knew how it all came about. I am so frightfully busy these days that I can never get to London to my Club and hear the gossip. So far I have found the articles in good taste and fairly dull, though under the surface, to those who knew a thing or two once, there are interesting points. For example, it is clear that Alex as well as you did not think that Monty fought Alamein 2 as well as he might have done; but no reference is made to the famous secret and personal telegram. It is also interesting that, for the first time that I can remember, the point is rightly stressed regarding Alex's orders to retain as many German troops in Italy as possible. You will also have observed that whereas these were the orders to Alex and very important orders too, which were received by him from the Combined Chiefs of Staff representing the Allied Governments, Winston sends him a telegram wanting to know why he does not get on faster. There is great material for your book on Winston concealed in that matter; also much entertainment to me, knowing how privately and amusedly Alex was contemptuous of that telegram. Of course he never said so. Shall we say that he had a very 'balanced' view of Winston. Winston knew this and disliked it very much. The Winston–Alexander relationship was of the utmost interest as demonstrating the characters of the two men. It will never be written. But oh, how W. tried to *dominate* him, as he tried to dominate everyone else, and failed and how it disturbed him.

On the subject of the Auk–Monty controversy over the 'Plan of Campaign', I still think you have not got all the picture. I fully accept that the Auk believes that Monty pinched his plan and gave him no credit for it at the time; also that Monty did not believe he had pinched the Auk's plan; so that both have been telling the truth as each sees it.

I can think of half a dozen ways whereby these apparently conflicting views can be perfectly reconciled.

A change in a High Command much resembles a change of Government from one party to another. In strategy and in politics I have seen the same thing happen time and time again. The in-coming Power produces a plan and honestly believes it be its own brand new invention, whereas it is so very like that which was on the stocks when the old Power went out, that the latter claims the new Power has pinched the old Power's plan.

I could write you an essay on this, with direct reference to the Auk–Monty affair. But, alas time is not at my disposal.

Have you ever thought of the similarity in character in certain ways between the Auk and Neville Chamberlain on the one hand and between Monty and Winston on the other?

The Patient and the Impatient. The former desiring to see everything worked out on paper in very great detail, before he studies it and gives his decision; the other the 'half-sheet-of-paper' type, who wants the conclusions first and refuses to deal with details of the plan on paper, going into that chiefly orally, after he has got his h-s-o-paper.

You say, 'This plan which Monty found in existence . . .' The questionable word is 'found'. I'll bet you half a dollar he never found it. Nor was he told of it, nor shown it, as such. Any attempt by an ill-advised staff officer to tell Monty that his *predecessor* had made up a plan, or, worse, shown him a 'plan-appreciation' of 27th July, approved by his *predecessor*, especially if it were a lengthy and detailed document would certainly have led to that ill-advised officer's instant dismissal on the grounds of disloyalty (to Monty). Any senior officer would have known this.

Along these lines is the clue to the apparent mystery. Though that is a 'half-sheet-of-paper' and not the full story.

Have I ever read Ambler? Yes. You told me of a book of his some year or two ago. It is not my line of 'thrillers'. Certainly good of its kind, but not my kind. I do not like what I define as a 'thriller', but only the true *Roman Policier* (French), where there is no love interest, and where the detective (official or lay) slowly works out the clues as to the murderer. Any sort of novel, or fictional adventure stories are not my cup of tea.

Oh yes, count me insane in your way, please. But not quite as odd as an old lady who demands my joining a Society which she alleges to be approved by St. Thomas Aquinas, who clearly states (her allegation) that we shall find every one of God's creatures in Heaven, having been granted eternal life. Fancy a Heaven where one pushed one's way through infinite forests of seaweed (and yet 'there shall be no more sea!' Rev.) thrusting aside hordes of every sort of animal from diplodocci to unicellular polyps, ants, termites, etc. etc. I recognise that the poor lady does not mean 'God's creatures' which is everything, or even 'God's living creatures' or, if she thinks about it, 'those dumb animals which Man has domesticated'. She really means those cats (I have a reason from her letter to exclude all but 'cats') which she has known in this world. Even so, I fear her translation of St. Thomas Aquinas, of which she gives me chapter and verse, is wildly inaccurate. I wonder if she realises that that gentleman did not write his stuff in English.

From R. W. Thompson   13th March, 1961
I have run into a bad patch of syntax, and cannot write a sentence that makes sense. Whether this is the effect of striving to help the children through their end of term exams, and the effect of Mel's preoccupation with Tacitus, I don't know. But it's depressing. One knows exactly what one wants to say, and it just won't come out right. But work is the only answer . . .

Meanwhile the wires are getting red hot with messages stirred up by the North–Alexander axis in the *S.T.*[1] . . . Basil L.H. has now sent me a foolscap typescript of his notes on 'Suppressions and Omissions' in article 1 of the series. These agree, but add to, my own conclusion. L.H.'s 'Tanks' has all the breakdown stuff on Alam Halfa and Alamein, as also the official records. How North–Alex can write that Monty's 'overwhelming strength' was an 'illusion' is baffling to one and all. But I suppose 'overwhelming' could be an arguable word. Also Von Thoma's[2] evidence in regard to the faked map is not in accordance with the chaps who interrogated him. In any case Von Thoma was serving on the Russian front at the time of Alam Halfa.[3] But Rommel knew that the map was faked. Luckily for Monty he had to strike where he did, otherwise the 22nd Armoured would have been a dead loss dug in 'hull down', and the 8th Armoured most certainly destroyed. However . . .

But now the Snow stuff[4] demands urgent attention. As you know, Bernard Paget, Blackett and others held and hold very strong views on Cherwell's[5] influence. Lord Brand shares them in the financial field, and I have various private papers in regard to the Tizard–Cherwell struggle. All this from my point of view is far more important than the

[1] Private Papers, B.H.L.H.
[2] Von Thoma, German General.
[3] Alam Halfa, famous battle in the Western Desert, Second World War.
[4] *Science and Government* by C. P. Snow.
[5] Lord Cherwell (previously Professor Lindemann).

rights and wrongs of Alamein 2, and if you can throw any light on any of its aspects I shall be most grateful. (I haven't seen any of Snow's stuff yet.)

In spite of working badly on Winston I am not thinking badly (although one supposes thinking and working should be closely linked?). Never was child more truly father to the man. He must have been shockingly lonely almost up to his father's death—perhaps always. He was driven into the 'nursery' and into himself, always glimpsed as that 'pale little ghost' in the shadows, 'Poor little Winston', 'wretched little whipper-snapper'. 'What on earth will he do! He only plays with soldiers.' Such phrases abound from Clara Frewen, Leonie Leslie, Blanche Hozier, whose daughter Clementine 'poor little Winston' would marry, and many others. He barely knew his parents. They seem to have had no time for him at all—not for him personally, or for anything but the social-political rat-race in which they were so involved.

So I began to think that his egocentricity derived from all that. He was forced to live in and with himself, save for Mrs. Everest. (Brookie was, of course, a latter day Mrs. E.—and so perhaps were you!) As you say about Alexander, Winston had to dominate, and could not in that case. But he also had to have a Mrs. E., and with Mrs. E.—or all nurse-maids—a child adopts a dual attitude compounded of dominance and submission. But I shall be getting into deep water, if I'm not up to my neck already.

Mel is now recovered, and we both bless this patch of good weather. As for you, take care, double bar the doors and windows, for these monopoly boys when threatened know no rules of 'warfare'[1]. . . . I regret that Ambler cannot be your ally in this . . . I find him singularly free from sex and sadism. In *Justice in Deltchev* he does convey very skilfully and with great force the workings of certain phases of the Communist machine. No girls! Meanwhile the children are reading Brett Young's *The House under the Water*, a minor victory for television. I think I shall read some of his books myself. A greatly under-valued writer, I always think.

And now to the struggle! The buds are bursting, the birds are singing. Why not I? Pretty soon you will be in the midst of the 'hedgehog' season, or thereabouts.

From Sir Desmond Morton   19th March, 1961
'Syntax diffusion' is a strong side of temporary mental exhaustion . . .
I am perfectly sure that your frightful experience must have caused you every sort of nervous strain.

---

[1] Desmond was involved in a hopeless attempt to prevent the powerful chemist-medicines ring from suppressing a new discovery by an Italian, which could have brought health to many at very low cost. No chance.

The Snow stuff is really frightful. Do I know anything about it at all. Most certainly, a very great deal.

Of course most of the basic facts are correct, though a number of minor ones are not. It must be difficult to be a novelist and a scientist at the same time.

I have only read the first two Articles, which really say little that is not publicly known. The third about the bombing of Germany will be most interesting.

The so-called Tizard–Cherwell struggles were over before 1940 in so far as public warfare was concerned. It is nonsense by the way, to say that no one knew the Prof.'s origins or parentage. I met his sister. It is equally nonsense to say that the Prof.'s figures of German air-strength *before the war*, were nearer right than what the then Government knew or believed. They were nearer right than what *Tizard* was led to believe, from whatever source he got them. I could never find that out, by the way. The true figures were well known to the Government, and turned out to be absolutely correct when it became possible to analyse them from German Official Documents after the surrender. BUT the Chamberlain and previously the Baldwin Government kept them a deadly secret. Politics again.

I take no sides, though Tizard was far more often right than the Prof. But Winston liked the Prof. and did not like T.

How tired I am getting of all this washing of dirty linen in public. . . . I am so bunged up with work that I hardly notice the good sunlight . . . The hedgehog still sleeps, and the Blackthorn is out . . .

From R. W. Thompson   20th March, 1961
The fog of war begins to clear, and with it my tortured brain . . . Saturday it was my brithday (57!), and I bought myself a fiver's worth of books . . . for the last two years I have been starved of reading— apart from ghastly quantities of research, which, although enjoyable is not the kind of reading necessary to bring the operator into the necessary keyed up frame of mind to create. Thus I have starved myself of input—rather like expecting a car to go without petrol—apart from starving my 'cultural' (if any) growth.

I shall now, I know, begin to work properly, no longer writing the same thing forty times in forty different ways, the last worse than the first. This, may be, is what is meant by 'Hell'. But you are more of an expert on that than I. I see that new editions of the *Screwtape Letters*, together with an *I Lucifer* are recently on bookstalls. Indeed, man has seemed to have a certain rather unusual awareness of the Devil lately (I hope it is no sin to give the demon a capital. It slipped out. I don't want to placate him.)

How I agree with you about all this dirty—and miserable—laundry.

The breakdowns of Alexander continue to arrive from historians, all shocked. I am shocked. Why on earth did he do it!... Only more soil shovelled over the facts. Oh these generals ...

And Snow. I've never been able to make out *why* he writes the novels he writes. Certainly, they are very good, but it fills me with horror that a man can—and desires to—fill his mind for months on end with such curious, dim, pedestrian people. One knows that they exist, but what will be discovered by setting them moving?

As for Tiz-Cher[1] controv. What passes for my intellect, as well as the heart I know I possess, puts me all on the side of Tiz. I do not like the sound of the Prof. from any angle. I don't imagine he was precisely your own cup of tea. If ever you feel when less jaded with it all, like telling me anything about him and Winston I am certain it will be of aid. But I do not press you. There must be a moment when the books are closed, however good the prospects. There is so much one will never know about Winston (or anyone else) that I shall be fortunate— and very clever!—if I make the best of what I have and know. The stars move in their courses with me now. Whatever happens I am resolved that I will add no jot of obscurity to these issues. My task, whether or not I succeed, is by however little to blow some fog away, even a whisker or a wisp.

A-propos Winston, and my newish nursemaid theory about the English (not patriarchy, matriarchy, but Nannie-archy, or Nanniery? vital need of British, having been Nanny-ed to Nanny others, hence painful vacuum nowadays in the soul, or whatever). Read funny poem by Herbert on subject:

> Some Nelson's in the bath today
> Some Shelley in her lap;
> And when I think on this small star
> How many mighty men there are,
> I call for wine and drain a jar
> To England's noble Nannies.

(A.P.H.)

From Sir Desmond Morton   10th April, 1961

Have you seen the articles in *The Times* on the Lindemann, Tizard matter? They are infinitely better than the Snow exaggerated misunderstandings. The best of all is a criticism of the book by A. J. P. Taylor in the *Observer*. This is curious, since the bloke who wrote *The Times* articles did not know both L. and T. during the wartime controversy and served on the famous committees, whence, indeed he understands the row better than Snow, whose propensity for writing novels

[1] Sir Henry Tizard and Lord Cherwell.

has outshone his scientific physicist's mind. Taylor knew neither; but has somehow guessed the truth even better than *The Times* man.

The drivel that no one knew what Lindemann's origins were. Snow did not know, that is all; anyone else who cared to enquire could have found out. Taylor reminds me that, apart from having met L.'s sister, I also met his brother who was a perfectly good Brigadier in the British Army.

Of course, L. was more than 'difficult'. He was a man whom it was very hard to like and who seemed to go out of his way to cause dislike of himself by anyone whom he, L., rightly or wrongly regarded as a rival or in any way a danger to himself and his career. Fortunately for my own peace of mind, he was intelligent enough to realise from the outset that I myself was neither. So we got on remarkably well. Not that I ever fell in love with him. But for some reason, rather like W.S.C. himself, L. used to regard me at times as a rather good sounding board of what the British people thought, and used to consult me on relevant matters. He seemed to find this useful.

Equally, of course, Tizard was a much better physicist than L., though both were high above the average.

The important point is that L. was a frantic snob and alarmingly ambitious, while T. was a most charming man and quite self-sacrificing and self-effacing. Hence, as always happens in such cases, the former gets what he fights for for himself, while the latter is overlooked. That is Government and political life.

Anyone who tries to write that type of history and, if I may also add, the type of history you are trying to write about W.S.C. must first undergo a full course of Reality, in what constitutes political life. Otherwise he will completely misunderstand motives and actions, especially those of the politicians and quasi-politicians who come into his narrative.

To be a 'politician', you need not be an M.P. or even a candidate for such a job. A 'politician' is an attitude of mind, and is one of the excuses for coining the word 'statesman', to describe someone who, at least, can at times rise above such an attitude.

L. was a 'politician'.

It comes to me to suggest that a remarkable definition of 'the perfect politician', would be any man or woman who, before saying or writing anything and before taking any action calculates in his own mind the effect of his thoughts, words and actions on his own aims and career.

You could probably better that definition and I do not say that there has ever existed a 'perfect' politician. But the matter runs along those lines.

After all, Machiavelli admirably defines the perfect politician in his book *The Prince*. Mercifully very few men even approach the beau (?) ideal. I am pretty sure that if she was capable of abstract thought, my cat Jezebel would approach as near to it as did Napoleon Buonaparte.

It would be interesting to conclude at what epoch of his life W.S.C. became a 'politician' in that sense. There was certainly a time when, even if he had already made up his mind to enter politics, which he probably did very early, he had not yet become a 'politician'.

What you say about your search for background is not Greek to me, but pure Aztec. However, I expect you know what you mean and I hope you find it.

From R. W. Thompson   17th April, 1961
Sometimes you do have the oddest thoughts! I look back upon nearly 18 years of this correspondence—every now and then in its early stages —and wonder if anything has given me so much heart and help over all that period. However deep in the depths I managed to burrow a response from you invariably lightened my wilderness. In these last two or three years, of course, your letters have been a delight and instruction of a different order. I wouldn't 'swop' you and your letters for any other comparable commodity. You may regard yourself as very much responsible for the best things I write, and be completely absolved from a hand in the worst.

Nevertheless I have wrestled with my 'Greco-Aztec' background to Winston. No wonder you do not know what it means—I scarcely knew myself, except that I wanted to put in a kind of curious conception of a foundation cum thesis involving brief background nineteenth century and my own particular view of Winston. Often these tortured efforts do not survive into print, but I have found that more and more in these last years some such preliminary orgy is necessary before I get myself right into the job, and running smoothly. Nature, I think, provides comparable instances of the original root and/or branch withering away when the luxuriant growth finally comes into its own.

As for Lindemann–Tizard, naturally I have consumed every word and comment avidly. Few things throw more light on the dangers inherent in W.'s choices based on his personal likes and dislikes. This you have emphasised very strongly over the last two years. It is one of the reasons why I do not think he can measure up as a 'statesman' with Balfour, Asquith and Lloyd George. He has affinities with a medieval monarch. But then, I doubt whether any great egocentric could ever be as great a servant of a nation as those who serve ideals, principles, peoples, outside themselves. Hence, perhaps, Acton's dictum about power corrupting. Certainly the individual is corrupted.

Lindemann emerges as an unlikeable chap, but of course with his own kind of brilliance. His fault was exactly that of Winston—the desire for power. It all begins to help me to steer a course through all the strategic bombing fact and fiction when I come to it. As for A. J. P. Taylor . . . I am ordering his new book today. It is terrific to be able to order a few books at last, and I telephoned for Hankey's First World War effort immediately, and also for Charles Snow's Godber Lectures. Best to see what he actually did say to his Harvard audience.

Meanwhile this small spider sits at the centre of a slender communications web, and the system lately has been burning up with comments on the remarkable North–Alex effort, and why. Basil, I understand, is harrying North 'all round the compass'. Quite apart from the Alamein rights and wrongs, and I agree with the Official Historians and Basil that 1st Alamein was the fundamental turning point of that part of the war, North's (or Alexander's) stuff on Cassino is odd to say the least. They (he) appears not to have read Mark Clark's[1] excellent and documented record.

But all that is of general interest to me, and does not intrude upon my present thoughts. What am I trying to do? Not write a biography, not a political commentary, certainly not another Second World War commentary; but a 'profile' of the piece of earthbound 'cosmonautery' known as Winston Spencer Churchill. If my view is not unique enough, true enough, exciting enough, if it does not cast a new light on new facets to bring that man into focus that is different, more human, more sane than the present picture, then I shall have failed. Pieces like your asides about the nature of politicians, a hundred and one small, casual things you say, are of immense help.

And now I must write to old Dr. Linnell,[2] who has enclosed to me the 'Incomparable Boney's' latest letter. Boney, by the way, has been suffering from a wretched cough all winter. He remains irrepressible: 'The Commonwealth is now a zoo in which the keeper, through his lack of foresight, has got himself locked up with the monkeys.' A wicked, but wonderful old man, and of course a very good man of most rare character.

By the way, I was somewhat shocked to hear of a violent defence of Snow and attack on Lindemann by Sir Philip Joubert.[3] Not an hour earlier I had briefly consulted a piece by Joubert, written ten years earlier, in adulation of Winston and his brilliant choice of, guess who! Lindemann.

My innocence is constantly startled in this way. I hope I don't grow out of it.

[1] Mark Clark, U.S. General, U.S. Commander in Italy, Second World War.
[2] Dr. Linnell, leading physician circa 1900 and onwards. Friend of many leading political figures.
[3] Air Chief Marshal Sir Philip Joubert de la Ferté.

If I have been your 'stop and pray' for the last eighteen years of your life, it is a wonder you have still remained standing. A feebler rod and staff I cannot imagine. However, as long as you are still standing, and kicking and fighting all lies and nastiness, loud cheers from the prop, and '*non nobis gloria*'!

'Queer thoughts'. If only you knew half of them, I should be ashamed. Still we cannot be responsible for our thoughts, only for those which we accept and nurse. I disagree with the views of modern trick cyclists who seem to be trying to prove that no one is responsible for anything. But I do not agree with the psalmist, whoever he really was, who speaks of the Devil *qui rudens quasi leo, circuit, quaerens quem devoret.* For the Devil, whatever *he* is, is a spirit and can therefore offer thoughts to the unwary. Moreover there are apparently plenty of ordinary men and women who merrily do his job for him.

You have something in the suggestion that 'lust for power' equals 'politician'; but what a difference between 'lust for power' and praise-worthy ambition. Looks the same on the surface, but is really as different as a china egg is from the genuine hen-fruit.

And if all that is not better double talk than your Greco-Aztec, try the latter again. Actually yours of 17th is beginning to enlighten me for the first time.

As to profiles, do not forget the stout lady attempting to go through a swing-door, and being advised to 'try sideways', who replied, 'Lor' bless yer, I ain't got no sideways.'

Boney's wisecrack is superb.

I know Joubert well. Was fellow subaltern in gunners. I saw him taught to fly by Cody. He is really a very good chap and clever; but I would never go to him for an opinion on a scientist, or on anything save the actual job he was running at the moment, at which he would be very good indeed. But alas, he is now too old to do anything, like me.

I liked your remark anent your preliminary orgies before getting into a job; 'nature provides comparable instances of the original root withering away when the luxuriant growth finally comes into its own'.

These things are called, in horticulture, suckers! I feel there is a useful analogy hidden in that fact. Let the plant grow on its own proper roots, and do not graft onto a common variety!

I began this letter on 18th April. It is now 23rd, St. George's Day. For the last three days I have not had a moment in which to continue and end this letter, being engaged in compiling an enormous memo for the Minister of Health, with a view to slaying dragons.

I only end like this to demonstrate the sudden and unexpected claims on my time, apart from the daily crises at one or more of the hospitals for which I am responsible, daily crises at home. I am going to have the back wall of the house pointed. Bridget Killeen[1] has got it into her head that this means making the kitchen triangular, to which she naturally objects.

From R. W. Thompson   7th May, 1961
Your last letter, as usual, had its gems of wisdom half hidden in the ramifications of the Governorship of the Hammersmith Hospital. Certainly, there is no more—or even less of—a sideways for Winston Leonard Spencer Churchill than for any old lady, however dimensional. But meanwhile I am on top of the job. Suddenly the puzzle—like a map one looks at trying to form sea into land and vice versa, fell into place. Of course, here it was, like something buried in stone, only to be quarried. Only! As though the sculptor were merely a mason knocking bits off rocks. I knew what I wanted to find inside—or that there was something I had to find inside, but where was it? Now, that is done, and the rest goes steadily on, an ordered pattern growing upon proper foundations. No profile. No portrait. Perhaps, simply an exploration of a man from a point of view.

How such statements may make you cringe with embarrassment for me. And yet, did I not attempt such Everests, of what use would I be. When you think of all you know, and of the vast wildernesses of all that I don't know, you must blench, like John O'Dreams—if it were he who blenched. Or merely that Richard D. of G. of the 'hideous mountain' on his back to mock deformity. (Shakespeare, as you will have gathered, is a kind of garbled song in my head. But a brave song, and one that often sings.)

But what days of riches are these. So much stuff at last coming from many directions. Hankey's books—*The Innocence of Colonel Hankey*, the O'G roars in wonder. Can you *believe* in such innocence. Oddly I can. For innocence is the kind of end product of knowledge and understanding. (I hope I'm not talking an awful lot of rot, round and round a tree [of knowledge] which is you. If I am, you will, I believe, forgive me as always.) And then there is A. J. P. Taylor, a dangerous man, a sparker of many thoughts, a most valuable man used as spice, with his *Origins of the Second World War*. But I find de Gaulle the man, above most of them, who saw W. L. S. Churchill, who knew that given grandeur, then such a man could not be surpassed. In May and June 1940 there was grandeur enough, or he fashioned it into grandeur with words. But *Gloire* was never there; not de Gaulle's *gloire* anyway. And if there were no grandeur then for Winston, what then? Where could he make his heaven? Not, most assuredly, then or ever, 'in a lady's lap'. But in *making* grandeur, much of it counterfeit, an alchemy of words. Hence

[1] Bridget Killeen, Desmond's name for his old cook.

Greece and much else. And the 'born journalist' war correspondent idea—if there is no story make one.

But I see that old Baillie Grohman and Heckstall Smith have come up with a book on the Greek adventure, making it out the saviour of 'The Middle East' while admitting it lost Cyrenaica and brought R. to the gates of Egypt. One can make an argument for almost anything, and the trouble is that no man can say the argument invalid. For 'ifs' are not much good to anyone, least of all to an historian even as poor as I am.

I think upon you with a kind of anguish these days. I had a discussion with Basil Liddell Hart and the U.S. historian Forrest Pogue last Wednesday, Sir John Eldridge[1] intervening especially on Italy. I came out of it rather well.

But oh what do *you* know; what riches; what a wealth of 'unguess' lies beneath your unruffled exterior. About Lindemann. I don't see how I can avoid the conclusion that Lindemann was the most powerful single influence on Winston, perhaps from even before 1930 onwards to the end. And not 'science'—just anything. Germany potato patch, for example, according to H. E. Brand. If ever Churchill had something approaching a *real* friendship surely it was this. You have told me almost nothing about it, and you must know more than anyone else alive. And why should you! I don't complain. I merely observe that here I grope, praying to chip off the right piece of stone from my block of granite and reveal something *new* in the shape of the man.

How do I set about being worthy of some of your thoughts? I am no journalist . . . I have a distaste—a genuine distaste—for asking questions, especially personal questions. But I chase Churchill through the archives of the spirit, horrified and fascinated, even sympathetic. If even a glimpse of the man behind the myth is uncovered it will be worth doing, for a myth grows out of greatness, and its dispersal can only serve to reveal the true greatness out of which it grew. If that makes sense.

From Sir Desmond Morton   9th May, 1961 (begun)
If you have solved the problem of Winston or even of how he *used to* tick, you are a genius. Maybe you are. Why not? I never cringe with embarrassment for my friends, even if they are charged with unspeakable crimes. I rush into the ring, roaring like a dozen dragons and two St. Georges.

One may appear to be cynical, and yet be a Saint. Vide my good friend St. Thomas More, who cracks latin jokes about it, 'True indeed, the King's Grace has shown me marked favour of late, but yet know I well that if my head could gain him but one more castle in France, it would be stricken off.'

[1] Lieutenant-General Sir John Eldridge.

France. On that line, I had a chat with Harold Macmillan last week. He tells me that when he asked de Gaulle what would happen to France were he to die or be assassinated, Charles replied to the effect that he doubtless would soon either be slain or thrown out by the French. The moment he was forced to abuse the Constitution he would go voluntarily. But, said he, 'Make no mistake, the French already wish me gone. I know the French people. What they always really basically desire is to be ruled by a single man for a short while. Thereafter, for a short while, they long for no rule and to be able to roll with release in the ultimate mud of absolute chaos.'

Of course, de Gaulle is perfectly right. What the French have always wanted ever since Napoleon I, is a monarch, with power to be only a figurehead for nine months in each year, during which the French would have three Prime Ministers for three months each. For the remaining three months in each year, all reasonable Prime Ministers having been guillotined, the monarch would have power to rule absolutely, until the French found themselves another bunch of avaricious politicians.

Constitutional monarch for nine months. Dictator for three. AND and BUT your French monarch must be quasi-holy, of the ROYAL blood. You do not shed that again.

You intrigue me deeply by calling Maurice Hankey innocent. It sounds like nonsense, as though he did not know the facts of life— political life. Such a suggestion would be terrific nonsense. The parabolic cat would laugh so much that it would split itself in half—worse than little Audrey.

But when you say that Innocence is the end product of knowledge and understanding, I take off all my hats to you, even the inner skull cap only worn by Bishops.

Lawks! (vulgar, admittedly), how I knew Maurice, Captain R. M., Brevet Lt. Colonel. Older than I, of course, but in many ways, quite inimitable, though humourless.

By the way, your friend Winston is now right 'out'. He makes no sense any more. Poor old s.o.b. His principal private secretary during the latter part of the war, now Sir John Martin, Deputy Secretary to the Colonial Office, was in America on business of State. He visited Winston on the Onassis yacht. W.S.C. had *no* idea who he was, and at one juncture thought he was Pug Ismay!!! Two people more utterly different it would be hard to find. Apparently the poor old man has more or less forgotten details of his own past; but remembers with great sense and lucidity what the daily papers have been talking about during the past week. He is thus the complete opposite to most old men. He would be. But frankly he makes no sense any more.

It is rather frightful, humanly and humanely speaking, is it not?

Those of us who live long enough will all arrive at the same misty glory of forgetfulness. Have you ever thought how perfectly useless a memory really is, save for a few worldly ends and as part of Purgatory and Hell?

Duncan Grinnell Milne's book contains more truth about the doings of Winston and Roosevelt with de Gaulle, than I have seen published anywhere. He calls the book *The Triumph of Integrity*, and then fails to show what particular integrity belonged to de Gaulle. No matter, he has blown a lot of fuses on W.S.C. and Roosevelt. Moreover he has really got somewhere when he suggests that the hatred of Roosevelt and the chief American statesman for de Gaulle was pathological, erected through their utter horror over the moral and military collapse of France. All their secret thoughts and far-off policies were based on France holding out against Hitler. (History; Lafayette etc. Also 'Good republican France', 'Horrid monarchical England' 'Why, curse it, she even has colonies. French colonies? No sirree. France is carrying on a republican mission in certain backward territories—they are not colonies. England, God curse her, she is exploiting the poor naked savage for her own advantage')!

Anyway, when all this bust up with the pop-bang blow up of Paris–France, then the name of everything French became anathema. Christ! they had to think again—and quick. The God-dam limeys were sticking it. All upside down. Why Hurrah, their boss-boy, Prime Minister they call him, he's half a good American. Hope still. Let's work it out.

Meanwhile for Chrissake keep all snail-eating sons of so and so's of Frenchmen out of the way.

But, of course, you have realised long ago that the above was the true psychological background to the general situation.

Why the present President's father became so unpopular in America as well as in England, was (a) he gave away through sheer arrogant stupidity, to H.M.G. what the line of thought was—as per above—in high places in the U.S.A. and (b) he told the American Government to go right on thinking that way since they were right and it was going to pan out.

Oh non-no no! The Churchill–Lindemann relationship was never real friendship. Each recognised the use each could make of and be to the other. There was no more real friendship between them than there is between Winston and Onassis today.

Winston's nearest approach to a mutual friendship (leaving out his immediate family) was, in recent years, Brendan Bracken and Barney Baruch. Largely because neither of these quite notable men had any illusions about Winston. You can put Beaverbrook in next. The Beaver only liked Winston as a sparring partner and vice versa. Winston was never as close to F.E.[1] as to the Beaver, because F.E. slightly despised him. He could out argue Winston on any subject at any time.

Your own words. How right. You chase Winston through the archives of the spirit, horrified and fascinated, even sympathetic. Beautiful! But I would put 'fascinated' first, then a curious mixture of sympathy and horror. Something that has been so enormously great, and yet, at the trial, has failed its own greatness, and so is now left without understanding of the memories of greatness. Not quite right, but on the way.

You are one hundred per cent right. What was the man like behind the myth, which he himself knew and believed to be himself?

Love to all. My next address may well be Execution Dock, or Little Ease.

Hamba Gashlé!

From R. W. Thompson   23rd May, 1961

The scourge of the family man is upon us this year with a vengeance . . . violent flus, colds, and what you will. Schools over a wide area have been reduced frequently to little more than twenty-five per cent attendance . . .

With my woolly head and wheezy chest I have been labouring, considering with a combination of intellect and emotions (is it possible to consider by any other means?) the actual *beginning* of it all—I mean It, the conflicts, unresolved of the twentieth century. Not by contrivance my reasoning produced the year 1895 (or late 1894). In that year Japan, to the consternation of the Western World, beat up old China in no time at all, and set Germany, Russia, U.S.A. and Britain racing to stake claims. Naval power took on new aspects, and was no longer the prerogative of Britain. Japan, furious at German–Russian interference (Shimonoseki?) built up her fleet and bided her time. U.S.A. was clearly a Colonial power, whatever she might say etc. etc.

I won't go on. But that does seem to me, not the 'origins', but a true beginning. And in that year our Hero embarked upon the adult world, via U.S.A. to Cuba, thence to his oddly conceived regimental duties in India. Curious that Winston and World War should *show* themselves in the same fateful year—or am I too far-fetching?

Your letter of the 9th was absolutely grand, feeding my hungry mind. And alas for poor W.S.C., how tragic it is that such a man, however merely mere man, and weak withal, should end so: the Gorgon's Head, you have it there. And think of men like Russell and Shaw, lucid, producing, thinking to the end. That is a tragic measure. But the alternative for the likes of Winston (and de Gaulle and Jeanne d'Arc) to the Gorgon's Head is the stake or the cross.

[1] F. E. Smith, later Earl of Birkenhead.

All that you say about U.S.A.–France–Britain is wonderful stuff to feed into my mills. I haven't yet read Grinnell Milne. I think he is being poorly treated by the Press. As for Attlee—I have the Williams book,[1] have thus far glanced through it, and shall do so again with care. But how Attlee bores me to excrucation, if there is such a term. His humour, if that is the word, crawls more slowly than a four-ounce tortoise tethered to a ton weight. Now and then he says something amusing. By accident, one feels. Even hilarious . . . Admirable man, I'm sure.

The fact is I don't think I'm going to come upon any real truth about Winston or Roosevelt by way of old Clem. I get more out of half a thought of yours.

I am also exercised about the ambivalence of Germany through the nineteenth century—and even now—towards US. There was the Hanoverian liking, liberalism against the Prussian disliking, the slow growth of Anglophobia-philia, mixed love-hate, I suppose in more modern terms.

And this first expressed by Schiller (1780s, I think) came back into currency with Wilhelm II in those portentous 1890s. That, for my money, is the decade where it all begins, including W.S.C. as an adult. If adult can ever be a correct term in regard to the infant-giant Winston, the only man—in Boney's potent phrase—he ever knew to pass from first to second childhood without maturity intervening. Gosh, I am provided with *bon mots* by the score by my friends, mainly yourself.

Another very valuable point about your letter was your straightening up of my thoughts on the Lindemann–W.S.C. relationship. I see at once how it was, and how all these relationships varied, Beaverbrook, F.E. etc. and why. Leaving Baruch and Bracken more or less in unique roles largely, as you say, because neither had any illusions about Winston.

Reading your last letter through again I curse my fevers for preventing me from writing before—for all I knew—you were on your way to 'Execution Dock'. As for Hamba Gashlé—what in Heaven or earth is that?

From Sir Desmond Morton   27th May, 1961
I return the Neilson MSS. I knew about him. As you say, nothing new, and anyhow, 'and so what?'

*   *   *

How right you are, there is nothing to 'Hate' in Winston—a few things to dislike and even deplore. It is a perfect waste of time to try and prove what any thinking person (one per 50,000 of the popula-

[1] Francis Williams, *A Prime Minister Remembers.*

tion?) now knows perfectly well as to what he was. The interesting question is how and why did he become what he was, when his blood brother was a very decent gentleman, rather stupid, save over American Finance, Stocks and Shares and took no interest in any of the things which Winston lived for? Genes, hormones, upbringing and education—(environment was identical for the two)? But so wildly differing a psychology.

Anyway, perhaps you'll find out one day and tell us.

Everybody has had the cold–flu–bronchitis here, and would be recovering were it not for the bitter north-east wind which is slowly killing me, but not quick enough.

Still there is asparagus and gull's eggs . . . On Tuesday I have to dress up in a top hat and so on to aid the Monarch open a foundations stone or lay a new ward block or something at Bart's. What a waste of time. And no food going either.

P.S. Hamba Gashlé, strong 'h' in Hamba and 'shl' in Gashlé pronounced as a click and sucking noise, is Zulu and means 'au revoir' or literally 'Walk' (away) 'smoothly' (happily, safely, carefully).

From R. W. Thompson   5th June, 1961
I am somewhat poor in spirit in the aftermath of all these flus and things, moving mentally and physically at snail's pace, but moving. Oddly enough my book began to go really well last week, and the whole story I have to tell is clear ahead. I am fortified, rather than otherwise, by never having seen, heard or read any conclusions or assessments of Winston from any quarter, remotely like my own. Yet, curiously, I feel that somehow I have dreamed and thought myself inside that man. It is, in fact, the first time that I have devoted months of my life to such a task—the attempt to understand somebody else.

Do you remember, a long time ago, I wrote to you suggesting a kind of 'bogus-maleness' about Winston? I didn't know quite what I meant, and neither, I think, did you. But the line of thought begins to work out. I have never studied a man who remained, in many ways, so much a child—not an adolescent, but a child. I don't think he ever loved, or was capable of loving, a woman—or perhaps anybody. Mrs. Everest, his mother, his wife, his faithful servants, represented his needs. And throughout his life he always had one or the other or their equivalent. But I cannot find a real 'power' man in Winston. He lacks malevolence, the naked evil essential to such a role. Shakespeare's Richard III—now there is a power boy, and at once (or so it seems to me) you can fit Stalin and Roosevelt into that kind of frame. Not exactly, of course, but they fit. As for Hitler, too much the psychopath to put in quite that class.

But as a 'power man' Winston remains a child in such company. His dream of power, like his dream of being a general, is a child's dream of being 'an engine driver'. It is an end dream—no work, no apprenticeship, no Machiavellian scheming; simply, miraculously, one IS. But such dreams do not come true. Winston could never achieve the kind of 'naked' power of which he had idly dreamed. For it was idly. He had never considered exactly what power meant. And he was never to attain it. His triumph and tragedy was, in a sense, that he was a better man. There were chinks in the armour of his egocentricity. When he had power in 1940 it was not his own; it was England's, because in that 'hour' he was England, and England was Winston. It was power 'in his own right', even in the sense that Roosevelt and Stalin (not to mention R.III) wielded it, had it, conceived it.

When Winston was no longer 'England' his power was an empty shell. This he did not understand. But in being an expression of a people in that period he lost, for a little while, his total egocentricity. In the act of expressing some force totally outside himself he was not that egocentric.

When it began to wane, he waned. At the end, recognising clearly all that he had done, naturally England rejected him. They had rejected him even as early as 1941 in truth. Henceforth, as you once remarked, he became aware—suddenly—of power. It was, you wrote to me, almost a 'schizophrenic trick'—his sudden realisation of power. But, in fact, as I see it this happened to him at the moment when he realised, briefly, the meaning of personal power and no longer *had it*—in the sense I am now writing. Hence he behaved like a 'bastard' (if you'll forgive me). Hence sacking great men whenever and wherever he dared, hence bombing (I don't want to go too far, and won't—I'm just thinking aloud here, but not in my book). In sum it is only when Winston's fortunes and England's fortunes coincide that he is at a pinnacle. The pinnacle is not *his*, but he is at the summit of it, its voice and expression, even its image.

But this makes him human. I couldn't possibly write a book like this about any of the others. I should be able, I think, coldly, to regard their malevolence, their nearly absolute evil. But I would not be able to understand it, or sympathise with it, in my heart. It would be, merely, a phenomenon. But Winston isn't a phenomenon. He's a person, a ruthless, egocentric adult-infant, demanding of life and all about him, a spoilt child at that. Terrifying, of course, as any infant with even half a giant's strength must be. But, at the core, someone one can feel for, be sorry for, weep for—bless, in the end, and pray perhaps nunc dimittis . . . thy servant who was too much his own servant, serving himself, but *did* serve a people.

His fate now is written in his 'stars'. If he lived long enough he was bound to revert to senile childhood of age, to go full circle. Impossible to imagine such a fate overtaking a de Gaulle, for example. If Winston had had—or deserved—the luck of Alexander [the Great]—or even of Rupert Brooke (if you see what I mean) he would have died at the end of 1940. That story would have been truly heroic in caste. It would all have made sense, and had the qualities of an epic. After that, alas, the bright vision fades. 1941 is horrible—it is all horrible, until in 1945 it becomes sad, and finally pitiful.

I hope all this conceals somewhere some truth to sort out more clearly. I live with it, and because of that you will forgive me. There is no one else to whom I could write like this, and it is of inestimable value to me to be able to do so. If it is drivel, it is even more important to put it down. But somewhere in the heart of it all, not easy to find, to sift, there is, I believe, a truth about Winston. Meanwhile he goes down on paper, and I am certain, lives. Whether it is the real Winston, only God could know, but he makes sense in this context.

What a curious thing is breeding. Winston with nearly all his out-ward qualities through the 'dam' (except for looks). Marlborough and Churchill much more a projection of his powerful imagination. Winston is American. That's where he belongs, and in his early days (up to thirty-five–forty) he knows it. After that he becomes ambivalent, wondering at times on which side his bread is buttered. The trouble is that his energies were too canalised away from emotion. He was a man who (to be balanced and be truly great) needed to love a woman passionately, and actually, or be in a battle once a week. As it was nothing filtered all that off. Sublimation is something else. Winston sublimated nothing. He let his emotional (and psychic) energies pour through the wrong tap.

Having burdened you with all that, failing even to hope thus far that you did get a 'drink and a bun' at that Nurse's wing at the time of your attendance upon H.M., and failed to get anything horrible, such as a cold. And, as you say, there is, or was until a week ago, asparagus. But not, in these parts gull's eggs, instead the wily plover.

And now, I must strive to fight out of the cotton wool enclosing such brains as I possess (and in this you have already helped me greatly by being on the other end of this typewriter), and work. Blessings upon you and your House, and our combined love . . .

From Sir Desmond Morton   10th June, 1961
Heartened by having won my war with a Professional Association, which in my just wrath I called a Trades Union, but proportionately depressed by hearing that all my contemporaries nearly have either gone mad or died, I am in sober fettle and can the more appreciate your letter of 5th June.

Frankly I am in awe of your thoughts which seem to me to carry much colour of truth. I have just been lunching with Jo Grimond[1] and his charming wife; also present her mother, Violet Bonham Carter,[2] daughter of old Asquith, who recalled that the last time we had met was at Chequers in the war, where apparently I had corrected some of her views about Winston. She gave me credit for far more wisdom than ever I have possessed, and something like the gift of prophecy, which I have never had.

Anyway we spoke much of those days and even earlier when her late husband, Maurice Bonham Carter was Asquith's Private Secretary. Many tales of villainy and heroism were unfolded. You would have enjoyed it.

Indeed I was resistant to your words that Winston had something of 'bogus maleness' about him. But now that you have corrected those words to 'bogus-grown-upness', and continued on the theme, I perceive you have a very interesting theory and line. In fact, I am pretty sure you have begun to uncover something very like the truth.

It still wants a lot of working out; but you will not forget his own account of his dream of success; to unite (or if you like *reunite*) England and the Empire with the United States. Indeed I do not think it was like Hitler's dream of uniting the world under *his own* domination. As you say, like a child he dreamed of being the author of great things, the architect of great buildings, but not necessarily their owner. His admiration of and desire to rank with his great ancestor Marlborough, was not really founded on a desire to fight and win great battles and to play at soldiers, but because having done so, Marlborough mixed with the great ones of other countries and was those countries' arbiter, though he did not rule them.

He needed his constitutional Monarch to be the symbolic ruler, and above all his Parliament to rule, while he was the great adviser, the great maker of plans, which others should carry out.

This is not quite your line, but think upon it. That he was never able to face absolute reality in great affairs and was thus always a dreaming child in part, is true, I feel sure. He nearly did so, or had to do so, when he was turned out of power in 1945. That is why he never really forgave the British people for that act; for the dream taking charge and not doing what he had dreamed it should.

Yes indeed he did serve a people but by serving himself. He served a people therefore, as it were accidentally (to his own way of thinking, were Winston ever capable of thought of that kind).

I suppose that self-analysis must always have been impossible to

[1] Jo Grimond, prominent Liberal politician, Leader of the Liberal Party.
[2] Lady Violet Bonham Carter, daughter of Asquith.

Winston. How could it be? When all his acts were dreams and the dreams seemed to come true? Were they not *his* dreams?

There is a Jungian interpretation of all this. He never saw what or what he did, as reality. When the dreams began to take charge and had a life of their own, he was struggling all the while to dream again as the dream should be.

If cotton-woollyness produces thoughts such as you have set down in your letter, sometimes in very great words, may I recommend you to get a dose of flu once a fortnight.

Winston, the brilliant, great, imaginative, ever-dreaming child, whom no one ever taught to control his imagination, or to be disciplined or to think of others! But, and here is the great question! Why did not they? Why did not those who said in his boyhood and youth how horrid he was, why did they apparently do nothing about it? *There* is a question which simply *must* be answered.

I do not know anything about his youth. But I can ask myself what emotions he created in others, not only in me by any means, when he had become a man of power. The first was *Entertainment*. Far above anything else. 'Admiration' of a kind, well second. Genuine 'Affection?' I am horrified to find that I think the answer is NO.

When he was out of power in the 30s, he was exactly like a child whose toy is broken. He ran to anyone for comfort, thus inspiring the same pity (akin to affection) as would the child with its broken toy. If the passer by happened to help mend his toy, or, better still, give him a new one, he ran off happily to play with it, with no sense or need for gratitude to the kindly stranger.

It begins to fit.

Of course, this is not the whole story. No man can be dissected into one single object. Every man is intensely complicated. But I think the dissection has indicated a very important part of the watch indeed. Perhaps the main spring.

I shall keep your letter.

Salutations to you and to Mel, and to all at the Mill, where something of value is going to be ground out.

P.S. Vague relevant thoughts. Important to keep in clear perspective the difference between 'childlike and childish'.

'When I became a man, I put away childish things'.

What would a 'man' be like who did not put away all childish things and possibly was never child-like?

From R. W. Thompson   19th June, 1961
Your grand letter of the 10th arrived to delight and stimulate me at a time when my wretched 'intestinal tract' was behaving as it almost

always behaves when I am under the tensions, inseparable from mentally 'biting off more than I can chew', and biting it. When this book is done I shall have to face that situation squarely and seek the best advice I can get. Meanwhile I am more or less recovered, having filled in the time by a burst of reading and writing voluminous notes.

Power and freedom are both strange states to ponder. I see that Sartre said yesterday in the *Observer*: 'I think the desire to retain power comes from already possessing it.' This fits in with my thoughts on Winston's sudden change of behaviour in 1941. Again Sartre said: 'Everything depends on the situation. No one is born with a desire to seek power or to shun it. It's a man's history that makes him move one way or the other.'

Certainly the whole power problem in regard to Winston is complex, but less complex, I think, than with many others. I find his total egocentricity helpful. His Narcissus tendencies appear to me very great, and his inability really to understand anyone else stands in the way of his greatness. Yet, against this, he is one of the very few to have 'understood', or had a flash of inspired insight, about de Gaulle. I would class his support of de Gaulle as one of Churchill's greatest acts, not necessarily politically, but as a man. I think in all the circumstances he withstood that Calvinistic masterpiece Cordell Hull, and the sinister Roosevelt with considerable courage and tenacity. True he wobbled a good deal in the years, but he seems to me, with my limited knowledge of what really went on at Teheran and Yalta, to have stuck to de Gaulle pretty bravely. Indeed, even though it may be held (by me) that he 'sold Britain down the river', (having first 'saved it' in 1940), he most certainly had a hand in preserving France as a European power. For that he must have very great credit. But of these things you know a great deal.

But why did people tolerate Winston, especially in the early days? As you remark, it is a vital question. Indeed it is remarkable how widely 'cads' are tolerated in all walks of life. The great mass of 'decent' people are extraordinarily sensitive, disliking 'trouble', disliking to be forced to say very unpleasant things. But if you examine closely, let us say, the predicament of Lord Roberts when this unwanted young and precocious 'Puppy' forced his way into his tent and to his table, what are you going to do. 'Icy silence' achieves nothing. Referring to him directly in the most opprobious terms appears to pass unnoticed. Does Roberts order an orderly to throw the young man out? He is, after all, an aristocrat, and at a pinch 'a brother officer'. Indeed, it becomes clear to me that whether you are Lord Roberts or Hugo Baring,[1] sharing quarters, or Haldane, having his shoulders climbed

[1] Hugo Baring, Churchill's brother officer in India during the early years of Churchill's career.

upon, the only thing you can do with the Winstons of this world is to resort to violence. Well, no one likes to do that. They may be too old—or smaller! They are almost certain to dislike brawling. And then, there are always the servants.

One sees this incorrigible cad simply helping himself to drinks, since no one offers him one, seating himself comfortably, putting his spoke in here, there and everywhere. And presently impossible to ignore, you have to say something.

As an exercise on a much lower level, try getting rid of that impossible . . . Randolph. You, no doubt, could do it much better than I. But it forces you (or me) to behave in a manner we do not like. We do not feel that 'civilised' men should resort to such words or deeds. So the 'Cad' is in a strong position if he has a thick enough skin.

But Winston, thick skin or not, is sustained by a definite goal. He is not being a cad simply for the sake of it. He demands freedom from his earliest days. Now, this may seem a very reasonable, even admirable, desire, until one realises that freedom is unobtainable except at the expense of others. Years ago I gave tongue to the pronouncement that 'aristocrats and tramps' were the last refugees of individualism. I think there was much truth in it. Both, of course, are more or less extinct today, but they have their counter-parts appearing here and there in other guises. Now, nothing infuriates a man more than someone enjoying something at his expense, and revealing to him in the process that he does not possess what he has led himself to believe he possesses. I'm afraid that is shockingly expressed. But I mean that he pointed out to Baring and Barnes and his brother O's at Bangalore that their freedom was a myth. They were tied by 'duty', by the myriad strings of convention, by (even) a desire for security, the security of a safe military life. Winston had no ties and no scruples. A scrupulous adventurer is an absurdity, as extinct (if it ever existed) as the dodo—or a scrupulous woman. For, in her nature, a woman cannot even conceive of being scrupulous. It would threaten her survival, not to mention the 'race'. Again, I think that a man instinctively disparages the qualities which make another man dangerous to him, and by the same token instinctively flatters the qualities which may render such a man harmless.

But Churchill is disliked, even hated to excess by many, because he was a traitor not only to his class, but to true adventurers. The dice was too heavily loaded in his favour. He didn't start from scratch. He didn't intend to abide by the rules at all—and it is said, truly, that there is honour among thieves. But Winston had no scruples at all. He wanted the best of all possible worlds, and because of that, in the end, he failed. It was the 'loaded dice' that in the end defeated him, as in the end it will defeat any man.

Of course, you are wonderfully right when you name the emotions he created in others when he had become 'a man of power'. He could then be regarded in 'isolation'. He was no longer climbing upon the backs of his contemporaries, no longer threatening their positions, no longer drawing attention to their self-imposed limitations, twanging the bars of the cages in which they had thought they were free. So 'the first was "Entertainment".' So you wrote in your letter. I think this is a terrific statement, revealing an insight which knocks all others into cocked hats. In that piece of perception there is a world of understanding of what I believe to be the real Winston. The more one thinks of it the better.

There is Winston at the height of his ambition, and what men feel observing him is 'first Entertainment'. It is a most terrible indictment of him, and in my view it is the unmistakable truth. But I must get down to hard writing to repair the ravages of my ailment—not that the time was not well spent in reading, assessing, all essential to my task. Indeed, brakes must be applied, either by myself or by nature. For this quest of mine must not be jeopardised by speed, even though a certain speed is essential in many ways.

I find it infuriating in life that wisdom comes at the end instead of the beginning. Imagine what a world we might have if we were born wise, our wisdom maturing, say, in our twenties, continuing, say, to fifty, and thenceforth dwindling. Instead of the reverse. But, why should I grumble, for it is because of this that 'words' have 'changed the world', or would have changed it had they not been always 'too late'. If wisdom came in youth deeds would have rendered the words of age unnecessary.

I believe that men like yourself and Alex Cadogan helped Winston all you could because you realised, perhaps not in concrete terms, that only a combination of a 'cad and a gentleman' might get into the 'game' with any hope of success against the Hitlers, Stalins and Roosevelts. One has only to imagine Asquith playing such a part, or even to slide down the ladder at speed, a Baldwin. Not a hope in Hell, as they say. Finally, I envy you your lunch with Jo Grimond and Violet B.C. I see no one these days. My own fault.

From Sir Desmond Morton   21st June, 1961
Non nobis sed Tibi gloria, Domine! You will note that I put capitals before certain words, so that you may not suppose I am offering *you* the glory.

My Islamic friends, all of whom are of the old persuasion and speak classical Arabic, which, alas, I do not, but wish I did, remind me that in that tongue there is no word for the English 'Thank you', as addressed to another human being. There is indeed some horrid modern equivalent, but to the old in the Faith of Peace, no thanks are due to anyone save God alone. Hence '*Al hamd'ul Illah*', is the due equivalent of 'thank you'. Literally, 'All praise to God' (alone)! A very good thought.

This introduction is to enable me to retain my humility and reject firmly all the laudatory phrases you habitually use towards me.

Sartre's statement in the *Observer* is largely nonsense. Perhaps he was thinking in French. I can see half a dozen possible French translations of the quotation, each of which would have a different emphasis.

To say, in English, that the desire to retain power comes from already possessing it, is ludicrous. How can one 'retain' anything one does not already possess!

If he means that anyone who has power and so has tasted its delights, tries avidly to retain it, then he is talking sense, as known to anyone, not only politicians, who has ever held power. *L'appétit vient en mangeant.*

But when he says that no one is born with a desire to seek power (or to shun it), he is talking *utter* nonsense. The merest tyro in psychology, philosophy, morals or metaphysics or ontology will laugh like an emptying bath at such drivel. The contrary is the truth. Every man and every woman—and, in its own degree, every brute beast—is born with a desire for power. Some with an overwhelming desire akin to mania; others with so little that it is hard to trace it. But all have it. All ambition—even rightful ambition—is a manifestation of the power-seeking-urge. Try reading Adler.

Freud, Adler, Jung. The first called his power-urge, sex; thereby meaning something very special and recondite, not what the *Daily Mirror* calls 'sex'. Adler, improved on that with his 'Will to Power'. Jung, just dead, and the most remarkable of the three, sought the causes of this varying but universal urge in human beings.

If you want something older, try the Book of Revelation: 'Through lust for Power fell the Angels'. I know the English translation of the Greek gives that as 'Through Pride . . .' But anyone (even Enoch Powell, Minister of Health, but a great classical scholar) knows that the Greek word used is not the equivalent of 'Pride', but of 'lust for power'.

Lust for power is the Devil in person, the final temptation of even good men. (Even the temptation of God himself in the flesh! One of the reasons I believe that the Christ is True God and True man.) The world, the flesh and the Devil. The world signifies its pleasures and excitements. The flesh we all know about. The Devil is that inborn lust for power.

But when you come down to wondering why X or Y or Winston manifested such an *inordinate* lust for power from the very beginning, you are up against a fascinating mystery which Jung, with all his wisdom and his symbolic 'Archetypes' never solved satisfactorily. A Narcissist most certainly, and that alone is usually a sign of great power-lust—developed indeed and intensified by actually enjoying it: enjoying it in more than one sense of the word. His confession to me once that a real sense of physical danger (or a belief that he was in physical danger would be my gloss) gave him a thrill like a sexual act, is deeply interesting psychologically in this respect.

The reality was of course that his own belief in his invulnerability and the after sense of having courted danger successfully, being unscathed, gave his power sense an enormous boost. Symbolically he had 'conquered death'.

I am not quite ready to agree that Winston's support of de Gaulle was a sign of his greatness. He supported him very grudgingly; but did so, because (a) he 'found' de Gaulle before anyone else (in his own thoughts), therefore de Gaulle became 'his'; (b) because he had the wit to realise that de Gaulle was a card in his, and not the American, hand; (c) because he really did think that a France was necessary to a balanced Europe, which Roosevelt in his aversion to all things French, after the 'let-down', did not. But Winston would never believe that de Gaulle was really the 'goods'. To him de Gaulle was all there was. Winston never believed that de Gaulle in person would rule France after the war. He thought de Gaulle would be swamped by clever French politicians, and was always trying to winkle such out of France in order to replace de Gaulle by them. He stuck to de Gaulle because he failed to find an older soldier, let alone a known French politician to take his place and he could always make some use of him as an offset to some of Roosevelt's cards. These last were clearly of another pack altogether. Nevertheless, with these reservations, he did 'stick to de Gaulle' and thereby helped (but did not know he was doing it) to preserve France, which he wanted to do.

Actually de Gaulle embodied most of the things which Winston thoroughly disliked. A genuine soldier, without political experience, who became overnight a successful politician and, in fact, defeated the expert politicians at their own game. A man who never boasted about it, but who tried to maintain inviolate—although a politician—a strict code of honour and ethical dealing. A politician who actually announced publicly what he stood for, and never suffered for such a dreadful breach of the modern political code. And finally, a man who told Winston in impeccable and polite French—as good as Winston's English—to go jump in the lake, when W.S.C. asked, begged, and ordered him to do something against his moral or ethical principles. Worse still de G. used to explain, as to a child of twelve, why the proposal was against his moral principles.

This last, of course, was a bit hard for anyone like Winston to swallow, since it made it clear that in de Gaulle's opinion, Winston had *no* principles whatever.

To my unregenerate self, this was astonishingly funny. Hence part of my Entertainment.

Yes indeed! You have seen an immense vision when you describe on page 2 of your letter why a cad given certain other advantages, according to the century he lives in, 'gets there'.

Curiously enough, I have just had a letter from an old, greatly admired friend of seventy-six, who is a person of the highest integrity and learning, wondering why it is that in these days as in others, the cad succeeds, while the decent 'gentleman' gets left behind. My correspondent, who was not thinking of himself in the least, he being no competitor in the Government Power Stakes, answers his own question much as you answer it. But it is an interesting matter for thought. It is even interesting to think out what constitutes a 'cad' and what, a 'bounder'. I also find it most interesting to remember before the First World War altered so greatly the structure of society, that a cad or bounder was quite definitely 'not received' and ostracised by that very valuable and solid (sometimes stolid) 'upper crust' of the County family type, which provided the 'ruling classes'.

Though only a lad at the time and just a young man, I can well remember that among those who firmly thought they knew 'how a gentleman should behave' there was really astonishing liberality of thought on such matters. Wealth and nobility of blood was not enough, while on the other hand, relative poverty or 'lowly parentage' by no means stood in a man's way if he was 'one of nature's gentlemen'. A man or woman might 'have to be received' through being a peer or the son of a peer; politicians ditto; a few wealthy 'cads' ditto; but they were never admitted to personal friendship or intimacy. The really good Men's Clubs regularly blackballed otherwise suitable candidates for membership, who were not 'gentlemen'. Some 'cads and bounders' had to be invited to great receptions and balls, but were never invited to dine privately or to 'weekends in the country'. Even in my day before the First World War, an officer of the Army or Navy who presented, even accidentally, a dud cheque, who was concerned in a divorce case, or who got into minor trouble with the police for, say, being drunk in a public place or was concerned in any newspaper scandal, was instantly required to resign his commission, and was never heard of in society again.

All rather snobbish, I have no doubt; made worse in that a grandson of the Duke of Marlborough could be a howling cad and get away with it to a great extent on the excuse that it was 'for the sake of his mother'. Even so there were plenty of houses in which Winston as a young man would *not* easily have been received, and those not the noblest by any means.

By the way, I suppose you know what disease killed Lord Randolph Churchill? There seems to be no physical trace of it in his descendants. A frightfully dangerous and unpleasant subject; never referred to in the books.

However that may be, Winston as a boy, youth and young man must have been a howling cad, but never in matters of sex or money; only in selfishness and disregard for anyone's feelings but his own. He had a lot of charm, it is clear, and was sometimes so outrageous that he caused a sort of *Schadenfreude* (untranslatable from the German) and 'entertainment' so long as the person 'entertained' was not a victim of his characteristics. As the child wonder and the youngest Cabinet Minister etc. he learned to alter somewhat his caddishness and reserve it for 'business', i.e. his own advancement in his chosen career of politics as a road to Power. He began to realise the meaning (and value to himself) of what he had seen in ducal palaces, the manner of a Grand Seigneur. These two psychological developments made him far more acceptable. This developed further; and perhaps it is fair to say that he carried the two traits to great perfection as time went on, hiding the caddishness under the Grand Seigneur; but never losing the former and using it when he felt the need.

This is merely confirmation of all that you say in your second and third pages. It is beginning to take shape.

But one must always remember—I—as well as you—that one cannot dismiss any man whatsoever, as simply as all this. Any man is a much more complicated creation than this.

How far and when and in what was Winston absolutely genuine and 'grown up'? Broadly speaking you are certainly right in saying that he cannot be regarded as a fully integrated grown man at any time. But I am sure you will at the same time realise that he was not wholly and at all times a complete Actor, playing the part he had conceived and previously noted for himself. He had moments of doubt, of human weakness and of sincerity, which were not in the script. Try and trace some of these. You will get further great illumination thereby.

Reverting to 'cads'. It is fascinating to see today how many such push themselves into high places, while many others, seemingly even more gifted, and who are not cads fail relatively to do so. What special sort of cad is the successful one? By 'cad' I do not mean a really evil man. Napoleon was not only a thundering cad, but was an evil man. Curiously enough there is some evidence that as a boy and young man Buonaparte was not a cad at all, nor was he evil.

It is all psychology. What makes that half-spirit, half-brute beast-

Man behave as he does? A great friend of mine who has studied psychology deeply and continuously (NOT psychiatry, but human behaviourism) for fifty years, and who is internationally regarded as a master of his subject, confessed to me that he is still merely a schoolboy in his subject.

Note. One kind of 'cad' kicks a man when he is down. Never, never, did Winston do that. He would get his enemy down all right, and why not? But he would then leave him and forget all about him. He would never dream of picking him up, however. Verb. sap.

Look after the intestines. Be good to the young. They can un-consciously teach us all much psychology. To Mel and yourself a profound salute in all sincerity.

From R. W. Thompson   2nd July, 1961

I awake these days before the dawn to that miraculous orchestra of bird song. With our windows wide, an enormous apple tree extending to within a foot of our windows, with forest, meadow all round, wonderful music is our morning delight. Small birds, wrens, pippets, tree climbers, tits, of course in droves, practically stand on our chests, their beaks going in that peculiar trilling, throats vibrating, quite fearless. All the larger birds remain in the background. In the hour or two of half sleep that follows old Churchill, young Churchill makes shadows through my mind from the previous day's work, and the evening 'homework'. This morning I wondered whether it might be true—in the sense of not creating a false impression—to believe that there could have been in him a kind of national—or international—Oedipus, through his blood 'marrying' his mother's country, yet not quite sure, not 'killing' his father, torn between admirations, aggrava-tions, ambitions, ambivalences. Perhaps, like a moth to a flame, feeling a compulsion to 'flirt' with his mother's country—dangerously.

But I don't want to drag Freud into this, and on your sound advice I shall read Jung. Knowing very little about these things I had for some years felt Jung to be the soundest thinker in that field. But—how does one find the time for all the reading necessary to the equipment of even a half-educated human being! It has always astounded me that almost everyone one knows under the age of thirty appears to have read 'everything', sloshing quotations all over the place in reviews, word perfect in the Greeks, the best of the Latins, not without acquaint-ance with the sages of India and China, able to recite the essays of Montaigne, word perfect in Montesquieu, and playwrights in five languages, ancient and modern. It beats me. When one gets older it seems one has to read the bare fringes of things, the gaps yawning like abysses on every hand. I worked out once just how many books a man could read, say, in fifty years of adult life at a rate of, say, three important works a week. It appears that chaps, like Tynan for example, have doubled this before the age of thirty!

So I am a clod; but not with too great an inferiority complex. (Perhaps too little?) At any rate I have just completed the first third of my book. I know that it is good in parts. I shall not read it just now, but press on with Part Two, which will bring me in another 35,000 words or so to 1940 and Part Three. But this is not a history of anything but, I hope, Churchill, and then not exactly a history, but an exploration of an odd kind, certainly of a different kind. Perhaps it will spark off some younger people to think on lines which might otherwise have remained invisible.

Your words in regard to the death of Lord Randolph rather suggest something really fell. I know no more than Winston's own description in his life of his father. What he writes there I imagine to be consistent with a particularly horrible cancer—or even more horrible syphilis. Your remarks about the children of the next generation would point to some such conclusion. But surely a man would not breed knowing himself in such a condition which, one supposes, must have been congenital, like the scourge of the Bourbons. Marlborough might well have suffered the ravages of the 'pox' in his life and times, and that might account for the failure in the male line thereafter and 200 years of nonentities. The same can be said of the Julian family until Caesar.

One of the ways in which your guidance is of tremendous value to me is in the prevention of loose thinking to which, I am aware, I am very liable. I have a great many ideas. I throw them off, not deeply considered I fear, at times. And you put them back on the rails. Thus power and 'pride'. I perceive from several letters and remarks in the past that you have a liking for Enoch Powell, and since he has the misfortune to be a politician, he must be a very considerable personage in your view to gain your admiration. It is good to know that such men exist in that muddled field.

I am clarified on 'cads'. I hesitate to apply the word to Churchill, for I don't really think he was a 'cad'—in many ways a complete cad, in others not. The word could be misleading. I believe I was thinking fairly straight on that, and have coped with it satisfactorily. It is my hope, and belief, that it will be clear to any reader of my book that I have deep sympathies with Winston. Otherwise I could not write about him at all. I don't believe in works inspired by hate or love in that sense. Love of the work, but not of the person. That must lead to as biased a result as hatred. One must, however, sympathise in the true sense, if one's characters are to live. For in all of us is almost all possibility, and we punish and snarl most severely at those crimes of which we *know* ourselves capable. It is only when we are confronted with an Eichmann that the mind boggles. Killing is useless, even an absurd mockery. We kill those who kill (although I believe we should not), we punish thieves, rapists and the like. We punish ourselves. We condemn gossip because we love gossip, and above all we envy the tramps and the free, and hate them when they do not suffer as outcasts of society as a result of their tramping. How dare they be outside the herd, and still enjoy its comforts, break its rules and seek their protection. Winston was even more naive than I—which is saying something.

Your guidance is most helpful. Steadily pieces of the puzzle fall into their places. Eric O'G wrote a terrific letter this week inspired by the publication of those last Roosevelt documents re. his private messages to Joe. This makes Eric a supporter of my *Price of Victory* argument with which he had not quite agreed. Of course, he sees the whole strategy from an Indian and Middle East angle, a most valuable angle if one has a contact like you to correct 'bad steering'.

From Sir Desmond Morton   7th July, 1961
I agree with you that it is difficult in these days to call Winston a 'cad'. It would be incorrect. On the other hand, he was certainly capable of the most caddish actions at times. I firmly believe, nevertheless, that his own story of his escape from the Boer Prisoner of War camp was the true one, and that Haldane (the General, not the S.O.S. for War) was quite mistaken in the version he used to tell. I have heard both stories first hand from W.S.C. and Aylmer Haldane. You would suppose that it would be impossible to produce two such different tales. I think it goes to show how highly trained men, who would be supposed to be competent observers of a very exciting action in which they took personal part, can honestly make gross errors of fact in their accounts of the same incident.

Anyway, Winston's and Smuts' stories complement one another. Here again I have heard both from the fountain head.

From Sir Desmond Morton   11th July, 1961
I have just read *The Spanish Civil War* by Hugh Thomas. You need *not* read it in so far as W.S.C. is concerned. It is a brilliant, painstaking, lengthy piece of careful research on its subject.

But, as it were, in passing, the author mentions casually that at a certain date, Winston was clearly pro-Franco from his public utterances and at a later date had swung (back) to supporting the Republicans.

During the period concerned, 1936–1938, I was very close to Winston, and can say without doubt that Mr. Hugh Thomas is fundamentally wrong, not understanding the mentality of a politician like Churchill. Thomas *does* understand the mentality of the many

Spanish politicians about whom he writes. They were men with a burning abstract ideal—different men, different ideals; God, Church, Monarchy, Anarchy, Communism etc. It is the Spanish habit really to be activated to death by such ideas. It is *not*, generally, the British outlook, and is not the Churchillian outlook.

In such very minor part as he played in the House of Commons or directed thereto by his letters, Winston was not in the least swayed by a desire to support either the Nationalists or the Republicans, because of *their* ideals. His motives, probably in this order, were (a) how to find a stick wherewith to beat the Government (of this country) in public in the House, and (b) which side in Spain ought to win in respect of the consequent advantage to *this* country, in international politics.

Do you get my point. It is essential you should, if you are to understand the mind of Churchill.

In so far as Spain itself was concerned, his real attitude was not 'A plague on both their houses!' but 'What can I (and we, later) get out of the whole business?' 'I' meaning 'I' in his political ambition to turn out Baldwin or Austen [Neville]; 'we' meaning the British international policy, which is of course linked with the former.

On the former issue, if the British Government of the day was showing weakness in its policy anent Spain and was being criticised therefore, in Parliament and the Press, Winston would criticise in the House, quite independent as to whether the 'weakness' shown would benefit Nationalist or Republican Spain.

It is a matter of history that the then British Government havered and fiddled and looked quite ridiculous in its policy towards the Spanish Civil War. That was of course Winston's opportunity with his great oratorical gifts.

At one time he bitterly condemned the bombing of Barcelona by Franco's forces (actually the German and Italian Air Force detachments). Actually at that time he thought it was to Britain's advantage that Franco should win—and swiftly. But what a splendid line of attack. Bombing civilians, who played no part in the war. (Didn't they just!) Bombing them too with arms which had reached Spain from overland thereby nullifying the futile British Government policy of a sea blockade etc. etc.!!!

Don't you go and make the same sort of mistake.

It is perfectly true that when he became Prime Minister, or even before, when he became First Lord of the Admiralty, in war times, Winston did constantly and earnestly pursue one real objective and one only, which was to win the war. That is all quite different. But is why he was so great a *war* leader, and so much less so as a peace-time P.M. or even earlier, Cabinet Minister.

From R. W. Thompson 13th July, 1961

Your guidance on Winston's attitudes to Franco are of the greatest value, and especially, as you point out, that he in fact shares an attitude that one might properly term British. Sometimes I wonder whether the British can ever stir themselves to believe in any thing, ideal, place or people other than themselves, and now that all that wears a bit thin they are left bewildered, in a vacuum, unable to believe even in God —any God.

But as for Winston, he certainly believed in something, if only himself, and whatever he could from time to time identify himself with: the British Empire, mid-Victorian model, winning the war, Union of the English, s.p's etc. But always—or nearly always—with Winston. In finishing Part One in 46,000 words I feel that I have begun, as Priestley would put it, to ride the elephant instead of being somewhere in the darkness—suffocating withal—beneath the animal. At last I am no longer beneath. Now Part Two, the politician and writer, about 35,000, I think, followed by Part Three, 1940, 41, 42— and thence, I believe now, mainly an epilogue. For I have a feeling to end my book on a high note, and not to drag myself or the reader through a weary anti-climax we all know so well. What it amounts to is an attempt at an assessment of Churchill as a person and personality, and his impact upon his times in that light. Ambitious—mad, possibly, but I'm deeply committed. I live with it, and because of that, if my portrait is not true or absolutely clear cut, it should be readable, and it must give new leads. At least, I hope so. Thanks to you I have avoided scores of booby traps, although how many I shall fall into—or will clout me about the ears—heaven alone knows. One must take chances with work like this, otherwise, nothing.

Your point about Winston's attitude is emblazoned on my mind, not to be forgotten. How I wish, sometimes, that Englishmen *were* anarchists, Monarchists (anything rather than Fascists or Communists), anything so long as they were something! Somehow there is an absence of PASSION—about anything. I wrote somewhere in my book that Winston never lacked passion, but was a stranger to compassion. I think that was in considering his attitudes to the killing of tribesmen, the burnings of villages, and so on, on the frontiers. But if that is true he also never asked for compassion. He may need it now, poor old man. But not in his vitality.

... Winston will be on my plate for months... Frankly to commit oneself totally to such a job as this demands all one's energies mental and physical ... A good many writers of my age believe that such jobs are almost impossible to tackle after the middle forties. That must depend on the chap himself. But it does take a terrific lot out of one ...

I heard from old Jack Linnell, a contemporary of Winston's, a great neurologist in his day, I believe, and still a kind of G.O.M. Consultant. He tells me that when he was at Westminster Hospital sixty years ago (sorry, *London* Hospital) 'it was generally accepted that it (Lord Randolph's death) was due to G.P.I. (General paralysis of the insane), a disease starting as a rule some ten to fifteen years after primary infection of syphilis'.

The old man writes much more, including many symptoms, many of which were present in Randolph. It is right to know these things, for I think it is clear that Winston at the time knew a good deal about it. It must have made a deep impression . . . At any rate, there it is in the background of one's thoughts and attempted judgments.

From Sir Desmond Morton   16th July, 1961

You are right about the British, as a whole and probably a large majority, being unable to believe really and truly and seriously in anything, and that includes God. But it is not only the British. The great and only cement that holds men and nations together is belief—a common belief—in something. A wall without mortar, however formidable it may look, falls down at a push lacking mortar to keep the bricks together.

Winston did believe in God, though he was not Christian, on his own argued confession and admission. His God was akin to 'the Lord' of the Jews, but further away and quite incomprehensible to Man. It was the Theistic belief common in the period of the great John Duke of Marlborough. A God who did create the world and all that is, but who is so detached therefrom that no access is possible. His favourite quotation about Death, was 'To sleep, perchance to dream'. But he did not think much on these things, so far as I know. He had great courage and would face such an idea without a qualm. He was quite illogical on abstract matters—a complete extrovert.

He was not 'mad' by any sort of acceptable definition of madness. On the contrary, I should say he was firmly and rigidly balanced on the pedestal he had created for himself. It is you who are engaged in describing that pedestal. It sounds to me as if you had really begun to conceive it, whether rightly or wrongly only time will show.

I frequently hear from people, who know my past connections with Winston, little stories of no importance in themselves, about him. I can nearly always tell at once whether the tale is true, at least in its foundations. But I cannot see why I can do so, and can say, 'Oh yes, that is Winston all right', save of course that it is 'in character'. On the contrary, I can equally say to myself, 'No, that story is imaginary. It is not Winston.'

The other day someone who knew him as well as I have done, and who was personally present at the affair recounted, told me of the affair, and added, 'Why on earth did he do that?' I had no difficulty in seeing at once why he did *that*. It was perfect Winston. A perfectly reasonable act, given his own way of looking at things, though sheer lunacy if done by anyone else.

That does not mean that I (or anyone else) could always tell what Winston's reactions would be. But as soon as the reaction occurred, one saw that it was Winston.

Nor does it mean that Winston's reactions were always right. Far, very far from it. I would say that by and large, Winston's reactions were just as likely to be wrong as right. One interesting thing is that I am sure his immediate reaction was more likely to be, at least sensible, than his second thoughts. I always found this very interesting.

What a mercy it is for us that Winston did not always get his way, whether it was a first thought or an afterthought. As a Roman Emperor, with practically no curb on his actions, Winston would have been a Caligula or worse, and quite properly had his throat cut.

I do not follow your 'absence of passion' in Winston. I do not understand. Equally incorrect to my mind would be his possession of passion without compassion, unless you explain, though that at least allows him passion, of which he was very fully possessed, save possibly great sexual passion. I think, however, you are talking about passionate pursuit of an end, and that your letter refers to the British people lacking passion, not to Winston. On Winston lacking *com*passion, I could agree, if you explained that his compassion was really passing sentiment. He was desperately sentimental, but there was little depth to it. He could view the results of German bombing in the East End with tears rolling down his face, and they were quite genuine, not put on for effect. But the moment and the sentiment passed rapidly.

Certainly true heartfelt compassion cannot exist without passion, but a passionate man may well lack compassion.

The word and idea of passion comes from the Latin root meaning suffering. Compassion also, but from 'to suffer with' someone else's suffering. 'Sympathy' comes from the exactly similar Greek words as produce the idea of compassion from the Latin. Can it be that Winston lacked sympathy with others? I rather think it can. I have always remarked on the apparent inability of Winston to put himself into the mind of another person.

From what I have heard too, your Dr. Jack Linnell has got the truth about the death of Lord R. and the cause.

Basil L.H. has asked me what I think of his article on Haig in the *Sunday Times* a few weeks ago. I am writing to tell him that unfortunately I think it excellent. It is not without interest to note that Winston's mind changed about D.H.[1] From a neutral or even hostile

[1] General Sir Douglas Haig, later Field Marshal Earl Haig.

attitude, Winston developed a very considerable admiration for D.H. Why was this? I think he always admired his (D.H.'s) obstinacy, had no real objections to D.H.'s frightful intrigues (after all, Winston was not a stranger to intrigue) but having cast in his lot with Lloyd George, Winston was naturally hostile to anyone who might endanger that great, but crooked? man's position. But when D.H. 'brought it off' the fact that he had succeeded outweighed everything else in Winston's mind. 'The end justifies the means' (a remark never made incidentally, by Ignatius Loyola or the Jesuits) would be a motto thoroughly approved by Winston, I suspect. I have a vague and possibly erroneous impression of having discussed this aphorism with Winston years ago at Chartwell. He was astounded to learn how it came to be attributed to the Jesuits and persisted in claiming it to be a very sound and good remark. I think Winston was about to use it in a speech until I dissuaded him, pointing out incidentally, that if he did and attributed it to the Jesuits, he would be liable to a penalty for Libel, as a result of a case brought by the Jesuits against some politician in the nineteenth century where an English Court, proof being brought, immediately accepted the uncontrovertible evidence and found the statement untrue, malicious and libellous.

The facts of course, as I expect you know are that in a famous written work on moral theology, Ignatius Loyola, arguing the end was *never* justified by the means, adopted the Scholastic method of argument, which begins by asserting the proposition it is intended to disprove and then disproving it. Hence his thesis began with the words, in Latin, 'It seems the end justifies the means', going on to show by every sort of argument that this was true. Thereafter he demolishes his own arguments one by one and ends with the statement. 'Thus it is clear that the end does *not* justify the means employed to attain it.'

However, the fact that he had written the first words was good enough for Henry VIII's and Elizabeth's propaganda machine. Modern newspapers could get some tips in the art of misleading the public were they to study the Council Rolls of that period.

From R. W. Thompson   29th July, 1961
... Your letter of the 16th was, as always, illuminating on Winston, helping to lighten certain areas of darkness or dimness, and throwing up new and interesting shadows. As to the presence of passion and compassion in the same heart and head—or the one without the other— I shall have to sort that out. Compassion certainly could not exist where there was no passion, but I feel that the reverse could be true.

However, a certain set of events have made me feel that Winston felt compassion for his father—not perhaps during his life time, but when, a very few years later he went through his papers and wrote the life of Randolph. Having received some more scurrilous muck about Lord R. through the post from the U.S.A.—which has shocked me deeply (it is also scurrilous about Winston, a literally filthy lie built upon a basis of truth) I read W.'s life of Lord R. again with great care. As a result I regard it as his finest work. Not because it is better written, but because, as I feel it, knowing such things as I know or think I know, it gets away from Winston and reveals a genuine devotion to someone outside himself—to wit, his father. I cannot help wondering whether, without Winston's work, Randolph would have enjoyed a tenth of his reputation, whether his name might have been lost along with a number of estimable politicos of his times. But in writing his story Winston has done both his father and himself a great service.

Before I go on with that theme and the libellous muck, Basil L.H. wrote to enclose me some interesting stuff, and said that he had a long and 'intensely interesting' letter from you in regard to Haig, and 'most illuminating'. It is about time your powerful illuminations shed their revealing lights . . .

. . . first put Neilson in touch with me, and I have his book, as you know. Now Neilson's secretary has sent me the muck that shocks me so deeply. It purports to be an account of Lord R. contracting syphilis, and a lot of filth from the pen of the infamous lecher and liar, Frank Harris. All this printed and photostat-ed under the signature of 'N. W. ROGERS', according to Neilson a judge and a research physicist. It is all about ten years old.

Together with this beastliness which throws (or does not for me do anything of the kind) doubts on Winston's birth, there is an anti-Jewish angle . . . and there is a letter from Neilson stating that Churchill's great grandmother was a Jewess. I don't like this kind of thing at all, and these people have made a great mistake if they imagine I am out to denigrate Winston in any way. You know, only less well than I know myself, exactly what I am trying to do. But even if I loathed Winston, which I do not, I would do my utmost to protect his name from this kind of dirt. But I expect you, with your long experience, will know more about this kind of thing. I have been uneasy for some time about the sources or inspiration of these people's pursuit of Winston . . .

I have the stuff here, and would send it to you without more ado, but I am ashamed even to have received it, and I feel therefore that it is an insult to send it to anyone. On the other hand, perhaps something should be done. I don't feel that a 'Pontius Pilate' on it may be quite right. I haven't mentioned it to Basil, or to anyone else, and perhaps I may be making too much of the ravings of a bunch of cranks. But there have been some dangerous bunches of cranks loose in the world in our life times.

All that has spoiled my letter. I dislike to tell you on the same page, that Franky is now recuperating fast, at home again, and longing to cycle and swim—and must not.

From R. W. Thompson   30th July, 1961

In my upset frame of mind over the wretched stuff from Neilson's 'ghost' about Winston I forgot to tell you something which may amuse you: I picked up a first edition of Winston's *London to Pretoria* in Cambridge this week. This consists of his despatches to the *Morning Post*, and yet another version—the very very first—of the armoured train episode and the escape from the model schools. This makes my fifth from those present, and second from Winston himself!

But there is, it seems to me, a small passage in this book more revealing of that Winston I try so hard to discover than all the 'facts'— facts are fearfully misleading anyway, even (or it may be, especially) when 'true'.

This short passage seems to cast a light on Winston's behaviour as a young man with Kitchener, Roberts and his exalted 'seniors'—here goes, in his own words:

> Pretoria: November 30, 1899.
> The bitter wind of disappointment pierces even the cloak of sleep. Moreover, the night was cold and the wet clothes chilled and stiffened my limbs, provoking restless and satisfactory dreams. I was breakfasting with President Kruger and General Joubert. 'Have some jam,' said the President. 'Thanks,' I replied, 'I would rather have marmalade.' But there was none. Their evident embarrassment communicated itself to me. 'Never mind,' I said, 'I'd just as soon have jam.' But the President was deeply moved. 'No, no,' he cried, 'we are not barbarians. Whatever you are entitled to you shall have, if I have to send to Johannesburg for it.' So he got up to ring the bell, and with the clang, I woke.

To me, that's authentic Winston. I like it very much . . . Hope you haven't seen it before.

From Sir Desmond Morton   31st July, 1961

. . . I wish I knew what specially appealed to you in Winston's dream, which is certainly great fun. But you may have got more from it than I do.

You will have noticed that the 'despatch' is dated on his 25th birthday. He had been captured by Janie Smuts on the 15th November and did not escape until December 12th. So I suppose his dream took place in the P. of W. camp. But I do not know why his clothes were wet.

All details are valuable to the interpretation of dreams, and an expert psychologist, which I am *not*, would make all sorts of things out of this dream, I have no doubt.

One very important technical point. You quote '. . . provoking and satisfactory (sic) dreams'. Is that copied right? Or should it read '*un*satisfactory'? I am taking it that you copied wrong, omitting the 'un' by mistake. If I am right, I can explain why you dropped the 'un' —a Freudian error. If however, you did not drop anything and it should read as you copied it, it is of deep interest.

What great phrases he could make even at the age of twenty-four/ twenty-five. Look at the first sentence. Magnificent! 'The bitter wind of disappointment pierces even the cloak of sleep.'

For the rest, his 'unconscious' certainly betrayed much. He would (knowingly) wish to go to, and have speech with, the topmost men, (Kruger and Joubert), the political and military leaders. But the clues are in 'breakfast', 'jam', 'embarrassment', 'marmalade', 'whatever you are entitled to you shall have', 'Johannesburg', 'barbarians'.

Of course it is authentic Winston, but how do you interpret it?

Minor differences of interpretation can be given, depending on facts I do not know for certain, but several things stick out a mile. It is largely a wish-fulfilment dream. *He*, Winston, wanted to be sent to Johannesburg as a P. of W., if his plea to be treated as a journalist and non-combatant and thus released, failed.

He had friends in Joburg and believed firmly he could escape more easily from there than from Pretoria. It was much nearer British lines. (This he has freely admitted later.) 'What you are entitled to you shall have', needs little interpretation in the light of the above (as a wish-fulfilment).

'Embarrassment' and 'barbarians' go together. Winston had already become unpopular with certain British circles for asserting that the Boers were far from being a set of 'bloody stupid farmers, whom we would soon bring to their senses'. Anything helping to prove his views would be important to his unconscious.

Behind all this was the wish that he, Winston, could be a means of stopping the whole war and offering the Boers most liberal terms of settlement, which he himself actually helped later to accomplish, helping to get the Boers regarded as honourable, civilised men with a really sincere motive behind their actions. In fact at the time of his dream, he was inclined to prefer the conduct of the Boers to that of his own side.

There's lots more.

By the way, don't tell me your dreams, or I shall be trying to interpret them.

For heaven's sake do *not* send me the libellous, and at least partly ridiculous, muck about Lord R. I don't want to see it. There is absolutely no doubt that Winston is the legitimate son of Lord R. and his wife. What is true, I fear, is that Lord R. did either contract or inherit a certain disease, from which he died. Obviously neither Winston nor his brother acquired or inherited that disease in its direct effects. That more indirect effects may have persisted, is a matter of scientific interest only, in connection with the proximity of genius and unbalance.

*   *   *

I am so glad that Basil Liddell Hart evidently found my comments useful on some stuff he sent me about Haig. How I agree, not with the words exactly, but with the thoughts behind them about 'facts'. Facts are actually of immense importance, as well you know, but it is the interpretation of those facts which is even more important.

That is why I have regrettably used some disrespectful words about 'journalists', meaning thereby those many persons who acquire a small fact and turn it into a 'sensation' by their interpretation, if not by direct lying.

With affectionate greetings to your whole barnyard.

From R. W. Thompson   2nd August, 1961
I am answering your letter at once mainly because it is difficult just now to work steadily on my book, and I am using whatever time I have to check various pieces of stuff and develop draft notes. First I must assure you that I had no intention of sullying your portals with the muck with which I have been insulted . . . I felt, on the other hand, that you should know that it had been sent to me, and have some idea of its content. I dislike even to put it in the post and will register it back to U.S.A. without taking a copy. I have never had the slightest doubt about Winston's birth, and as I read the whole background of his childhood I find it, and his attitude to his father, greatly to his credit.

I find the typing of the 'dream' is correct (except that you have not quoted back to me the word 'restless' between provoking and satisfactory [no 'un']). My interest is partly in the form of expression, which strikes me as very much Winston and at an early stage; secondly as revealing—or casting some light—on the side of his character that enabled him to intrude upon others, his seniors—Roberts, Buller, Kitchener, for example—and observe their evident embarrassment with seeming nonchalance. It was partly this attitude which induced me to use the word *hubris* to try to describe this kind of especial pride, more often the curse (or prerogative, or a characteristic) of princes. Here he appears to be dreaming such a situation. He is very junior, a prisoner to boot, yet it is his hosts who are discomfited. 'Jam' is peculiarly 'un-English' for breakfast, and marmalade is even a kind of class symbol. Kruger and Joubert, one feels, are anxious to appear as 'men of the world' etc. etc. Jam is therefore a fearful gaffe.

The dream is dated his birthday, but in fact it took place on the second night at the halting place on the march to Elandslaagte. In another book, and another despatch, Winston says that he stood one hour alone in the pouring rain, hence his wetness and chilled limbs.

But I have fortunately provoked you to confirm views I was forming, and even arguing a night or two ago, that Winston had considerable sympathy with the Boers as people, fighters, and in their national ambitions, exclusive of their 'apartheid' attitude of which he did not, even then, approve. In fact, his political link up in 1904 with the 'pro-Boer' faction of the liberal party, his preferment at Christmas 1905 to Under Secretary of State for the Colonies by Campbell Bannerman all points in that direction. And Marsh's memories tend to confirm it. Indeed, Randolph also although by no stretch of the imagination a 'liberal', that is in the tradition of Cobden, Mill 'and those kind of chaps', was often very liberal in his attitudes, and I think genuinely so. I think in many ways his friendships of those days are at least as interesting, and illuminating, as his enmities. For Balfour liked him on the one hand, and Asquith on the other. They had a far better opinion of him (although neither one of them believed in any great political future for him) than Haldane or old Sir William Harcourt, for example.

*　　*　　*

I am a bit of an anarchist myself . . . I first read Kropotkin while languishing in a military hospital, and had at the same time the unique opportunity to discuss him with the old Marchioness of Salisbury who kept me company at my 'elevenses'. Herbert Read also appeals to me. Like you, I have always imagined this to be a 'free country', or at least 'aiming' at so great and glorious a distinction.

My 'barnyard'—how right you are—thank you for your affectionate greetings . . . Basil, by the way, has a piece about Berlin in a weekly called *Today* on 14th August. He is very sound, I think.

From Sir Desmond Morton   5th August, 1961
I think your interpretation of Winston's dream is excellent. Now knowing that it actually took place before he got to Pretoria and after his capture, I can both modify and strengthen the interpretation.

You did quote rightly 'provoking restless and satisfactory dreams'. I think that interesting since the idea of 'restless' and 'satisfactory' together seems to me to be unusual. One would normally call restless, *un*satisfactory, since one of the chief objects of sleep is rest. Alternatively I, myself, but I am not Winston, would have written 'restless *but* satisfactory'. However, since he wrote and meant 'satisfactory', it is clear that the dream was 'wish-fulfilment'. Our interpretation therefore stands enhanced. All that you go on to say about Winston's attitude towards the Boers, sounds to me first class and true. There is little doubt in my mind that Winston's political attitude has always been more 'old fashioned Liberal' than Conservative or Tory. We know when he elected so to declare himself by crossing the floor of the house, but it has always seemed to me unfair to assert that he only did this through believing that it was likely to lead to political promotion for himself.

Far from a repudiation of all that his father had stood for, it was in fact a confirmation in his belief in his father, who, as we know tried to form a cave of Adullam against the Tory element of the day, and might, had he lived, actually have done the same thing as his son—but that is only speculation.

There was a very difficult mentality in the entrenched supporters of 'The Establishment' in those days, who were apparently certain that they alone were right in everything and everyone else was wrong in everything. The Tory party of the 1890s would certainly have regarded not only Harold Macmillan, but die-hards like the late Tops Selborne,[1] as out and out Socialists!!! It was impossible for them to believe in the honesty of any 'gentleman' (as then mentally defined) still less a member of a titled family—unless he was already bound by long and genuine Whig tradition—being or becoming a Liberal. Why, Liberals were 'psalm singing, chapel going folk, rich tradesmen, lawyers, and so on', who were properly the servants of the Tories.

The matter of 'hubris', anglicised with the adjective 'hubristic' is interesting. When I was at school and learned some ancient Greek, I was told that the Greek word was not only untranslatable, but that its exact connotation was most difficult to express in modern times. The Greek Lexicon offers 'insolence', but it goes on to admit that that is bad. As I am sure you know, and certainly Mel does, it was applied in Classical Greek (from which alone we have borrowed it) to persons who offended the gods in a peculiar way. Seemingly the gods approved of a certain measure of hubris, but when that hubris grew too great, they reacted by causing all sorts of misfortunes to happen to him or her.

I have often wondered whether the ancient Greeks really distinguished between the two sorts of emotions we, in English, call 'pride'. The French recognise these two by different words. We only do so by the context. It is not only good but necessary that a man or woman take a certain sort of pride in his job, his family and so on; but a man who is proud, overproud or arrogant, is to be avoided as a rule.

As I understood it the Greeks would only ascribe hubris to a man who was very rich, very successful and did not appear to have a care in

[1] The Earl of Selborne, Minister of Economic Warfare. Personal friend of Churchill and Desmond.

the world apart from his own self-advancement. Hence the very opposite of meek and humble.

Such a man became an object of envy to the gods, who punished him for his '*hubris*', by a series of disasters in this world.

My English dictionary is too small to include 'hubristic', so I do not know what is said in official English today about the adopted word. I know how I sometimes use it myself, but I may be wrong. I am sure that there cannot be anything to admire in the idea. A great classical scholar admired my use of it in answer to a question: 'What on earth are your Postgraduate Professors doing?' (in regard to a line of policy they were unanimously adopting). My reply was, 'It follows logically from their hubristic attitude towards anything that is not Postgraduate research'.

That, therefore, *may* be a correct use of the word. If so, I would find it difficult to apply *hubris* to Winston.

I suggest that Winston never saw any embarrassment on the part of Roberts, Buller,[1] Kitchener etc. when he intruded upon them. He would, however, see the embarrassment of the dreamed Kruger and Joubert in the circumstances of the dream not only for the reasons you give, but because also in his secret mind he wanted to show that they were just as civil and 'gentlemanly' as any English gentleman.

However, my only advice is to make quite sure what is precisely the modern content of the English word as borrowed from Classical Greek. I believe that in modern Greek, the word is quite simply translated, but it is not from the modern Greek that it is borrowed.

From R. W. Thompson   14th August, 1961

August has been horrible . . . I worked fairly well yesterday, but the truth is that I am horribly depressed. This is (I hope) a natural upshot of the last few weeks, the need for a real holiday with all cares forgotten, and a replenishment of the mind. As the O'G so often says, 'hard thinking is the hardest work there is'. Sometimes I almost believe that it is the only work. And if one has an agile mind plus a certain amount of talent nothing is more simple than to do all the things that come easily. But once one realises that hard thinking is the only way to fulfil oneself there is no escape; absolutely none. It is impossible to go back. And I think there is substance in the O'G's contention that Winston never did any hard thinking. Why should he? As he thought, he was outstandingly brilliant. He thought he didn't need to—and he didn't . . .

In these more or less enforced periods when I am unable to work steadily Winston grows in my mind and imagination—for I can never be free of him until I have written myself free. It doesn't matter whether I should write about him, or can write about him, or whether

[1] General Sir Redvers Buller, South African War.

171

I have anything to contribute from my outside angle; what matters is that I am caught up in it, and must go through to the end. There is no escape. There is always an illusion after such periods as these that they are a godsend; that had I worked straight on much that has matured would not have done so. But in that way a man might 'wait' through years to know all that he might know, and do nothing.

I find that I like Winston in his Edwardian years . . . I imagine Randolph is working away, and I should think too that it will be a great deal better than many people think. For Randolph, as impossible as his father (I imagine) from a personal point of view, is steeped in political background, has all the 'archives', letters and what not, at his disposal, and knows his way—or *a* way through those labyrinths. Such work is not for me. I have neither the time, money—secretarial resources—for such a labour. What I am trying to do is much more on the lines of Philip Guedella's portrait, *Mr. Churchill*. My book, I hope, will be readable by a wide public. If it has any merit this will be due to any creative insight I may have. If I have not then it will be merely another 'hack' job. But I pray not.

There is something to be said on the physical side for Winston's contention that the Tory party moved away from him, and not he from them. After all Balfour did lead the Party out of the House in a body at the end of March 1904 during a Churchill speech on cheap food. It was a unique incident, and damned rude to say the least. Derby walked back to Mount Street with Winston that night, and didn't think his behaviour very odd. Neither did Dilke—or even Joe Chamberlain. Joe had done much the same thing in the reverse direction.

But in a sense Winston was never a serious minded politician in the sense of A.J.B., or even Lloyd George. He was much more a kind of super Max Aitken,[1] but not seeking that kind of power. His at least was a dream of some grandeur. And he wore his heart too much on his sleeve.

Your *hubris* guidance is valuable. 'Insolence' is, in my feeling, a large part of it, an insolence of excessive pride. And I believe Winston *did* offend the gods in a peculiar way. Again your suggestion that Winston did not see the embarrassment he caused when intruding on such men as Roberts, Kitchener, Buller, but that he did dream Joubert's embarrassment for the reasons you give. In fact, he said in the House he regarded these Boer farmers as the equivalent of 'country squires', and disliked the British common soldier 'pushing them round'. In his mind they were a kind of 'local gentlemen', like a military or civil rank bestowed upon some citizen of a remote colony.

. . . I would like to explode like a bomb, to rush off somewhere and do something wildly exciting, and come back renewed—like Korea.

[1] Later Lord Beaverbrook.

But may the Saints defend us from any such possibility, although why they should bother with us any more I really don't know.

But I refuse to burden you further with my jaded spirit. I must chain my mind to the task, and hammer out the thoughts—hard thoughts. I don't blame Winston. He could always 'get by', even if his dreams were not where his rainbow ended.

From Sir Desmond Morton   21st August, 1961 (begun)
                                                   ended 24th August
I am a little poggled by your query as to what 'the enigmatic Esher was meant to be doing'. I have forgotten in what connection I mentioned him in a recent letter. Possibly it was his presence at the Doullens Conference[1] in 1918. If so, he was meant to represent the Cabinet of that day, and his instructions were to agree to anything that Haig agreed to. The fact that he did nothing except burst into tears—presumably of sheer nervous tension, for there was nothing of a sorrowful nature to affect him—did not matter, as when told to do so, he appended his signature to the document which was an Anglo-French agreement to make Foch Generalissimo of the Western Front, with defined rights.

My other possible reference to Esher was his truly magnificent Report—at least, it is called the Esher Report,[2] and he was Chairman of the Esher Commission, which reported in 1910 (I think) and which, the report being approved by Parliament and the Crown, set up the modern system of Defence and the Committee of Imperial Defence, the General Staff of the Army and other useful relevancies.

If it was in any other connection I mentioned him, you must remind me. The Esher I am talking about was of course not the present Viscount, but his father who died in 1930.

A really very very great man was Archie Wavell. I have just refused to 'review' a ninety-seven-page book by Brigadier Bernard Fergusson called *Wavell, Portrait of a Soldier*: my reason being that I was an immense admirer of the man as was nearly every decent person who ever came into contact with him. Fergusson was Wavell's first A.D.C. and subsequently a close friend of his for sixteen years until Wavell's death. The book is merely a mixture of anecdotes about Wavell, endeavouring to show what a supremely kindly gentleman he was. These anecdotes are nearly all trivial. They would be invaluable to any

[1] Hankey, *The Supreme Command*, vol. II, p. 787.
Doullens Conference, 26th March, 1918, following tragic news. 'The news was about as bad as it could be for the right of the Third Army had been stove in and a breach made between it and the Fifth Army.' So it seems there was something to cry about. Desmond attended as A.D.C. to Haig.
[2] Esher Report on War Office Reform.

proper historian writing a proper biography of Wavell, which is well overdue. Moreover only a person who was an Army Officer of pre-First World War vintage, would really appreciate their meaning and context, while there is not a word about Wavell's other greatnesses.

I see the *Daily Telegraph* this morning gives a 500-word comment—hardly on the book, though provoked by it; but on Wavell, producing matter which is not in the book in any way. The note is highly laudatory—of Wavell, not of the book; and does just mention that he was a victim of Winston's temperament. That is to put it very mildly. I think that the first time I ever deeply disliked Winston and realised the depths of selfish brutality to which he could sink, was when he told me, not only that he was getting rid of Wavell from the Middle East, but why.[1]

I remember telling you some time ago that Winston was 'afraid' of Alexander. I stick to the phrase, though, to be understood, it requires explanation. I also said that Alex was the only soldier, sailor or airman, of whom he was thus 'afraid'. That last was wrong. Wavell was another.

My analysis (subject to review always) is that Winston heartily disliked any person whose personal character was such that he could not avoid, most unwillingly, feeling respect for that person. Winston's overweening desire to dominate resulted in a feeling of inferiority in regard to anyone who was not in the least afraid of him, and never would be, and in whose character he could not see any flaw. Were there such a flaw, Winston could always attack that flaw and close his eyes to other great qualities.

Naturally any such person must be either a rival or in a position to do Winston some potential harm. (That such a person would never dream of doing Winston harm, never entered his thought-processes.) 'If you have power, you use it', would be his unalterable expectation.

Persons of such immensely high character and also extremely good at their job, are rare. One does not find them easily among politicians. But there have been a very few high officers of the Armed Forces who really answer to that description. Both Wavell and Alexander are examples. I know of no others active in the last war. Jack Dill approached them, and was consequently got rid of by Winston. He did not however equal them, for though his personal character was as high as theirs, he was not so great a soldier, while he showed a weakness of which Winston took full advantage, of being disturbed by Winston's unjust criticisms.

In that connection, Winston never forgave Wavell for a personal

[1] Desmond described to me how Churchill had walked up and down his room, chin sunk on chest, glowering ferociously, and muttering, 'I wanted to show my power!' over and over.

174

telegram the latter sent him during the evacuation of Somaliland by us. Winston had tried to force Wavell to hold on to Somaliland. Wavell, who was not only adamant when his military mind was made up, but could argue his case unanswerably, had agreed that he would make a fighting retreat, as, indeed, he had always intended. When the casualty list for that retreat was received at home, Winston demanded to see it and found that 'only' (his words) 1,800 casualties had been caused in the British Forces concerned. He sent a personal telegram to Wavell, accusing him of 'breaking his word' and other allegations amounting to a charge of pusillanimity. Wavell merely replied, 'Butchery is not the mark of a good tactician'.

Winston raged, but could think of nothing to say in return. Moreover, the ill-concealed satisfaction of all three Chiefs of Staff and others who saw this reply, did not do anything to mitigate his fury. And, of course, he knew in his heart that Wavell was right and that his own telegram was—to anyone but a person like Wavell—unforgivable.

I think you are quite right in saying that Winston was not a serious politician like some. I doubt if the idea of ruling in order to *serve* the people of his country was ever clear to him. To him, politics was an intensive game, highly competitive, in which his side won or lost a 'chukker' as in polo (a game of which he was very fond and played well in his youth and even middle age). If you won, you had the satisfaction of winning, you got a 'cup' to be held for a period (power), and you received the plaudits of the multitude—or at least a majority thereof. If you lost, you failed to gain these things, but you lived to fight another day. In fact, he played it for a game, with little, if any, thought for the good you might do your country. You might have a policy, but that policy was calculated to appeal to the voters, so as to get a majority; there was little thought given to the broader issue, whether the policy was the best thing for your country, or made progress, or made a majority happier etc. etc. Naturally, in war, with a united nation behind you, these considerations mattered little, since any policy must basically be to win the war.

It is fully understandable that in modern democratic British politics, a politician is bound to consider what policies and laws he can get the people to accept. The honest statement can be made, 'There is no doubt we must *aim* at doing so and so, but the people will not be with us until we have done thus and that, to educate them to accept the so and so.'

But this attitude is acceptable since the politician truly aims at doing that which he thinks is best for the country as soon as circumstances allow him. That is why F. D. Roosevelt was such a good politician in internal affairs for his own country, the U.S.A. In private conversation he used to say quite openly, 'I must get public opinion educated before I can do so and so and must even *seem* to lag behind public opinion in what I say, until it looks as though the people forced *me* to do what I know is proper.'

'Slick' if you like, but sound leadership for a country like U.S.A.

A politician like Winston, who was notoriously bad at home politics, cannot even begin to think in that sort of way. An individualist of an extreme sort, looking on politics as a game, which he has to win, and not as a duty to be performed for the sake of others, he was always quite certain that what he wanted was right (first error in approach), thought that anything was right which was calculated to get votes (a confusion of thought on the meaning of 'right'), and tended to pay no attention to the views of the people when he had got power (the dictatorship mentality). I speak and think of Winston in power or aiming to get power in peace-time, where the issues are nothing like as simple as they are in war.

Naturally it requires far more space than I can afford here to discuss the details of behaviour and attitude of anyone, let alone so complicated a person as was W.S.C., but I think I have set out reasonably the bare bones of what I feel about Winston's attitude towards politics, which is a complete confirmation of your own views, in so far as I can see.

From R. W. Thompson   30th August, 1961
My questions about Esher reflected the lack of order in my mind as I emerged from the miseries of the 'guests' and midsummer. In future I am going to devise some means of 'skipping' midsummer, going somewhere to build sand castles—as Winston used to do, in the manner of Vauban. But not attempt to work.

Hankey is rather unnecessarily mysterious about Esher, and that may have sparked my feeling. He uses Berthelot's phrase: 'I am everywhere, I am nowhere' to describe him, and states (quite wrongly) that Esher never had an official job. Of course he did, dozens, but he preferred to flit about behind the scenes, especially in Paris. He seemed to know everyone, and was adept at making swift and witty assessments of various characters—*vide* Derby[1] as Ambassador. At any rate, Esher's papers will not be available until 1981—period, as the Americans say. According to Randolph they will be the most intriguing papers of all. We shall not care!

But I feel that people like Esher were one small manifestation of the Edwardian scene. They enjoyed a friendship and familiarity with the Monarch which, I think, did not recur in quite that way. On top of that was the remarkable lack of knowledge, even of interest, in foreign affairs. It was a wonderful happy hunting ground for anyone who did care. So there he was 'flitting about' behind the scenes, being mysterious.

[1] Earl of Derby, Ambassador to Paris, 1918.

The tears at Doullens are new to me. Not exactly in character, but reasonable in view of the stresses and strains of command at the time.

George V nevertheless was pretty close to Grey, and quite obviously liked and valued L.G.—so do I, the more I know about him. In some ways he's a nicer man—an easier man to understand—even than Balfour, or Asquith . . . Our Winston is the only comparable citizen of the age, and as a 'one man show' Winston wants some beating. But he *is*—and always was—a One Man Show. L.G. was not. Winston's behaviour at the Admiralty in 1914 is the real Winston, the best Winston in many ways. Brilliant, foolish, brash—actually likeable. He wants to be First Lord and man of action combined, wielding the Navy (commanding the Cruiser Squadron in his mind on those 'grey seas') while defending Antwerp in person. Asquith was obviously enchanted—and dismayed at one and the same time. Of course, it wouldn't do. He went on like that, the everlasting adolescent.

Did you ever read that piece by James Gould Cozzens about the Quebec conference? Winston 'often grumpy, half a mind on his brandy-soured stomach and throatful of cigar-flavoured phlegm. Grimacing, Mr. Churchill must taste, too, the gall of his situation . . . at the last word, impotent'.

There is another passage, so true I think: 'The object could not be simply to concert a wisest and best course. The object was to strike a bargain wherein both high contracting parties had been trying, if possible, to give a little in order to gain a lot. Since, in each such arrangement, someone must come out on the short end, and since no subordinate could risk being the one, chiefs must meet and agree.'

Hence the Summit and all the silly summits, and the useless (almost) Foreign Ministers. A thing of the past. Perhaps they always were—think of Grey,[1] fishing in Hampshire, knowing as much about Europe and its troubles as one's maiden aunt in Guildford, or better, Cheltenham. I remember the book shocked me at the time—some ten years ago. People thought it blasphemy. Now they don't. Times are changing. People are beginning to question all kinds of things as the shadow darkens.

But there is another short piece. (Please don't be bored by me—it helps so much to write things like this, and look at them) about the essential adolescence of the Winston's of this world:

'They were boys in mind only. They had the means and resources of man's estate. They were more dexterous and much more dangerous than when they pretended they were robbers or Indians; and now their make-believe was really serious to them. You found it funny or called it silly at your peril. Credulity had been renamed faith.'[2]

[1] Sir Edward Grey, Foreign Secretary in the Asquith Government, 1908–16.
[2] *Guard of Honour*, James Gould Cozzens.

There's much more. I think it's very good indeed. I have just had a letter from the aged Linnell asking me to take tea with him and P. J. Grigg with whom he likes to yarn over such things. Linnell asks, do I know about the 'junketings' at Teheran, of Winston teaching Stalin to dance the Horn pipe? I don't, but how I wish I did. They might well have got to that by then. The Americans, as usual, are the only sources for that kind of thing.

Several people have written to me about Wavell and Fergusson. Connell is working on the full length official biography with all the help of Lady Wavell and the private papers. He'll do a good job, but it's a pity in a way that he too is 'involved'. Better to be uninvolved. I regard Wavell as one of the most noble men of these times. Of course Winston couldn't stand him, a living mirror. He wouldn't look in that one . . . You are the only one who really understood all about that all the time, and I doubt whether many do now—except me, because of you. But then I live inside Winston's skin, and sometimes I want to scratch like hell.

I see that Mendelsohn's book is nothing to do with me. I doubt very much whether anyone else is tackling such a peculiar and 'impossible' job as mine. So much the better. Impossible or not, something will come of it, portrait of a man-child amok now and then. His attitude to politics is and always was exactly as you say. He makes tremendous speeches about Land Values, Women's Suffrage, Home Rule, but life begins for him at the Admiralty in 1911. Politics is simply a vehicle on which to ride to power. L.G. fights for his Welfare State, thinks it out, constructs it, and leaves it as a monument. L.G. thinks inside the munitions problem of the First W.W. But Winston is always a wild tactician . . . No sense of strategy . . . Never prepared to think things right through. Oh Gosh, one's heart bleeds to think of the mess up of the Balkans in the First W.W. If only Grey hadn't been such a clam! And not only Grey. If only we hadn't sent all those men to France, and remained a maritime power and won the war. In a curious way Winston never forgot. He knew—or sensed—the way for Britain. But Kitchener had killed that—forever. The trouble with Winston was that once he got an idea he would never let it go—hence Norway, too late; Gallipoli, too late (too little) . . .

Now we have a black and white world—what absolute rot. Like a horror comic. I read T.L.S. lead piece with great interest on all these chaps thinking away—if you can call it thinking—in the Rand Foundation, Princeton and so on. Incapable of making an Appreciation on the level of a G.S.O. 3—so help us all, oh G.!

Mel is in Holland. I have a minor dose of gastric 'flu. The children play in the sunshine. I live indoors with Winston, and you my friend, so far beyond my deserts, help me by letting me do this, like an old char-woman easing her stays, ordering a pint of stout, and just saying what is in her mind. Now, I don't feel a bit like an old char-W., but it is wonderfully helpful just to put things down. Your name is blessed in my house.

From Sir Desmond Morton   8th September, 1961
Since receipt of yours dated 30th August, I have been engaged in many battles taking all my time. This may be the 'holiday season', but the Ministry of Health takes no holidays from its idiocies . . .

A bricklayer having arrived, who was a gunner with the non-Wingate Chindits, and who has surprisingly, quite the right views about Vinegar Jo, Wingate and others, with the correctly huge admiration for Bill Slim, I have to keep away, lest we should gossip of those things and prevent the pointing of the wall.

I may return to this in connection with Winston. Meanwhile, on your letter, go carefully about 'Winston is always a wild tactician—hence the failure of the Dardanelles. No sense of strategy, or an ultimate object or what for'.

First, pray don't mix up strategy and tactics even subconsciously. A wild tactician, certainly; frequently a crackpot strategist. Of tactics he had little understanding, and less appreciation; never comprehending that unless tactics were correctly and wisely planned and perfectly carried out, the overlying strategy must get into difficulties and very likely become impossible. On the other hand, he may have had the wildest strategic ideas at times, he always had a strategic idea and ultimate object very clearly in mind. Of course that ultimate object may have been wrong, unattainable and certainly, like many things about Winston, only seen as a delectable vision and thoroughly badly worked out.

Whether in war or any other great enterprise of peace, strategy and tactics must go hand in hand, and both must be thoroughly worked out from every angle. Whether the strategic objective be limited, or in stages, the attaining of the strategic objective can only be achieved by these means.

This was quite beyond Winston, but it would be an error to suggest that he never had a strategic objective. His trouble was, figuratively speaking, that the moment he heard of the internal combustion engine, he began talking about voyages to the moon, even when the motor-car had hardly begun to exist and the aeroplane was only a pipe-dream.

Continuing the parable, he would start by setting everyone to work finding out what minerals existed in the moon, and how it might be possible to dominate the earth from the moon, without bothering about how to get there.

You mention the Dardanelles. I think it would be dangerously wrong to blame the failure of that enterprise in the 1914 war to Winston.

First, the plan which he sponsored warmly was not his own idea in the first place, but was backed not only by the Admiralty and Admirals, but also by the Cabinet—doubtless persuaded by his excited oratory. There was most certainly a great strategic objective. The capture of Constantinople, the knocking out of the Turks and the consequences of being able to attack the Central Powers from the East as well as in France, together with the hand-link with Russia from the South.

On the tactical side, the appalling error was made by Admiral de Roebeck,[1] who elected to withdraw when victory was in sight. Have not you read Morgenthau's book[2]—the U.S. Ambassador to Turkey in those days—where he recounts in detail how the German and Austrian Ambassadors came to him, asking him to look after German and Austrian affairs, since the Turks had just told them that they had only one day's more ammunition left for the forts, and they were as good as out of the war; that the British Navy would be through next day. That was the day de Roebeck elected to chuck it, *not* having the naval tonnage which his written orders allowed him.

Now *that* Dardanelles business, the first naval attack, may be laid at Winston's door, for reasons given above. The subsequent futilities cannot be, even though he may (have) pressed for them; if so, he was not alone in doing so.

Of course the Norwegian entertainment in the Second World War was far too late. It should have been carried out in September–October 1939 or not at all. Moreover, it should have been only an extended raid to destroy the Norwegian iron port for Swedish ore *and* the railway leading to the Swedish frontier. These could not have been rebuilt by the Germans for at least one year or even more. Hence they would have been in a colossal mess for iron, when the Baltic froze over in the winter 1939/40. The effect might have been tremendous and produced with little loss—if it was a raid of this kind, and carried out as stated according to timing.

Winston saw well enough the strategic aim; but the timing, which comes into tactics, was beyond him. Again, the idea of a raid and the short term strategic purpose, was insufficient to his uncontrollable imagination. He *would* dream of occupying Norway and attacking the Germans from that base. Ways and means to do this, got no consideration.

Yes, incapable of making an appreciation as taught at the Staff College; only capable of seeing an end and expecting someone else to

[1] Admiral Sir John de Roebeck, commanded the Dardanelles Fleet, 1915.
[2] *Secrets of the Bosphorus*, Henry Morgenthau.

produce the know-how. To his mind, nothing was impossible, even the moving of an immovable object by an irresistible force.

I was much interested to be reminded by reading *The Road to Mandalay* just out, by John Masters, of the part played by Winston in connection with Orde Wingate, the Chindits, Vinegar Jo and Co.

I wonder where John Masters got hold of the telegram (it is true enough) which he sent from the Ottawa Conference[1] suggesting that Bill Slim be replaced as C. in C. Burma by that unbalanced individual Wingate, in which he called Wingate the 'Clive of Burma', and said everyone was calling him that, when, in point of fact, Winston in a burst of private oratory, invented that (quite inapplicable name) himself.

The whole business was one of Winston's worst typical perform-ances. I have no private papers now, but the long story is mixed up with his relations with the President, his own idea of strategy—and, for once, tactics—the British justifiable hatred and horror of that England-loathing murderer and gullible liar, but very brave man, Stilwell[2] and his utter ignorance of India and Burma, the Far East and the British generals out there, Slim, Stopford, Messervy and others. That was one (I think the only) occasion when the British Chiefs of Staff jointly and whole-heartedly warned Winston that if he did not lay off, they would publicly resign en masse and say why. He laid off, but not before he had caused much damage and lost many lives unnecessarily.

Incidentally the death of Orde Wingate must have been an act of divine providence. Wingate's Chindit idea, as originally conceived, was brilliant in a limited way and for a limited purpose. When it had been heard, it should have been accepted and turned over direct to the area Commander, Slim, for action and control, Wingate being put under most comfortable arrest in a private lunatic asylum.

But Wingate and Vinegar Jo, who hated one another by the way, were both swashbucklers of the type which made an instant appeal to Winston.

Bill Slim's views on Winston, which he will never disclose publicly, are extremely fair, measured and sound. He hardly knew him face to face; but he had 'got' him to a fine point of decimals, giving the fullest credit for what he did to help win the war, with full admiration for his manifest virtues, but equal deprecation of his vices. He was com-pletely detached from any 'spell' cast by the presence of Winston and refused to receive any telegram from him, always passing them to the C. in C. India or Dicky Mountbatten to deal with, which was fright-fully clever if you think it out. Winston was not P.M. of India, is the clue. And how Winston hated him and all Far Eastern Generals.

[1] Desmond must have meant Quebec not Ottawa.
[2] General J. W. Stilwell, American Commander Far East, known as 'Vinegar Jo', owing to his sour disposition.

Fortunately the excitement of planning and carrying out D-Day for Overlord allowed Winston to forget the war in Burma, so that British–Indian troops could chuck the Japs out of Burma untrammelled by his interference.

That Burmese campaign has never had the publicity and admiration it mightily deserved. Of course the American history says it was American troops. Actually there were no American troops concerned —only Vinegar Jo and his admittedly American aircraft with 30,000 Chinese, none of which last ever did anything of any use in the North, were never where they said they were and claimed to capture everything from Myitkina to Mandalay, which is just as if Eisenhower had claimed to have won the battle of Alamein, and with the American Army.

By the way, you are not quite right in suggesting that George V 'liked L.G.' My dear, he detested him. The things he said when he came out to France in 1918!!! But I am discreet.

After all, George V was doubtless grateful for what L.G. had done to help win the war, but he was (rightly or wrongly) wholly on the soldiers' side against the politicians. Moreover, being forced by L.G. to promise to make enough liberal Peers to swamp the H. of Lords, if the latter would not accept the Commons Bill for confining the Lord's powers, was a matter he never forgave. Look too at the payment for honours business, which came after the war (First World) and ruined the Liberal Party.

Since the early days of Victoria our monarchs have fortunately seen the wisdom of not making friends with their politicians—or enemies, particularly actual or potential Prime Ministers. It must be a lonely life in many ways. That, by the way, is why Esher and George Arthur had such power, which was potentially wrong. Both were friends of George V and he used to talk to both with perfect and unwise freedom and listen to what they said.

I am certainly not bored with the quotations you see fit to send me. They are good stuff.

P. J. Grigg[1] used to be well known to me. We always got on all right. I tried to dissuade him from chucking his secretaryship of the War Office and becoming a politician, foreseeing what would happen. There is a man who could talk about Winston if he would.

From the comments—all adverse—Mendelssohn[2] should have stuck to his forbear's Moonlight Sonata. I hope indeed that it is not remotely like yours. I have not read it, and do not intend to do so. I am sure you must not make your book, whatever it is like, too long.

[1] Sir James Grigg, Secretary of State for War, 1942-5, a distinguished senior Civil Servant.
[2] Desmond confused Mendelssohn and Beethoven.

Do not keep on getting gastric flu. It is a rotten habit or a rotten gut. But by all means go on 'easing your stays'.

From R. W. Thompson   18th September, 1961
Like you I am addicted to bricklayers. I have found them among the most intelligent of my solitary audiences, luring me from my work when their ladders go past my window. Among them I have found gunners, long range Desert Group, infantry and so on, and nearly all with exceptionally clear ideas on what happened, and what it all might mean. In these last few days I have been wrestling in my mind with the problem of 'privilege', and the way in which it inevitably divorces rulers (even in quite low categories) from the peoples they are supposed to rule. Considering the travels of W.S.C. immediately prior to the First World War, his access to most of the private papers coming in from Embassies, his awareness of military planning through being on the sidelines of the C.I.D., he knew surprisingly little about the 'moods' of Europe. Perhaps more than most, but not nearly enough.

Do you remember the incident recalled by Lloyd George in July 1914? He had stated (and believed) that the skies have never looked more blue, when he met an Austrian lady, a normal traveller across the Continent from the edge of the Balkans through Europe to England. She was appalled. 'Do you not know,' she said, 'that Europe is on the brink of war? That the mood of the people of Europe wherever one goes is growing to fever pitch?'

I often wonder what statesmen and politicians would think of the world they have fashioned were they to travel now as ordinary people must. They might realise why so much that they say about 'The Free World' etc. etc. sounds like so much bunkum. What might Butler say if he had to enter his country through Harwich—or Dover; or Macmillan or Selwyn Lloyd think as they were rather roughly fingerprinted in Grosvenor Square and subjected to the callous and brutal reception of Customs and Police at Boston or New York.

They do not have the opportunity to feel the changing mood manifest on trains, in the behaviour of officials all the way down, spreading like ripples in a pool. Nor do they try to find hotel accommodation, and know the attitudes of the various people, helpful or otherwise. They do not jostle with the crowds in the squares and boulevards, nor sit in the cafés.

For my part I have crossed more than seventy frontiers since the war (between 1945–51), and was startled by the difference in what I experienced from the Arctic to the Black Sea, and from France to China, from what, according to statesmen, I was meant to be experiencing. Where it was alleged I should find enemies and no help at all, I found friends and courtesy. In three countries alleged to 'hate' us it was impossible to doubt the real admiration and affection in which Englishmen were held. I remember one wild night, particularly. I was driving a Mercedes Benz from Paris through to the Black Sea, mostly alone, and on this night I had decided to strike off to follow the rugged road through the hills on the Hungarian–Serbia border. My tires were badly worn, and it was said in Zagreb that shell splinters on the usual route through to Belgrade meant up to ten bursts! On my lone journey (it was wild rugged country and a wild night) wolves charged the doors of the car as I came down into the valleys. In the midst of nowhere my two back tyres went pop. I inspected carefully in the almost pitch darkness, my lights off not to attract attention. All at once I was surrounded by dark armed figures, materialising out of nowhere. '*Ingleski*' I said hopefully. The result was astounding. I was hugged. Almost I was wafted through dangerous frontiers on a wave of love of the '*Ingleski*', in Roumania, Hungary, Serbia, Bulgaria and slap through a Soviet Armoured Division at Phillipopolis.

But I am, as too often, turning into a bore, running on and on. But it is true—and grave—I think, the way in which, even in the years before the golden world vanished, privilege cut politicians off from the world. Today I doubt whether there are more ignorant men on earth—what a pity Macmillan does not talk to bricklayers, and what a profound loss it is to him and to us.

As to the Dardanelles, far from convicting Winston, I believe that his idea was the only sound way to 'win' the war. It might even have prevented the Russian Revolution and 'changed the course of history'. He cannot be blamed for his persuasive tongue, for the failure of the Service Chiefs to back the project with all the strength possible. The commitment of the British people on the Continent of Europe was the death knell of a people and an Empire. It should never have happened. I don't like to blame de Roebeck too much either, for that wasn't the true crux of the matter. And how does one know that one's opponent is on the point of exhaustion? De Roebeck reflected, I think, the half-hearted attitudes at home. It had to be 'all or nothing'. It was instead a tragic and terrible compromise.

Meanwhile I have a most interesting precis of a paper presented by Leo Amery to Dill in Spring 1941, detailing the strategy Amery suggested Britain should follow. I have this paper because Lady Dill has let John Connell have a sight of Sir John's papers to help him in his life of Wavell.

Amery, of course, was a true Imperialist and that rarest of rare birds, a Tory intellectual (almost a contradiction in terms). He was also a 'Far Easter'. His views are very close to those expressed by Dorman Smith[1] in his earlier paper (written) in India. Dill approved—and according to Kennedy—so did the Chiefs of Staff. But not Winston.

I incline to the view that Dunkirk could have been the greatest blessing on earth to this country. Having lost the best of our blood and youth in W.W.1, we had the luck to have our army spewed out of the belly of the whale at an early stage, mauled but living. Never again. Now was the chance to realise that we were a Far Eastern plus an Atlantic and Med. sea power. But Winston, as you know much better than I, changed the priorities, wouldn't allow anyone else's ideas living room, etc. I must get Masters' book. He's always good reading anyway, and Winston on Wingate reveals him at his infantile-romantic worst.

I have clearly over-stepped the mark about K.G. V liking L.G. But surely Asquith in 1913–14 threatened the King with an immense increase in the peerage if the Parliament Bill was thrown out by the Lords? Of course, that horrible Maundy G business and L.G.'s implication through Davies must have sickened the King.

At any rate I press on too slowly, longing for the day when this 'Old Man of the Sea' is off my back. Two or three months yet, I fear, at this rate. But my mind is fairly clear. I know my course, and have cause to be grateful for my wise pilot 'in the wings', saving me from rocks I do not even see. That's you, in case you didn't know. In a world quite clearly directed by the insane (there appear to be so-called statesmen who still imagine an ancient exercise known as war, is still with us as a political instrument. So help us please God. For no human agent will.)

From Sir Desmond Morton   25th September, 1961
Many thanks for calling my attention to my odd mental confusion as between Asquith and L.G. in relation to George V. It was, of course, Asquith in 1913 who threatened to force George V to make rows of liberal Peers in certain circumstances. I ought to have had that clear, as curiously enough I myself might have been one of them.

Perhaps this needs a little explanation. I had a half-uncle who was very active as a Liberal and who had no children. He never got into Parliament, but was very active in the party. He and I were good pals, though I cannot say I was a 'good Liberal' in those days or any other. I was much too busy trying to become a good soldier. Anyway, when Asquith and his party whips were collecting names (they cared little who they got) for persons willing to become noble lords in order to vote on the Bill, should it come to that, my uncle Willy was asked if he would put his name down. As he had no children and believed I might become a politician in time, he asked permission and got it to put my name down instead as I was then over twenty-one.

[1] Auchinleck's Chief of Staff was sacked with his Chief in 1942. Virtually ruined, he changed his name to Dorman O'Gowan.

So there's an odd bit of history for you!!!

My real but obscure recollection to the point, however, is that when George V came to France, which he did on several occasions when I was A.D.C. to Haig, I saw a good deal of the Monarch and took him around once or twice, as well as overhearing conversations at Mess not meant for me! George V was remarkably indiscreet at times, especially when irritated. He made no secret of his great dislike for L.G. despite what the latter had done towards winning the war. He used to refer to L.G. as 'Thatt Mann', the Germanic pronunciation becoming very strong and was completely on the side of the 'Soldiers' against the 'Frocks'. There was one occasion when he gave me the most violent instructions on the telephone, which I naturally obeyed, to pass on a very rude message to L.G. (in England, the King being in France) through Stamfordham[1] who was also in London.

Apart from this, however, I have a recollection, now recalled, that at Mess one night he was inveighing against L.G. to Haig, and recounted how even during the war and not long before its end, L.G. was telling the King his plans for post-war legislation. The King demurred at something I have forgotten: whereupon L.G. had reminded George of Asquith's threat and blandly remarked that he could do the same thing.

That is what I had in mind and what caused my confusion. Anyway, the great point that, as a man, George V could not bear L.G. largely because of his extremely rude and uncultivated manner in private dealings, stands clear in my mind.

You have a particularly good point in the lack of direct contact between the head politicians and the thoughts of the people. But, like so many others of real importance, it is a matter which wants much thought and careful handling. Though of greater importance in international affairs than in home politics, where the lack of contact of a direct and human kind is somewhat made up for by newspapers and other machinery, there is, I think, a wider gap in knowledge and understanding in regard to foreign countries.

The reason for this is not perhaps difficult to find. In any country, democratic or otherwise, the rulers know that they must know as best they can what the ruled are thinking about. Thus they set up machinery to keep them informed, apart from the natural means. But when they turn to consider foreign countries, there used to be no similar special machinery apart from the Foreign Office and Diplomatic Service which is part of the latter. These read the foreign Press; but you and I know well that in many foreign countries, the Press of that country is not always a good guide as to what the people are really thinking. Moreover, each foreign nation has its own turn of psychology, which reacts

[1] Lord Stamfordham, Private Secretary to George V.

to events in a different way to what the English as a whole would do.

Although after the First World War it may be said that a special machine was set up to report what the hoi polloi in other countries was thinking, since it was recognised at long last that the said hoi polloi might be thinking on lines totally different from what their political rulers were thinking, or, equally important, might be thinking the same, it has been the custom of the Foreign Office and Diplomats to disregard anything said by this Special Service which ran counter to the trend of events and thought *they* were reporting.

That awful human trend, inevitably particularly noticeable in men of very forceful character such as leading politicians presumably are, of turning deaf ears to any information hostile to the policy they have decided upon or the course they wish to pursue, seems to be very strong among the English. This naturally applies to Diplomats and Foreign Offices who are the prime channels through which the Government makes up its mind on Foreign policy and expects to learn about foreign countries.

Believe it or not, before the First World War it was considered wildly improper for an Ambassador to have any contacts with the Opposition in a foreign country. Nor did his Embassy read any foreign Press save the official organs of the party forming the foreign Government.

Still, diplomats at least spoke the language of the country (in which?) they were serving, or most of them did. Hence a few of them acquired real knowledge of what the people were thinking. However, they risked their careers if they insisted too strongly that the Foreign Office might be wrong—and worse, if they firmly told their Ambassador he was mistaken.

Events immediately preceding the First World War in the Berlin Embassy are typical. The Ambassador was convinced that there would be no war. (It was just as bad before the Hitler war).

Before the First World War, only the Military and Naval Intelligence were convinced that the Kaiser was going to make war. They, however, were told that this was a political matter, and nothing to do with the Military or Naval Intelligence!!!!!

Turning to another of many aspects of this phenomenon. You and I have travelled a good deal in our time and in times of peace as well. We have learnt much about foreign countries and their psychologies, and what is more important, have learnt that there is such a thing as a national psychology. But look at our politicians! I mean the very successful ones, not every M.P. In the past some of them might also have travelled. But did they meet and talk with the hoi polloi? No, at best they met and talked with officials, other politicians and our own diplomats, all of whom for varying reasons, knowing that they were talking to a foreign politician took great pains to keep on the official line.

Did you know that when Gladwyn Jebb[1] was a young Secretary of Embassy in Persia, he had the initiative to travel home on leave to England via Moscow, without permission (which would never have been given). He spent some weeks in Moscow without telling the Embassy there (if we had one at the moment. I think we had some representation). He learned a lot of interesting background. He was as near as a touch dismissed from the Service, and it was only because the F.O. could not frame a respectable charge on the regulations as then existing that he got off with a temporary huge blot on his reputation.

Lawks! what tales I could tell you.

The Amery paper you speak of is most interesting. I had the honour to know Leo Amery well. Was it not Arthur Balfour who said quite kindly, 'I think Leo must be the cleverest bloody fool alive?' What he meant was that in his opinion Leo was frequently most devastatingly right, but never knew how to play his cards in the game of politics.

But what a criticism of 'politics'.

If, in anything I read, and my reading season of the long nights will soon be upon us, since I do much less reading in summer, there being no time, I come across anything of interest to you concerning Winston, I will not fail to let you know.

Meanwhile I did come across an interesting thing—nothing to do with Winston directly, but about the great Lawrence of India;[2] this is an obscure diary of a contemporary Indian Civil Servant. From this it appeared so clearly first that whatever great things Lawrence did in conquering and administering the Punjab, and however much he was worshipped by the Sikhs, Mohammedans and Punjabis, he was absolutely loathed by all his brother officers and especially subordinates. Secondly the reason for this hatred was perfectly clear. Certain similarities of character between Lawrence and Winston struck me immediately—only certain ones; but they were the causes of his immense unpopularity with the Europeans and justly so. Truly it is difficult to assess character through historical events. It is only by knowing a man well personally that one can hope to succeed, save by great fortune. However do not let that remark depress you.

Did you get anything interesting out of your meeting with P. J. Grigg?

From R. W. Thompson   2nd October, 1961
I fight the germlins besieging my too vulnerable carcase (I see I have scrambled 'gremlins'—perhaps aptly!) and your letters help greatly. I

[1] Sir Gladwyn Jebb, later First Baron, diplomat. Distinguished career in the Foreign Office, Ministry of Economic Warfare, etc. H.B.M. Ambassador, Paris.
[2] Lord Lawrence of the Punjab, 1811-79.

am convinced that I shall be as right as rain as soon as this vast 'aspiration' is off my plate. Have just read Claud Cockburn's new book, *View from the West* . . . He writes that a synopsis (upon which all publishers insist, and dole out considerable sums of money) is midway between a wild aspiration and a confidence trick. There it is. It always seems impossible, but since one has committed oneself one hacks and strives with one's whole personal inner reputation with oneself at stake. So, there is nothing for it but to win. But what a life! Setting up impossible cock-shy's . . . and then spending the next twelve months in hopeless—as it seems—(attempts) to knock them down. Meanwhile the 'considerable sums' inevitably dwindle, and there comes a day when time is no longer on one's side. Gremlins indeed by the million. But I shall prevail. I believe my idea of Winston is going to emerge. I wish it would go faster, but it won't. Every five thousand words demands up to seven or eight drafts before I think it says just what I want to say. But if I do what I set out to do it is a kind of small personal triumph; one more small victory over the 'impossible'. That's what is meant, perhaps, about it being necessary to work in a garret. For, why, unless one had to, unless one had so committed oneself in those periods of resurgent optimism that inevitably arise out of the trough of labours, attempt such bold projects! And if one did not, then probably one would doodle, perhaps amusingly, instructively (not me), spin—even toil. But not this kind of toil.

Eric O'G wrote a terrific new piece of chapter and verse re. Middle East, Greece, Valona etc. I feel the chips falling from his shoulders, his expositions growing more brilliant and lucid. He really should write a book about it all. But what a lament that such a fine mind, allied to such energies should have been thrown on the scrap heap before fifty years of age! Of course, it is always one's own fault. One carries the seeds of one's own disintegration, and why should anyone else weed the garden. Nevertheless, contemplation of the wasted 'misfits' is an unhappy exercise, for if only the world knew how to use its so-called 'misfits' it would have a reservoir of tremendous energy, enthusiasm and brilliance to draw upon. None of them—unless he happens to be an Alexander of Macedon—really gets used, or is able to benefit the world by his existence.

Have bought John Masters, but not yet read him. Have also bought Graham Greene's *Burnt out Case*. All this in a resolve to relax by night. But Churchill is a clinging type if ever there was one. What a pity his deeds—especially his misdeeds—always drew such extravagant praise or blame. It obscures the real man groping always for a vision that is not really true. What an unfortunate start in life he had—poor Winston! Such a child, spoiled of course—beyond belief; a child in giant's clothing. And you were neither nurse nor fellow infant playmate.

What a role. But you believe in something, and that is just what is wrong with the world—I mean most people don't. Not even in themselves.

From Sir Desmond Morton   Begun, 10th October, 1961
Too long since I got yours of 2nd October, before answering; but I, like all of us, have my minor troubles. My housekeeper has been ill, and is not too well yet, so have had to buy food and so on in addition to other work.

Your letters are always appreciated by your humble friend and servant to command and also most entertaining. I like the idea of a synopsis being midway between a wild aspiration and a confidence trick. Also there is much in common between a gremlin and germline—perhaps only a grimline between them—oh Lord!

My hat! Winston 'groping always for a vision that is not really true'.

That is brilliant, and I believe *is* true. I do not think he ever saw that vision which, even though it be 'dimly reflected in a mirror' (much better translation than 'through a glass darkly') is absolutely true.

I prefer to think that than to suppose that he did see that reflection at any time and then turn away from it. But *that* one can never really know. At any rate I know that he used to claim with sincerity that although he was not a Christian, since to name himself such would be dishonest, he firmly believed in the existence of God. A sort of Unitarian outlook. He said he was not a Christian since he could not believe that Christ was God, though he recognised him as being the finest character that ever lived.

I take it you will not attempt to deal with Winston's spiritual beliefs and outlook in your book. I do not think it would work. No one really knows what they were and it would be fatally easy to fall into very bad taste on such a matter. Actually, however, if one did know for certain, I think his outlook on such matters would throw much light on his character. It would be impossible to say when and how any action or decision of his was affected by religious or spiritual considerations; still less, whether any restraint he imposed upon himself was due to such. Mark you, I am not for a moment suggesting that Winston lacked moral standards. Far from it. He held and I would say, generally, followed very definite standards of behaviour. But as you will know the 'good Pagan' (if you ever read that interesting book) had a strict standard of morality, i.e. behaviour, but that standard was far removed from the Christian standard.

One of the objects of my writing this letter has not yet been achieved. You may remember our mention of Esher, the Lord. Esher, the Lord was indeed Chairman of the Royal Commission which sat after the South African war from 1902 to 1908 on Imperial Defence and produced the famous report which is called after their name and was the cause of founding the Committee of Imperial Defence, the re-organisation of the Army Staff system, though they failed to recognise the Naval Staff and it took the First World War to do that. But it was of course not Esher, either that one or his successor, who came out to the Doullens Conference in March 1918 which made Foch General-issimo of the Western Front after the Germans had broken through the join between the Fifth Army and the French; and who burst into tears of hysterical nerve strain at the said conference. I cannot imagine how I got it into my head that *that* was Esher. It proves my dotage. It was Milner. Quite a different party.

This was recalled to my errant memory by reading the official account of the bombing of Germany controversy which recently burst upon us, wherein it is mentioned in a manner of retrospect only and in no sense of contribution to the bomb-Germany affair.

★   ★   ★

Returning to the B of bombing. Air Marshals at my Club are furious over the Official History and claim that in very many respects it falls miles short of veracity. But the bombing controversy will never be satisfactorily resolved. You will, however, doubtless have noticed that there is new evidence that Winston was personally agin it, though as P.M. and Minister of Defence, he condoned it to begin with under pressure from the Chiefs of Staff. I honestly doubt if the Prof. came into the picture very much and am sure that whatever view he took, it actually carried little weight.

I am glad Eric O'G is getting a mellower judgment of things. To be thrown onto the scrap heap at the young age of under fifty is not conducive to dispassionate appreciation of causes, effects and the characters of those who seem to have assisted in the throwing, what-ever the true merits of the case.

As regards Winston, 'The evil that men do lives after them, the good is oft interred with their bones.' (Shakespeare W.)

Nowadays that is no longer quite correct about politicians. A man who has held great offices of State is the object of great controversy and abuse as well as praise, while he lives, and well after his death. At his death, it seems that all persons and Parties unite in saying what a fine fellow he was.

From R. W. Thompson   23rd October, 1961
I am now almost totally immersed in Winston, seldom coming up for air. Days run into days without my realising, and I shall be very glad at last to emerge. He is fairly easy to live with now, except when he

takes off on one of his obsessional flights of rhetoric. This trait appears to have begun in 1917—a crucial year if ever there was one, with U.S. coming back into Europe, and Russia revoluting!

We went down to Basil L.H.'s last weekend and had some interesting talk about tanks, and Winston's row with Albert Stern. That was remarkably revealing of his political caution at the time. But 1917 was the year when he first made contact with Baruch and screamed blue murder about the 'kind and gentle' Czar etc. Startled quite a few people.

Beginning to understand something of Tory party and Tory ways and means, so that I wonder whether it is possible in this country to be a Tory and a patriot—men like Amery may be the exceptions proving the rule . . . I don't like Tories . . . I don't think I'm a true blood-thirsty type.

Your letter delighted me . . . Did you see Kingsley Martin's rather good story? An American in crowded compartment of British train. Englishman tries to persuade formidable female to move her lap dog from the seat it is occupying to the exclusion of himself. Upon lady refusing for third time, irate Englishman hurls lap dog out of the window.

Lone American remarks: 'You goddam British beat me. You drive on the wrong side of the road; serve warm beer, and you throw the wrong bitch out of the window!'

If you are reading on after that, receive my thanks for reminding me that Winston was more a creature of 'hunches' and opportunism than a man with any clear idea of what to do with power. No, I don't actually attempt to deal with Winston's spiritual beliefs beyond a bare suggestion of the kind of God he probably had. In my feeling, he has one thing in common with m and lm classes in that the Monarch was in place of God, the symbol here on earth. Hence his nonsense about the Czar and his regime.

I agree about his moral standards, but they were very adaptable. I wonder whether a total egocentric actually *can* have moral standards— unless things go smoothly. Or, alternatively, his moral standards— bearing in mind the meaning of the word, were strictly his own. But if Winston were going to lose out then I doubt whether any moral scruples of a conventional pattern would have deterred him. But he was certainly not a man without moral standards and, therefore, as you point out, a moral man. (Not that you did point out that Winston was a moral man, but simply had the nature of a moral man.)

I find I must possess the official bombing story. I liked very much the long essay in the T.L.S. Of course, one never knows, nor is it worth speculation, what would have happened but for the bombing; what else would have had the priorities, raw materials, factory space etc. Perhaps the Battle of the Atlantic would have been won that much sooner. But it seems certain that German civilian morale was grossly underestimated, as well as von Speer's brilliance as a producer of goods of war.

From Sir Desmond Morton   Begun 30th October, 1961

Of course, these Party labels are now so mixed up and have so mightily changed their original significance and even principles that they are meaningless. I call down a plague upon all their houses! All the successful politicians nowadays are, with very few exceptions, professional politicians, who put Party before any sort of principles, and, when asked what are the principles of their particular Party, become quite confused if pressed.

The Party which is hopelessly muddled in its outlook is the Labour or Socialist Party. Its tenets, allegedly those of the Second (Socialist) International, bear no arguable resemblance to the latter's proposals, have no idea where they are going and, even if they admit to Socialism, differ wholly in their alleged tenets from the alleged tenets of continental Socialist Parties, who differ markedly between one another.

The old difference between Tory and Liberal, and the only real permanent difference in outlook which has now presumably disappeared, was that whereas the Tories, once elected, considered that their job was to govern (until thrown out) without further consultation with the governed: they were, in fact, elected, or so they considered it, to govern, the Liberals, when elected, originally assumed that they were elected by the people who understood what they wanted at the time of the election (probably a complete fallacy) and that they could only hold power if they were constantly in touch with the people, whose views would change according to circumstances. Should they feel unable to do what the people wanted, the Liberals would resign.

Whether this difference between the Tories and Liberals was ever real, is a moot point. But there is a clear and important difference in intellectual outlook between, 'I have been elected, because the people think I am the best person to govern', and 'I have been elected because the people think I am their best representative to do what they want in the matter of governance'.

You have to go back to the Greek City States to find the true application of 'democracy' as interpreted in an old fashioned Liberal sense.

I admit intellectually and in theory to support the idea that the person elected should be what the people think is the best person to govern, because the frightful complications of modern home and international relations are such that no ordinary voter can possibly understand them. This, undoubtedly originally Tory idea, should however be combined with a machinery of a liberal nature, whereby, if the people think the person they have elected is no longer the best person to govern them, that person should be compelled to resign.

Naturally I see the impossibility of such an arrangement; but it is the only sensible interpretation of 'Democracy' that I know. Actually, again in theory, I am very doubtful about anything one could call pure Democracy, and probably favour a sort of ideal feudal system, which it would be impossible to realise. However one can have a good gab-fest and talk nonsense about this sort of thing for weeks on end.

There is one thing I am dead against and that is, imposing by force on one nation a system of Government in force in any other.

I like your story about the 'lap dog' though I have heard various variants before. This one is the best.

You will doubtless have paid due attention to Winston's 'romanticism'. Fascinating in its childish appeal; infuriating as to the appalling mistakes it caused him to make. He really and truly believed these two-pence coloured and highly erroneous images. The superlatively courageous, courteous, urbane, masculine, Arab, terrible in his wrath, living an ascetic life in company with Allah, a camel, a spear and rifle, an arab mare and a Selukhi dog, jealous of his honour above all, like a medieval knight of chivalry, etc. This he really believed and nothing could persuade him to a balanced view, with a realisation that *en masse* the Bedu is a dirty, cowardly cut-throat, with very primitive passions indeed and about as trustworthy as a King Cobra.

His heroes—mostly and mercifully dead—were all Sir Galahads, or pure and holy women of queenly dignity.

He adored swashbucklers, whom he regarded in the light of d'Artagnans. Any sort of 'higher criticism' of the heroes and heroines of even recent antiquity, Florence Nightingale is typical, would drive him to frenzy.

I have often wondered what all this was about, psychologically. 'England with all thy faults I love thee still' was anathema. England had no faults, only wicked men had misled her at times. All Germans were Nahzees, all Italians organ-grinders, all South Africans Smutses, Americans, as a whole, bold frontiersmen living dangerously and so on. Why psychologically, did he yearn for a romanticism which has never existed save in the minds of romantic authors? There are lots of possible explanations, but I have not a single clue as to which could be right. Of course he hated any kind of life, action or thought that he would consider 'sordid'. Equally, he was the 'never-grow-up' type of boy that you have seen him to be. Nevertheless this particular trait was endearing. Have not we all in our time read Henty and with avid interest? The hero who after great trials always comes out on top and covered with honour. A set of novels which Winston would not put down when a new one came out, and which he read time and time again, were the 'Hornblower' stories. That was exactly his cup of tea. I enjoyed them myself. But to W.S.C. they were almost as a draught of pure wine to a thirsty man.

Actually there is something fundamentally of importance in this. Of course, he saw himself in all the heroic roles, does not a boy do this? But there is much more to it than only this. I regretfully agree with you that 'if Winston (thought) he was going to lose out' few moral scruples of a conventional order would govern his fight. But then, his type, if one dare to consider him a 'type' of anything, has a marvellous power of 'rationalising' i.e. finding a marvellous excuse for his own unmoral acts, which he could heartily condemn in others. Without being in any way what is technically known as a schizophrenic, he was a dozen or more different personalities at different times, which makes it immensely difficult to describe him. However you have set yourself that task and I wish you luck. In an ordinary man one would call these personalities 'moods'; but with Winston these 'moods' were those of a very great actor playing different stage roles and could not be called 'moods'. He was no Charles Hawtrey, superb in a single sort of character only; but he was like Charles Hawtrey in that you knew that each character was (Hawtrey) Winston unmistakably. Yet he was not completely versatile. There were roles and characters he was quite unable to portray. He could never be a clown or portray a madman, like Irving in *The Bells*. He had no interest in comedy, seeking always grandeur and magnificence but, let it be said, admired greatly demonstrations of the same trait in others. He would have willingly, I believe, have been Stalin, simply for the power that Stalin enjoyed, but he would certainly have demanded that Winston–Stalin and his associates should dress in the clothing of seventeenth-century boyars and would never have allowed his enemies to be shot in the back of the neck secretly in cellars. They would have been executed publicly by a scarlet clad headsman with an axe, possibly with very loud speakers playing the Dead March in Saul, and a clarion voice crying out, 'So perish all Starchil's enemies!'

In fact I doubt the Party would have stood him for long, or else it would certainly have changed its ways.

From R. W. Thompson   13th November, 1961
Your letters always seem to arrive with an almost miraculous sense of timing. I have been revolving in my mind the relationship between T. E. Lawrence and Winston, and it began to seem to me that Lawrence evoked feelings in W. different in kind from anyone else. Then comes your wonderful piece of 'prose' about romanticism. Winston and his 'noble Arab'. Do you remember his portrait of Lawrence? It is quite remarkable, 'the eyes of fire loaded with comprehension' etc. etc.

Lawrence seemed to be the embodiment of one of his visions. A piece of 'fiction' was there in the flesh. And Winston tried to make T.E. his own, not without some temporary success.

For a little while Winston had a real live hero in a pattern dear to his heart, and Lawrence didn't let him down when they went together to 'fix up' the Middle East. Such relationships are rare, for Winston reserved his true admiration for very few—apart from Lloyd George.

Your brief exposition of the Tory attitude was also valuable. And did you see Harold Nicolson's piece in the *Observer* yesterday? I liked it. It was remarkably straightforward. His simple statement that he hates Tories rang absolutely true, a straightforward hatred, as one might have for the Devil. He also used a phrase about Churchill I liked. He said Churchill said round about 1910 that 'All Churchills damp down at forty'. Curious. I had come to the conclusion that Winston expected to live about fifty years, and that in the 20s he was living a kind of middle-aged end pattern to a life. His mediocrity in peace was astonishing (for such a man). He was not so much a bad Chancellor, a bad War and Air Minister, but as mediocre as poor Inskip, whom he called the worst since Caligula made his horse Consul (or worse. Poor Inskip wasn't so bad in my opinion). Then suddenly Churchill pinches himself, finds himself alive and kicking and launches himself all over again, plenty of money, Chartwell, his personal 'General Staff' or 'Shadow Cabinet' or 'Focus' or whatever, would be an apt description. He then lives a brand new life with, as you once remarked, 'prodigious energy'.

You have also wonderfully crystallised my feelings about his peculiar passion for England. As Amery said, he was an Englander. He didn't understand the Empire. It was always a fiction in his mind. He was mid-Victorian even to his night-shirt. Gandhi was that 'naked fakir', and so on. His dream was England and he St. George. He was helpless and hopeless without a Dragon. Well, he got his Dragon, unhappily more than one, and the one who spoke in his own language swallowed him—whole. Alas for England and all the rest.

But Winston's cause was always Winston, and even England was no more than its essential piece of geography. St. George can't attack and kill a Dragon in 'nowhere'. At any rate, I too find him endearing a good deal of the time, but an awful and dangerous myth. Not that anything can be really dangerous any more. We and the world are past that. It remains simply to be seen whether enough men believe that they may be—or can be—'The Sons of God'. . . .

Strange how Churchill has become a living and growing person in my mind through all these months. Perhaps I don't know him at all, but I feel that I know him intimately, and I've found a common denominator in all those strange people who hate him with peculiar virulence: they're all pro-German or Empire Loyalists, unless, of course, chaps who have some personal cause. But they usually get over it. It's very difficult to 'hate' (and very wrong) a brave boy who didn't grow up. If the English weren't such pre-adolescents themselves it wouldn't matter anyway. Wells thought he was like D'Annunzio. But I won't have that. Not in the end.

From Sir Desmond Morton   23rd November, 1961
On the left of the front page of your last letter, of 13th November you wrote in handwriting, 'I would be enormously grateful for some "detail" on this. What would you call it? Who were its main and more permanent component—'. The trouble is I cannot relate this query to anything in your letter, on either page, and presumably this note must refer to something on the front page.

On the front page you deal with (a) Winston's friendship with Lawrence, (b) Nicolson in the *Observer* on Prime Ministers I have known and (c) Winston's possible expectation of not living more than forty years and the reaction when he found he did—and (possibly I have got it here) Winston's friends at Chartwell. Anyway, I have comments on all four.

First and easiest, I wholly agreed with Nicolson on the Prime Ministers, particularly L.G. and W.S.C. and Asquith. I think he dealt inadequately with others and never mentioned Bonar Law, if I remember right.

Second, the forty-year life expectation. I have never heard a single thing to support that from him (and at one time he unburdened himself with surprising fullness to me about things and himself in general), from his wife or any of his intimates. I am inclined to doubt it on the grounds that he never had a trace of fatalism in his make up, nor did I ever hear from him a single suggestion of superstition—even those non-serious half-superstitions which have often been current in elegant society e.g. throwing salt over your left shoulder if you spill it, sitting thirteen at table, lighting three cigarettes with one match. He was immensely healthy, took all sorts of risks to his health without a moment's thought and, as P.M., only showed slight neurotic anxiety if he got a cold which might interfere with his speaking voice—and who shall blame him for this, since he well knew that his speaking voice was one of his greatest assets.

Of course, he may have pondered deeply at one time on the cause of his father's death, and wondered if that would shorten his own life. I know nothing of this, chiefly because I did not know him until he was just past forty and Minister of Munitions in the First World War. Again, if you are right he would have passed his fear date and would be free of the imagined Fate. Still, it is so much out of character (or characters, for he developed several) that I knew that I should want cogent evidence before accepting (anything?) of the sort. You also suggest that fifty was the fear age. I knew him well before that and there was no sign of it. When he was in the doldrums politically, having quarrelled with the Tories over India, one of the facts supporting him was his youth relative to that of the senior Tory Ministers, whereby when they had dropped off the bough, he would still be there and in Parliament. Look at your dates again. W.S.C. was born in 1874 and was fifty in 1924. When he said in 1910 'all Churchills damp down at forty'—he was then thirty-six, it would be important to know the context. If someone had just told him that his uproarious political behaviour (Sydney Street or something like that) was strongly conducive to his being dropped, or to political unpopularity, he might have made this remark intending to convey that he would soon get more staid in his behaviour as a Cabinet Minister. Note 'damp down' not 'blow up' or anything like that.

Next, his apparent very great friendship for Lawrence. This can be commented on together with your point (if it is what you want) regarding the persons he got to visit him at Chartwell and at ?Sussex Square (I forget the exact name and number of his house in London at that time), it too was North of the Park on the opposite side from his present 28 Hyde Park Gate.

As for Lawrence, I am sure you have a somewhat exaggerated picture. I am very much afraid that Bob Boothby's statement on the radio a year or so ago was true. He said that Winston never had a friend, but that the three closest approximations to that state of comradeship had been Bracken, Baruch and himself, Boothby.

In agreeing with this general idea, I am not intending to criticise Winston, because in my view his character made him incapable of complete friendship [comradeship] with any other man. He had one or two great women friends, apart from his wife to whom he was devoted and towards whom he was most affectionate; but that is quite a different thing. While sexually he was most highly moral, he was wholly male and delighted in female society if the female was intelligent and liked him. He was also an artist and a beautiful (not necessarily pretty) woman well dressed and poised appealed highly to his artistic sense. He was highly eighteenth century in that.

Do not forget his similar love of colour, uniforms, the stage, a great show or procession.

Bob Boothby also said that with men, one must be either his servant, indifferent to him or his enemy. You could not remain his 'friend'—at least in Winston's own subconscious, unless that subconscious could regard you as also his servant. Not a domestic servant, but inferior, and of use to him.

The full truth, I believe, is that Winston's 'friends' must be persons who were of use to him. The idea of having a friend who was of no practical use to him, but being a friend because he liked him, had no place. I repeat that I honestly believe this to have been a subconscious process.

As regards the encomium Winston gave to Lawrence, you will find that he has given hardly less if at all less encomiums to or about other of his temporary friends. His friendship with Lawrence started as you know when the latter got him out of a political difficulty just after the First World War through his great knowledge of certain Mid East affairs. *Of course*, Winston adored meeting picturesque and even odd characters, particularly swashbucklers, which last Lawrence was not really, though both Winston and Lawrence himself thought he was, though actually he was something far more valuable. He had elements of real greatness, based on sincerity but certain terrible twists in his own subconscious prevented that greatness fructifying.

But, after Lawrence had so greatly assisted Winston over the Middle East and done his extraordinary act of joining the R.A.F. as a private, Winston forgot him until he, Winston, out of favour with the Government, began to look round for persons who could keep him informed about other things, e.g. the Air Force. He then got into touch again.

The people whom Winston got down to Chartwell between 1920 and 1939 were very varied—some have never caught the public eye, such as the Professor of History, whose name I am ashamed to say I have forgotten, but who gave him immense help over Marlborough (I've just remembered his name, Feiling). He was not a paid assistant, but helped out of sheer interest. F. E. Smith, Anthony Eden, P. J. Grigg, Louis Greig, Dyer[1] and O'Dwyer (at the time of his fight with the Govt. over India), Grandi,[2] Cartier de Marchienne, Bob Boothby, Jimmy Thomas,[3] half the men who eventually became his Cabinet Ministers when he was P.M., Duff Cooper, Willingdon,[4] any Tory M.P. who was restive about any policies of the Tory Government, Bob Vansittart,[5] 'Kitten' Wigram and many others, apart from such persons as Lindemann, Bracken of course, and Lawrence.

This astounding collection had two things only in common— Winston wanted and got something out of them of use to himself in the particular 'ploys' with which he was engaged at the moment; secondly that all were attracted by the fascination of Winston's speech, energy

[1] General J. H. Dyer, known for his firm action over trouble at Amritsar.
[2] Count Dino Grandi, Italian Ambassador in London.
[3] J. H. Thomas, Labour politician, Colonial Secretary, National Government, 1933.
[4] First Marquess of Willingdon, Viceroy of India.
[5] Sir Robert Vansittart, First Baron, Permanent Under-Secretary, Foreign Affairs.

and activities. They came willingly to hear him talk and to examine his ideas. Oh! another frequent visitor was Gwynne[1] of the *Morning Post*.

You must not get the idea that he was permanently surrounded by a specific 'Court' or even by specific 'Clients' like a Roman Senator, either at Chartwell or in London. It was all in a way quite natural. He used lunches and dinners in London in the same way he used Chartwell; but the guests at either or both depended largely on mutual convenience. Winston was 'courted' as he 'courted' others and he was most ready to see and talk to anyone whom he thought was worth talking to from his point of view. There was nothing like what your words, 'Shadow Cabinet', 'General Staff' or even 'Circle', which you do not use, would imply. Winston was the centre of an ever-changing circle—the changes being due to the fact that his particular interest in a particular subject, which was the subject of the person invited, changed, or temporarily lapsed. Similarly, if a subject, temporarily abandoned, was resuscitated, certain people who previously had been frequent visitors, but who had not appeared for months, would again be cultivated.

Winston was in no sense a Maecenas. He was not a rich patron of the arts, science, politics or anything else. He was not the centre of a circle, permanently composed of definite particles. He was self-sufficient, collecting particles into a sort of orbit of those whom he chose for a particular purpose and rejecting them either permanently or for the time being when they had ceased to serve his purpose.

This may sound hard, and it is difficult to know how to put my thoughts and conclusions into gentler words. In the light of what Winston was in himself, I can find any amount of excuses for what may seem a most heartless proceeding. It was not that, because he certainly gave all who knew him at least as much pleasure as they may have given him use or interest. He owes them no debt. Moreover there were few who were not fully aware of the nature of the process.

I could go on soliloquising or philosophising, but to no value.

You cannot blame a highly charged electro-magnet for acting as it does—attracting iron and steel filings when a current runs through its coils, and dropping them off when the current ceases to run. Equally you cannot blame the electro-magnet for not attracting copper, glass or paving stones. The magnet must behave in accordance with its nature, and *Naturam expelles furca tamen usque recurret* (Horace not Solomon, or you may chuck out nature with a pitchfork, but it will always run back).

My profound salutations to Mel, who is certainly enduring for your sake just as much as you are, which *is* friendship, and the sustained hope that both your sufferings may soon be ended satisfactorily.

[1] Major H. A. Gwynne, Editor of the *Morning Post*.

In spite of my lamentable incoherence your letter helps me in my pursuit of Churchill, as do all your letters. Henceforth for at least five weeks I shall be living with you and all that you have said to me. I think I would be wise to sweep away the mounds of books from my desk, clear it and my mind (oh, monstrous, happy thought!) and simply write—'like spirit writing'. There is so much to know, and so little. Enough is enough is enough. I face the end pattern of my book, 105,000 words behind me, dredged out of my dreams and oceans of word sludge, and if the pan is dry of gold, so be it. I 'panned'. My man is established in his context, and there is no going back. He cannot go forward. He never could. He could only wait for the world to have a time-slip backwards and 'catch up' with him. It did.

As I see it against the background of the twentieth century, all men are dwarfs. No one sees or dares to see and to face the challenge. It is in essence a Christian challenge, that all men are brothers. The ultimate simplicity. All the ancient concepts of national power are gone, and on the grand scale (in this little world of men) is the struggle for which Merlin strove to prepare Arthur, in vain. In Europe the civil war was bedevilled by the entry of the U.S.A. But they went away, content (one hoped) with their gigantic loot. But still threadbare Europe refused to see the nature of its own domestic struggle. Instead of striving to see the nature of the new Europe (even the new world) we reduced it at last back to 'tribal' proportions. Communism and Fascism were the two horns of the dilemma, pointing the problem and the challenge. It was not to choose one of the ways, but to know through these two manifestations the true choice.

Perhaps in those days from 1914 there were two men in England (it is barely possible: I do not say it was so), Lloyd George and Asquith, with between them (in Asquith's brain pan) the depth of scholarship, in Lloyd George the energy, the bold vision, almost diabolic. But in neither the courage. Had these two men been able to shake 'hands'— think of that! Merely to shake hands, like children—unless ye be as little children . . .

But they could not. Imagine Asquith with Lloyd George at the Peace Conference. Now, there would have been a team of men. They could have prevailed, even against the wolf-pack howls of what is called 'democracy'. L.G. alone could not—at least he could, had he been more than the man he was. But he towered among dwarfs even so, except for that ancient tribal chief, Clemenceau, who had played his last part—as chieftains should—and did. (And there was another chieftain in the wings, waiting his turn, and it would come! In England.)

Then afterwards, when the Europe that must arise was clear, these two again, Asquith and L.G. in friendship, could have repaired liberalism, re-fashioned it as the only Christian political concept to set against Communism and Fascism. Instead a dreary conservatism entrenched itself in mediocrity, in squalid tribalism, the outward and visible sign of primitive man, a badge of squalor to fight an equally dim and squalid labour party, barely whelped, wet and shapeless from a dreary womb. Over such puppets as these Hitler, Lenin, Stalin rose like colossi.

Yet in 1929 old Amery (the cleverest bloody fool in Europe, as Balfour called him) believed that Briand and Bruning, given one man of stature in Britain to stand at their side, could have refashioned Europe, and seen the nature of the European domestic struggle. But Lloyd George, the *one* man who might have filled that role, was under the surgeon's knife. There was no other. For Churchill was a bird of vastly different feather, head-dress 'n all.

The 'Round Table' never was. The hour of the tribal chiefs was dawning. Since Europe would not go forward it went back, until England (for Churchill, it was always England—This sceptred Isle . . . back to Hereward the Wake . . .) at the bottom of a pond, stagnating with the Tory millstone round its neck was back behind its ditch in an ancient posture. And thus Churchill was its man. He had never moved away from such a world. And it had caught up with him from behind, a back slip in time. This was Henry V and all the great music of Shakespeare in the tribal soul. For a moment he saw himself mirrored in the pool of England, and England in him, Narcissus Superbus!

I won't go on now. I let my thoughts drift off to you. Is it all rot? I don't know. It is me. Only poets and philosophers saw the nature of it, but not hard, not in political and economic terms.

And why not reduce it down? Did not Christ do that? For at the heart, when all the complex is cleared away one is back again at the simplicity of the beginning . . .

But first, a recognition of the nature of the 'civil war' in Europe would have been enough, a simple first step but too difficult for those dwarfs—which is us—or Lilliputians, ill equipped in our tiny natures to fight bigger battles for bigger things. So again the U.S.A. bedevilled the issue, and before civil war was faced, world civil war was upon us. Now, quite properly, it is 'double or quits' with humanity, to be or not to be, that is the simple question, whether to blow ourselves up, leaving perhaps some embryo to begin again, or to know that we are men in the image of God, and that if we can—like peasants—get our thoughts out of the dung heap, and soar like primitive man even as far heaven-wards as the Sun (as a beginning), we shall inherit the earth—along with our fellow men and neighbours.

And all we have is Churchill, poor Anthony [Eden], sage old cockatoo Macmillan . . . And, democracy! Few have much more. Many have less. It is not a hopeful prospect.

. . . Do not weep for me, nor sigh, nor wring your hands. I am as I am. I do my best, which is not easy for any man. Soon this mountain will be off my back, and I shall be as light as air. How I should love to laugh and sing and dance and play in the sun, in Mexico perhaps, on some ancient strand . . .

From Sir Desmond Morton   9th December, 1961
A very brief line in reply to your letter of 28th November. Not only am I unwilling to worry you further when you are on the last lap of your course . . . but I am overborne with work too, though of a totally different nature.

I am certainly complimented by your saying you will be living with me (in the spirit) for at least five weeks, and am more than content if any part of my spirit and lucubrations are of any use to you.

I am quite certain that the notes in your letter are not 'all rot'. There is vision behind them. Whether you can translate that vision correctly I do not know; but it is *your* vision and *you* must describe it.

You are abundantly right in my view, in rejecting as unrealities Equality, Democracy, the Organised Man etc. The truth, which is an attribute of the only reality, is along the lines of Caritas (since 'love' has now been reduced by the screen and stage—as well as modern novels—to mere sexual desire or intercourse).

Hence, descending to very great hope for the crowning of your present struggles with success.

P.S. Have just had a private lunch with Winston and Clemmie at Hyde Park Gate. I will not tell you about this until your present labours are ended, from fear of unsettling your mind, or perhaps even sending you round the bend.

From R. W. Thompson   15th January, 1962
I have been on the verge of writing to you ever since the New Year, but at the critical moment my typewriter has seized me and sent me off on wild excursions. Now, as we used to say at school, I've worked myself 'blue in the face' all morning, and have come up for air. Alas the task is not yet done, but the end is near. One is always over-optimistic, and indeed without an overdose of optimism one would never embark on such tasks at all. Christmas—colds and so on, took a minor toll, and cost more than a week of words. But all for the best; at least I always feel so. There are periods of digestion, and invariably I find that after a tantalising period of partial frustration something has

cooked that could not have cooked earlier. (I observe my digestion has become mixed with the cooking; no matter.)

But one reason why you have been slightly on my mind, as opposed to properly in my thoughts, as you so often are, is that I thought I detected a faintly anxious note in your last letter about this mammoth task. I can only say in re-assurance, if such be needed, that the reward of such tasks is largely—almost overwhelmingly—that one has pleased one's friends, above all those very few friends whose opinions are really valuable, not only in a personal way. Thus if you and Basil, and one or two others did not like, or approve this book, the rest of the praise or blame could be of no personal importance.

You above all will not doubt that it has been from start to finish an intensely serious undertaking. It has involved my whole mental and physical apparatus to the point of exhaustion. It will take me weeks to unwind. But recently I have begun to feel fairly happy about it. I know that I have said all that was in me to say. It is, of course, fundamentally a work of 'fiction' (that for your eyes alone!) that is it explores the unknown of a man's mind in a jungle of 'facts'. But what are facts? And are there 'facts' about the character and personality? I doubt it. Any job of real value—or to have a chance of real value— must be a work of intuition, and much hard labour. Ninety-eight per cent dedication and two per cent inspiration, I think someone once said. If so, I've gone over the hundred per cent with the inspiration side of the business.

And what have I done? I don't really know. I think I have written 'an intelligent child's guide to our times'—for the structure is true from mid nineteenth century to the present day. Whether you will recognise my Churchill only time will show; whether you will truly feel that I have been blessed with insight. I hope so, profoundly.

Another two weeks perhaps, and I shall be done. 135,000 words. Quite a big job. Mel typing furiously for extra copies. Bless her. And about her Latin with her infants. If they can't imagine 'O Table', like Winston, they'd better not say so! Soon I shall hope to know more of that luncheon party with my 'hero'—when my mind is beyond 'unsettling' . . .

From Sir Desmond Morton   Begun 18th January, 1962
I had thought I might be hearing from you about now, and hoped that it would be to say that the first draft of the BOOK had been completed, thus relieving one source of strain, even though that gave place to another. However, you are in sight of the winning post, so that having successfully leaped all obstacles on the course, your exhausted mount is unlikely to fall flat on its face on the run in, if you can hold him up.

I collapsed for a week with a mixture of flu, bronchitis and cold, but Tetracyclene kept me without a temperature and on my feet, to the immense detriment of my taste, digestion and good temper . . .

* * *

Any sort of history contains a greater or less element of fiction—if you use that word to describe a feat of the imagination. Some histories—most readable too—contain so much fiction that they are of little *historical* value. But rising above that is the far superior element of 'Art', which if possessed and used as intended by the human psyche, can give a far truer impression of probable historical fact than a catalogue of facts. So much more is needed than mere facts . . .

As regards your great work—of course you are doing it because you have felt compelled to do so, a fact against which the gathering of Lolly, however important in another sense, has little or no meaning. Rarely does any work of art 'done to order' and without the desire of the author to do it for the sake of doing just that, amount to anything but hack work. The desire to do some special thing is what makes doing it possible, and what makes the possibility of doing something really good and memorable.

My anxiety for you is born of the hope that you have done just this and that the information you have gathered from omnivorous reading and subconscious thoughts thereafter will have sufficed to call forth your natural skill to a superabundant degree. Naturally such work calls forth every scrap of energy in the person. Whether you have been granted some special measure of insight, no one can tell until they have read the book. From my friendship for you, I hope indeed you have, while thinking to myself that for *anyone* to write something profoundly arresting about Churchill, without access to the mass of secret papers of his own, which will eventually become available to his literary executors, would be a stupendous achievement.

True mid-winter comes on 2nd February in this latitude. Thereafter one can look up and not down, forward and not back, while the springs of life, half frozen by the gloom, dark and cold of our relatively northern and stormy climate, begin to flow again, slowly at first but ever more quickly as the distant song of spring is faintly heard.

May this spring be good to you and yours.

Affectionately as always.

From R. W. Thompson   18th February, 1962
I am living in a kind of twilight in the aftermath of my book. It's done—about a week now, but I did not write at once because in fact I was scarcely 'here'. The last months were a great strain, and our brief exchange of letters in January acted as a last catalyst—if that is the right

word. It broke the tension, and I went straight on to the end, to the last words, de Quincey's, not mine, for he was 'magnificently unprepared for the long littleness of life'.

All my heart and faith is in the book, for better or worse. It is my story of our times, if nobody else's, and of course you must be right when you say that whoever—Randolph is doing it—has the private papers will do the Churchill book. But I have done a book—not that book, naturally, but my book, because by looking at these things in such terms something new or different may be discovered, as perhaps to life's evitability or inevitability. That, at least, is one of the questions.

I sent the book away last week. Basil telephoned late last night to say that it is a *tour de force*. He wants me to stay with him when he has fully annotated it, and work on it for a couple of days. He did that for me with *The Price of Victory*, but this book is much more than that. Without you, however, it would never have been done, and my debt to you is beyond compute. I know you will deprecate this, even not believe it, but the inspiration one gives is not always conscious, and even I, in my small way, know how hard it is to realise that people imagine one to be someone so much 'bigger' than one is. Inside ourselves we know how very small we are, and perhaps in the end one is drained of all conceits, the vanities of this world, to the ultimate simplicity and peace.

Knowing you, and I remember so well walking with old 'Watty'[1] on a desolate beach in Jamaica, voicing our discontents, and through him knowing about you, and that this was a fact to be grateful for, to cling to. So there you are: you can't get away from it. You gave strength to that magnificent old human being, fully endowed with his brands of strength, and he handed on a light from the same candle. Do you remember, Arthur at the last and young Tom of Warwick, that truly beautiful piece of dialogue,[2] an intimacy so wonderfully expressed, and you know, even better than I, that Arthur felt—well, as all good men feel who have done their best. He was a King, and young Tom a page, yet they were 'equal', and yet not equal. And it was Tom who would bear that small flame to Warwick, shielding it with his life.

You cannot avoid having lit flames, and inspired others to carry them, even though they are not the flames you thought or intended to light. If we had not met I should not have done much of the work I

---

[1] Colonel R. P. Watts, retired, doing an observing and advisory job. He had known Desmond Morton for years. Like Boney Fuller, far into his eighties he was living life at first hand in far places.

[2] 'Arthur and Tom of Warwick', from *The Once and Future King* by T. H. White.

have done in the last twelve years, especially. I should have worked, of course, but not so well, not to such ends.

I have had rather a wearing week, but inspiring. I met Linus Pauling[1] on Friday with magnificent old 'Lord Bertie'. His facts and figures on the U.S. build-up of the means of shrivelling this island to a cinder, and a good slice of the world, are hair-raising. I understand from Basil that Mountbatten shares our fears, as also do some permanent officials of the Min. of Defence. Those brave kids in the dock made me proud again to be an Englishman. At dinner last Tuesday I had asked the First French Secretary to give me and my family French citizenship, to go there as de Gaulle came here. It is a horrible feeling to be a subject people. At least in France a man may be locked in mortal combat with the Devil for one's own soul and the soul of a Nation. I think England has mislaid her soul and her spirit—she has certainly mislaid God.

[1] Dr. Linus Pauling, leading U.S. physicist, Nobel Lauriate, 1952. He had flown from the U.S.A. to stand by Bertrand Russell and the young C.N.D. people in the dock at the Old Bailey. Bertrand Russell had asked us both to give moral support.

Index

Index

Abyssinian War, The, 75
Acton, Lord, 121, 136
Adenauer, 29
Adler, 126, 153
Africa, North, 91–2; landings in, 22; French, 93; campaigns, 40–1, 91–2, 93, 119–20
Agincourt, 61
Aircraft production, 42
Aitken, Max, *see* Beaverbrook
A.J.B., *see* Balfour
Alamein; First Battle of, 16, 42, 91–2; the real turning point, 127, 137; Second Battle of, 92, 127, 129, 131, 132, 182
Alam Halfa, Battle of, 131
Alanbrooke, F/M Lord, 14, 23, 54, 59, 83, 125; C.I.G.S., 14, 42; liked by Churchill, 48, 132; his diaries, 58, 74
Albemarle, *see* Monk
Alexander of Macedon, 110, 147, 189
Alexander, F/M Viscount, 11, 23, 61, 132; Churchill's dislike of, 69, 84, 129, 174; articles by, 125–9, 131, 134, 137; a despatch quoted, 128; his view of Churchill, 129
Alexandria, 93
Alfred, King, 77
Algiers, 28
'*Al hamd'ul Allah*', 153
Ambler, Eric, 128–9, 130; *Justice in Deltchev*, 129, 132; *The Nightcomers*, 129; *The Schirmer Inheritance*, 129
America, *see* U.S.A.
Amery, Rt. Hon. Leopold, 13; political memoirs, 45, 51, 64, 116; papers on

strategy, 184–5, 188; comment on Churchill, 196; Balfour's epigram, 188, 202
Amritsar, 199(n)
Anglo-French Union, 28
Ankara, 41
Anti-Semitism, 165
Antwerp, 89, 115, 177
Aquinas, St. Thomas, 130–1
Arabic language, 152
Arabs, the, 73; Churchill's picture of, 194, 195
Architects, 55, 56
Arctic, 183; trans-A. railway, 94
Armoured Divisions, 8th and 22nd, 131; Soviet, 184
Army Staff system, 191
Arras, 20
Arthur, George, 182
Arthur, King, 201, 206
Asquith, Rt. Hon. H. H. (later 1st Earl of Oxford and Asquith), 13, 14, 67, 82, 116, 136, 148, 152, 169, 177, 197, 201, 202; a comment on *The World Crisis*, 116; *Moments of Memory*, 123; and the Parliament Bill, 185, 186
Athens, 41
Atlantic (theatre of war), 91, 92; Battle of, 193
Attlee, Rt. Hon. Clement (1st Earl), 13, 14, 57, 144
Auchinleck, F/M Sir Claude, 11, 12, 13, 16, 55, 90, 109, 111, 128; his assistance to the author, 33, 36; Churchill's attitude to, 56, 91–2, 95; as inspiring

trust, 82–3; feud with Montgomery, 127–8, 129–30; his dismissal, 185(n)
Austria, 183
Audrey, Little, 141
Avon, Earl of, see Eden

Baldwin, Earl, 13, 132, 152, 160; his confidence in Morton, 10, 21; reluctance to hear facts, 21, 29
Balfour, A. J. (later Earl), 13, 15, 67, 136, 169, 172; comment on Amery, 188, 202
Balkans, The, 178, 183
Bangalore, 94, 151
Barcelona, 160
Baring Hugo, 150, 151
Barnes, 151
Barnett, Correlli, 88, 90, 91, 93, 95
Barts (hospital), 145
Baruch, Barney, 11, 13, 79, 123, 126; friendship with Churchill, 124, 142, 144, 192, 198
Basil, see Liddell Hart
'Battleaxe', 56
B.C., see Bonham Carter, Maurice
'Beaver', see Beaverbrook
Beaverbrook, Viscount, 13, 47, 172; and Churchill, 36, 38, 39, 44, 47, 59, 79, 142, 144
Beda Fomm, 41
Bedouin, 194
Beethoven, 182(n)
Begbie, Harold, 13, 93
Bells, The, 195
Beloff, Max; a letter, 67
Bessemer (steel process), 108
Birkenhead, First Earl of, 142, 144, 199
Blackett, Professor P. M. S., 13, 63; his feud with Cherwell, 47, 63, 131; co-operation with Tizard, 63
Black Sea, The, 183, 184
Blenheim, 77
Board of Trade, 28
Boer War, see South African War
Boers, The 166–7, 169, 172
Bomb, The Atom, 105, 117; U.S.A. and, 207
'Bomber' Harris, see Harris, Sir A.
Bombers, 115
Bombing of Germany, 133, 191, 192–3
'Boney', see Fuller, Maj. Gen.
Bonham Carter, Sir Maurice, 13, 58, 148
Bonham Carter, Lady Violet, 148, 152

Boothby, Lord, 13, 25; friendship with Churchill, 198, 199
Borstal, 87
Boston, U.S.A., 183
Bourbons, The, 158
Bracken, Brendan (later Viscount), 11; friendship with Churchill, 77–80, 142, 144, 198, 199
Brand, Lord, 13, 131, 140
Bridges, Sir Edward, 71
British Empire, see Empire
British people; lack of belief, 161, 162, 207
Broad, Lewis, 33, 34, 116
Bronstein, see Trotsky
Brooke, Sir Alan, see Alanbrooke
Brooke, Rupert, 147
'Brookie', see Alanbrooke
Buenos Aires, 36(n)
Bulgaria, 129, 184
Buller, Gen., 168, 171
Burgoyne, Gen., 55
Burma, the campaign in, 181–2
Burnt Out Case, 189
Business of War, The (Kennedy, J. K.), 38, 41q.
Butler, Prof. J. R. M., 52
Butler, Rt. Hon. R. A. (later Lord), 183
Byron, Lord, 49, 121

Cabinet Office, The, 46, 50
Cadogan, Rt. Hon. Sir Alexander, 14, 21, 71, 152
'Cads', 120, 150–2, 155–6, 157, 159
Caesar, Julius, 158
Cairo, 28, 41
Caldecote, Viscount, see Inskip
Caligula, The Emperor, 163, 196
Camouflage, 65–6
Campbell Bannerman, Rt. Hon. Sir Henry, 14, 169
Canary, the Grand, 93
Caribbean, the North, 22, 25
Casablanca, Conference (1941) at, 12, 59
Cassino, 137
Cats, 23, 131, 136, 141
Caudle lecture, 99
C.C.S., see Combined Chiefs of Staff
Chamberlain, the Rt. Hon. Austen, 16
Chamberlain, the Rt. Hon. Joseph, 172
Chamberlain, the Rt. Hon. Neville, 14, 72, 93, 97, 129, 133, 160; confidence in Morton, 10, 21; reluctance to hear

facts, 21, 60–1; replacement by Churchill, 93, 97, 98

Chartwell, 19, 28, 30, 80, 164, 196; Churchill's guests at, 197, 198–200

Chatfield, Adm. of the Fleet, Lord, 14, 39; views on a Defence Ministry, 43

Cheltenham, 177

Cherwell, Lord, 14, 137, 191, 199; opposed by Blackett, 13, 47, 63, 131; relationship with Churchill, 11, 36, 38, 42, 43, 48 passim, 133, 140, 142, 144; his graphs, 36, 38, 43, 44, 48; relations with Tizard, 131, 133, 134, 136; his origins, 133, 138; his character, 135, 136–7;

Chiefs of Staff, 12, 95, 184; Churchill and, 40–3, 47, 49, 50, 74, 77, 92, 96, 175, 181, 185, 191; American, 74; Combined, 92, 129

China, 111, 121, 183; entry of Western Powers into, 94, 143; industry in, 107

Chindits, 179, 181

'Chink', see O'Gowan

Christ, Jesus, 53, 190, 202

Churchill, Jack, (brother of W.S.C.), 79, 145

Churchill, John Spencer, see Marlborough

Churchill, Lady, 15, 79, 132, 203

Churchill, Lord Randolph, 94, 106, 107, 169; cause of death, 156, 158, 162, 163, 168, 197; a libel on, 165, 167–8; Life (by W. S. Churchill), 164–5

Churchill, Lady Randolph, 14, 15, 94, 145; Memoirs, 123. See also Churchill, Winston

Churchill Legend, The (Neilson), 63, 76

Churchill, Randolph (son of W. S. Churchill), 14, 77, 79; Life of Eddy Darby, 45; compared with his father, 106, 108–9, 110, 151, 172; His Life of W.S.C., 172, 206

Churchill, Roosevelt and Stalin, 76

Churchill, Sir Winston S., dislike of strong characters, 12, 47; treatment of Wavell, 75, 174–5; rejection in 1945, 22, 146, 148; three Winstons, 29–30; influence of American mother, 30, 48, 54, 69, 70, 83, 86, 94, 115, 124–5, 142, 147; Alexander's effect on, 36, 69, 84, 129, 174; relations with Beaverbrook, 36, 38, 39, 44, 47, 59, 79, 142, 144; attitude to Harris, 36, 44, 48, 84; the influence of Cherwell, 36, 38, 42, 43–8 passim, 131, 133, 140, 142, 144; his

feeling about soldiers, 40, 44, 45–6, 69; relations with Chiefs of Staff, 40–3, 44, 50, 74, 92, 96, 175, 181, 185; and bombing strategy, 42, 73, 191; criticism of his strategical ideas, 42–3, 44, 47–9, 115, 120, 179; relations with Roosevelt, 44, 48, 52, 54, 56, 64, 65, 67, 69, 74, 87, 96, 101–2, 142, 150; with Stalin, 44, 48, 87, 91, 101–4, 178; soldier-politician, 45–6; obsessive hatred of Hitler, 44, 47; sentimentalism, 48, 73, 120, 136, 163, 185; attitude to Unconditional Surrender, 12, 44, 48, 84, 87–8, 90; as a 'father figure', 50–1, 55, 80, 121–2; demands on subordinates, 51, 71, 198; the Myth, 52; his English style, 53, 167; early life, 53, 94, 132, 155–6, 189; his egotism, 53, 56, 65, 67, 69, 70, 71, 76, 106, 146, 192; and staff work, 51, 53–4; public speeches, 55, 56, 64, 82; his many-sided aspects, 67, 195; attitude to bribery, 68–9; as gentleman, 69, 70, 113, 115, 158, 159; and civil servant, 71; his superficialities, 71–2; knowledge of history, 72, 77; confidence in France, 72; as inspiring personal liking, 77, 79, 81, 84, 149; his essential greatness, 78, 81, 83–4; his courage, 78, 82; a consummate actor, 78–9, 156, 195; his personal friends, 79–81, 140, 142, 169, 198–200; political career, 82, 85, 169, 172, 175–6, 177, 178; his escape from Pretoria, 82, 85, 159, 166; moral standards, 86, 190, 192, 195, 198; soldier-adventurer-journalist, 88–9, 90; and U.S. support in N. Africa, 91–2, 95–6; emphasis on 'attack', 95–6; replaces N. Chamberlain, 93, 97, 98; attitude to Spanish Civil War; Franco, 97, 159–60, 161; failure to understand a new world, 106, 110, 123; 'the Voice', 115–6; religious beliefs, 117, 118–9, 162, 190, 192; veneration of Crown and Parliament, 118–9, 120, 192; limited aim in Second World War, 123, 160; extreme old age, 141–2, 143; and England, 146, 194, 196, 202; support of de Gaulle, 150, 154; attitude to power 137, 145–6, 150–2, 153–4, 156, 174, 195; an 'Entertainment', 149, 152, 155, 156; lack of compassion, 161, 163, 164; sympathy with the Boers, 167, 168, 169, 172; a dream and its interpretation, 166–9;

responsibility for the Dardenalles, 179–80, 184; the campaign in Burma, 181–2; attachment to romantic images, 194, 195–6, 202; life at Chartwell, 196, 197. *See also* Morton, Thompson, O'Gowan WRITINGS, 19, 21; *Life of Marlborough*, 14, 19, 21, 29, 39, 64, 67, 68, 89, 110; *Great Contemporaries*, 19, 38, 64, 67, 68; *Their Finest Hour*, 20q; *Eastern Front*, 38, 64; *The River War*, 38; *My Early Life*, 51, 56; *The World Crisis*, 64, 89, 116; *The Second World War*, 72, 77; *History of the English Speaking Peoples*, 90; *Life of Lord Randolph Churchill*, 165; *London to Pretoria*, 166

Cicero, 40

C.I.G.S., *see* Alanbrook, Dill, Ironside

Civil Service, The, 71

Civil War, 110; American, 47; Spanish, 93, 97, 159–60

Civilian Affairs, A Minister of, 50

Clark, U.S. Gen. Mark, 137

'Clem', *see* Attlee

Clemenceau, 14, 93, 96, 201

'Clemmy', *see* Churchill, Lady

'Clive of Burma', *see* Wingate

C.N.D., 207(n)

Cobden, Wm., 169

Cockburn, Claud, 189

Combined Chiefs of Staff, 92, 129

Communism, 87, 90–1, 114, 123, 132, 161, 201, 202; attitude to truth, 102–4; aims, 103–4. *See also* U.S.S.R.

Connell, John, 184

Conservative Party, *see* Tory

Constantinople, 180

Cooper, Duff, Rt. Hon. Sir A., 14, 75, 199

Corsica, 59

Cozzens, J. G., 177; *Guard of Honour*, 177–8

Crete, 42, 119, 120

Crimean War, 61

Cromwell, Oliver, comparison of Churchill with, 33, 34

Crowe, Sir Eyre, 14

Crown, The, 118, 120, 148, 192. *See also* Parliament

Cry Korea, *see* Thompson, R. W.

Cuba, 143

Cunningham, Adm. Sir Andrew, 12

Cyrenaica, 41, 140

Czar, *see* Nicholas

Daily Mirror, The, 153

Daily Telegraph, The, 67, 99, 174

Dakar, 98

D'Annunzio, 197

Dardanelles, The, 179, 180, 184

D'Artagnan, 25, 83, 120, 194

D-Day, 182

Dead March in Saul, The, 195

Deakin, Col. F. W., 14; appealed to by the author, 26–7; literary assistant to Churchill, 27, 28; his knowledge of Morton, 27–8q. *See also* Letters.

'Defeat before Dakar', 98(n)

Defence, Ministry of, *see* Ministries

Defence Staff, Chief of, 43

De Gaulle, Gen., 26, 76, 93, 142, 147, 207; Roosevelt and, 96, 142, 154; his estimate of Churchill, 139; and the French people, 141; Churchill's support of, 150, 154; character, 154; Morton's opinion of, 29

Democracy, 100, 193–4, 203

De Quincey, Thomas, 206

De Rerum Novarum, *see* Encyclicals

Desert Generals, *The* (C. Barnett), 88, 91, 93; criticised by Morton, 90

Desert Group, Long Range, 183

Devil, The, 133, 137, 153, 207

D.H., *see* Haig

Dilke, Sir Charles, 172

Dill, F/M Sir John, 14, 42, 93, 105, 184–5; C.I.G.S., 14, 41; disliked by Churchill, 48, 58, 174, 184

Dill, Lady, 184

Diplomatic Service, The, 186–7

Directorate of Operations, 41

Director of Military Operations, 15, 42, 114

D.L.G., *see* Lloyd George

D.M.O., *see* Director of Military Operations

Dorman Smith, Mag. Gen. E. E., *see* O'Gowan

Dorman Smith, Col. Sir Reginald, 43(n), 45

Doullens Conference, 173, 177, 190

Dover, 183

Downing Street, 40

Dragoons, A Captain of, 83

Dreadnoughts, 115

Dreams, the interpretation of, 167–8, 169; a Churchill dream, 166

Dumas, 76, 120

Dunkirk, 42, 95, 185
Dyer, Gen. J. H., 199

Eastern Front, see Churchill, W. S.
East India Company, 62
Economics, as a factor in war, 32, 59–61,
    73, 110
Eden, Rt. Hon. Sir Anthony, 13, 41, 43,
    111, 199, 203; and the Greek campaign,
    49, 93
Education, Popular, 108
Edward VII, King, 176
Egypt, 140
Eisenhower, Gen., 75, 182
Elandslaagte, 169
Elbe, R., 76
Eldridge, Lt. Gen. Sir John, 140
Eleanor, see Roosevelt, Mrs.
Elizabeth I, Queen, 164
Elizabeth II, H.M. Queen, 145, 147
Empire, 67, 76, 93, 161, 196; Union with
    U.S.A., 148
Empire Loyalists, 197
Encyclicals, Papal, De Rerum Novarum,
    114; Quadragesimo Anno, 114
Engels, 106
England, 207; Churchill's devotion to,
    194, 196, 202
Enver, Pasha, 14, 93, 96, 98
Equality, 203
Esher, 1st Viscount, 14, 116, 173, 176;
    Letters, 82; Commission and Report,
    173, 190; friendship with George V,
    182; a case of mistaken identity, 190–1
Eton College, 86
Europe, 105, 106; the unity of, 104
Everest, Mrs. (Churchill's nurse), 14, 132,
    145
'Execution Dock', 143, 144

Far East, see Pacific (theatre of war)
Fascism, 161, 201, 202
F.E., see Birkenhead
Feiling, Keith, 199
Feis, Herbert, 76
Fender, P. G. H., 82, 85
Ferguson, Brig. Bernard, 173, 178
Fighter Command, 10
Fisher, Admiral Lord, 14, 44, 82, 93, 94
F.O., see Foreign Office
Foch, Marshal, 173, 191
Foreign Ministers, 177
Foreign Office, The, 24, 71, 186–8

France, 10, 42, 72, 142, 183; and De Gaulle,
    154
Franco, Gen., 97, 159–60, 161
Free French, The, 28
Freud, Sigmund, 55, 79, 126, 153, 167; the
    Oedipus complex, 157
Frewen, Clara, 14, 132
'Frocks', see Politicians
Fuller, Maj. Gen. J. F. C., 14, 40, 43, 63,
    76, 137, 138, 206(n); assistance to the
    author, 36, 70; a conversation with, 75;
    on Churchill, 120, 144
Fulton, 102, 104
'Funny operations', 47–8

Galahad, Sir, 194
Gallipoli, 51, 89, 93, 97, 98, 105, 106, 178;
    the 'tea' story, 97, 99
Gandhi, 196
Gatehouse, Maj. Gen., 92(n)
General Staff, The, 173
Gentleman, The; the idea of, 86; and war,
    111–3, 115, 150–2; Churchill as, 69, 70,
    113, 115; and the dictators, 115; pre-
    1914 standards of, 155–6
George V, King, 177; and Lloyd George,
    182, 185–6
George VI, King, 97
Germain, George, 55
Germany, 59, 87, 88, 110, 143; revival of
    industrial power, 107; defeat of, 119;
    bombing of, 133, 191, 192–3; 19th-
    century ambivalence, 144
'Ghost' writers, 125(n)
Gilbert, Martin, 27; Life of Churchill,
    27(n)
Godber Lectures, see Snow (Science and
    Government)
Gorgon's Head, The, 143
Gort, F/M Viscount, 40
Gran Chaco, The, 25
Grand Strategy (ed. J. R. M. Butler), 52
Grandi, Count Dino, 199
Grant, U.S. Gen. Ulysses, 47
Great Contemporaries, see Churchill, W. S.
Great George Street, 22, 25
'Greco–Aztec', 136, 138
Greece, the (1941) campaign in, 13, 41, 42,
    73, 89, 140, 189; an error in strategy, 49,
    93, 120; catastrophic consequences, 110,
    114
Greece, ancient city states, 193

Greeks, The, 56, 73; modern and ancient, 120; literature, 157, 170–1
Greek Fire, 117
Greene, Graham, 189
Gregory, Maundy; the honours scandal, 185
Greig, Louis, 199
Gremlins, 188–9, 190
Grenville School, Clare, 36, 46
Grey, Sir Edward (later Earl), 177, 178
Grigg, Sir James, 178, 182, 188, 199
Grimond, Jo, M.P., 148, 152
Grohman, Baillie, 140
Grosvenor Square, 183
Guedalla, 116; *Mr. Churchill*, 172
Guildford, 177
Gwynne, Major H. A., 25, 200

Hackett, Francis, 35
Haig, Dawyck, 51
Haig, F/M Douglas (Earl), 20, 27, 173, 186; his Papers, 51; attitude to politicians, 53; article by Liddell Hart, 163, 168; Churchill's view of, 163–4
Haldane, Gen. Sir Aylmer, 82, 83, 85, 159
Haldane, Viscount, 14, 150, 159, 169
Halifax, 1st Earl, 14, 97
'Hamba Gashlé', 143, 144, 145
Hamilton, Alexander, 16
Hamlet, 74, 79, 84, 88, 89
Hammersmith Hospital, 23
Hankey, Maurice (later Lord), 14, 15, 60, 63, 137, 176; Morton's loyalty to, 24, 141; *The Supreme Command*, 15, 137; his 'innocence', 139, 141. *See also* Roskill
Hanley, 63
Harcourt, Sir William, 169
Harris, Sir Arthur (later Lord), 11, 15, 86–7; Churchill's attitude to, 36, 39, 42, 44, 48, 84; his obsession with bombing, 44, 48, 60
Harris, Frank, 165
Harrod's Stores, 46
Harrow School, 53
Hart, Basil Liddell, 25, 27(n), 86; a paper by, 59, 61; 'Military Competence', 66, 67–8, 71–4; *The Tanks*, 70, 74
Harvard, 137
Harwich, 183
Hassall, *see* Marsh, Sir Edward
Hawtrey, Charles, 195
Health, Ministry of, *see* Ministries

Hedgehogs, 67
Heenan, H. E., Cardinal J.C., 15; his tribute to Morton, 21
Hell, 142
Henry V, King, 202
Henry VIII, King, 81, 164; a comparison with Churchill, 34, 35
Henry VIII (Hackett), 35
Henty, G. A., 194
Herbert, A. P., 134
Higgins, Trumbull, 76, 92, 95, 97, 122; *Winston Churchill and the Second Front*, 76, 122–3
History; military history, 59; disease and, 63(n), 75; American historians, 76, 140; Australian, 98; the writing of, 99–100, 135; official history, 52, 98, 191
History of the English-Speaking Peoples, The, see Churchill, W. S.
Hitler, 32, 35, 37, 84, 94, 110, 114, 115, 152; his view of the Greek campaign, 119; 120–1; psychopath, 145; and world empire, 148
H.M.S.O., *see* H.M. Stationery Office
H.M. Stationery Office, 52. *See also* Playfair, Gen.
Hoi polloi, The, 187
Holmfirth, 63
Home Rule, 178
Honours scandal, The, *see* Gregory, M.
Hopkins, Henry L., 70
Horace, 200q
Hornblower novels, The, 195
House under the Water (F. B. Young), 132
Hozier, Clementine, *see* Churchill, Lady
Hubris, 168, 170–1, 172
Hull, Cordell, 64, 150
Humanists, 82
Hungary, 184
Hurricanes, 184
Hurricanes, 59
Hyde (Cheshire), 64
Hyde Park Gate, 198, 203

I.I.C., *see* Industrial Intelligence Centre.
'Ike', *see* Eisenhower
I Lucifer, 133
Imperial Defence, Committee of, 10, 14, 15, 173, 191
India, 150, 181, 198; Literature, 157
Industrial Intelligence Centre, 32; its purpose, 9; established by Morton, 20–1, 29

Industrial power, 106–7; in 19th-century England, 108
Industrial Revolution, The, 114; as a new force, 106–10, 115; causes, 108
Innes, Capt. (a portrait), 83
Inskip, Rt. Hon. Thomas, 15, 196
Intelligence Corps, 22, 24
Ireland, 16, 26
Ironside, F/M Lord, 48; C.I.G.S., 15, 41
Irwin, Anthony, 98
Irwin, Maj. Gen. N. M. S., 98(n)
Irwing, Sir Henry, 195
Islam, 93, 152, 188
Ismay, Gen. Lord, 15, 26, 63, 141; his book, 52, 54, 99; devotion to Churchill, 99
Italy; campaign in, 129, 137, 140; in Spanish Civil War, 160
Ivan the Terrible, 81

James, Robert Rhodes, 12; judgment on Morton–Churchill, 10–11, 12
Japanese, The, 41, 89, 92, 94, 143, 182
Jeanne d'Arc, 143
Jebb, Sir Gladwyn (later 1st Baron), 188
Jerome, Jennie, see Churchill, Lady Randolph
Jerome, Leonard, 15, 107, 121, 124
Jeromes, The, 105, 115, 124
Jesuits, The; ends and means, 164
Jezebel (the cat), 23, 136
'Joe', see Stalin
Johannesburg, 166, 167
John Duke, see Marlborough
Joing Planning Staff, 24, 41, 47, 50, 72
Joubart, Boer General, 166, 167, 168
Joubert, Air Chief Marshal, Sir Philip, 137, 138, 171
Jugo-Slavs, The, 26, 28, 55, 56
Julians, The, 158
Jung, 126, 149, 153, 157; his Archetypes, 154

K., Mr., see Kruschev
Kaiser, The, see Wilhelm II
Kennedy, President John, 142; on Churchill, 121
Kennedy, Maj. Gen. Sir John, 52, 54, 114; D.M.O., 15
Kennedy, Joseph, 142
Kiachow, 94
'Killeen, Bridget', 139
King, U.S. Fleet Adm., 15, 41

King Lear, 79
King Log, 50
Kings Lynn, 63
King Stork, 50
Kitchener, F/M Earl, 15, 88, 89, 94, 106, 166, 168, 171
Korea, 25, 94, 172
Kropotkin, 169
Kruger, President, 166, 167, 168, 171
Krupp gun, The, 61

Labour Party, The, 97, 193
Lafayette, 142
Land Values, 82, 178
'Land Warfare' (O'Gowan), 43
Latin literature, 157
Law, Rt. Hon. A. Bonar, 197
Lawrence of the Punjab, Lord; comparison with Churchill, 188
Lawrence, T. E., 67; relationship with Churchill, 195–9; character, 199
League of Nations, The, 73
Lenin, 99, 102
Leslie, Leonie, 15, 132
L'Etang, Dr. Hugh, 57, 63, 70, 75
Letters:
Deakin–Thompson, 27–8; Thompson–Wheatley, 24–6; Thompson–Morton, 31, 33, 35–6, 38–40, 46–7, 51–2, 55–6, 62–3, 63–4, 66–7, 69–70, 75–77, 81–4, 88–9, 91–3, 94–5, 97–8, 100–1, 104–5, 106, 106–7, 109–11, 114–6, 120–1, 122, 123–4, 124–5, 127–9, 131–2, 133–4, 136–7, 139–40, 143–4, 145–7, 149–52, 157–9, 161–2, 164–6, 166, 168–9, 171–3, 176–9, 183–5, 188–90, 191–3, 195, 201–3, 203–4, 205–7; Morton–Thompson, 31–2, 33–5, 38–9, 45–6, 47–51, 52–5, 56–62, 64–6, 67–9, 71–5, 77–81, 85–88, 89–91, 95–7, 99–100, 101–4, 105–6, 107–9, 111–4, 116–9, 119–20, 121–2, 122–3, 124, 125–7, 129–31, 132–3, 134–6, 138–9, 140–3, 144–5, 147–9, 152–7, 159, 159–60, 162–4, 166–8, 169–71, 173–6, 179–83, 185–8, 190–1, 193–5, 197–200, 203, 204–5; O'Gowan–Paget, 40–3; Paget–O'Gowan, 43–5
L.G., see Lloyd George
L.H., see Liddell Hart
Liberal Party, 85, 169, 170, 182, 185, 193, 202
Liddell Hart, Sir Basil, 15, 27(n), 33, 52, 63, 69, 70, 84, 86, 97, 123, 128, 204, 205;

assistance to the author, 36, 39, 51, 55, 84, 140; 192; paper on strategy, 55, 59, 61, 71–4, 88; on military competence, 66; views on Churchill, 66, 70–1, 84, 87; comments on Mexander articles, 131, 137; article on Haig, 163, 168

Life of Eddy Derby, see Churchill, Randolph

Life of Maroborough, see Churchill, W. S.

Lilliputians, 202

Lindemann, Prof., *see* Cherwell, Lord

Linnell, Dr., 63(n), 137, 161–2, 168, 178

'Little Ease', 143

Livy, 40, 64

Lloyd George, Rt. Hon. David (1st Earl), 15, 53, 67, 82, 84, 93, 96, 172, 183, 196, 197, 202; appoints Morton to I.I.C., 20–1, 29; his direction of 1914–8 War, 57–8, 85, 164, 178, 201; his character, 177; and the Welfare State, 178; and King George V, 182, 185–6

Lloyd George, Guillam, 85, 136

Lloyd, Rt. Hon. Selwyn, 183

Logistics, 73

London Hospital, The, 162

London to Pretoria, see Churchill, W. S.

'Lord Bertie', *see* Russell, Bertrand

Loyola, S. Ignatius, 164

L.S.D. (drug), 77

'M', *see* Morton

Macbeth, 79

McA., *see* McArthur

McArthur, U.S. Gen., 123

MacDonald, Rt. Hon. J. Ramsay; his confidence in Morton, 10, 20–1, 29

MacKenzie, Compton, 119q, 120, 121

Maclaglan, Victor, 29

Macmillan, Rt. Hon. Harold, 24, 141; 170, 183, 184, 203

Machiavelli, 136

Madras, 62

Maecenas, 200

Maestricht, 120

Magnificence, 87, 195

Mahrattas, The, 62

Mailer, Norman, 121

Malakand Field Force, 88

Malaya, 41

Maldon, 91

Mandalay, 182

Man of Secrets (Roskill), 24

Mao, 111

Marchienne, Cartier de, 199

Marlborough, John, First Duke of, 34, 54, 69, 70, 77, 115, 120, 147, 158; Churchill's admiration of, 148; and bribes, 68, 81

Marlborough, Consuela, Duchess of, 76

Marlborough, Dowager Duchess of, 76, 94

Marmalade, 166, 168

Marsh, Sir Edward, 15, 125, 126, 169; his devotion to Churchill, 80; Hassall's Life, 125

Marshall, U.S. Gen. G. C., 16, 41, 58, 75, 92

Marshall Hall, Sir Edward, 55, 56

Martians, 106

Martin, Sir John, 16, 141

Martin, Kingsley, a story from, 192

Marx, Karl, 106

Marxism, 99, 102. *See also* U.S.S.R.

Masters, John 181, 189

Maundy, G., *see* Gregory

Maurice, *see* Hankey

Mediterranean Sea, 185

'Mel', *see* Thompson, Mrs.

Mendel, the Abbé, 54

Mendelssohn (the Composer), 182(n)

Mendelssohn, 178, 182

Mercedes Benz, 184

Merchant adventurers, 94–5

Merchant Navy, The, 73

Merlin, 201

Messervy, Gen. Sir Frank, 16, 181

Metaxas, 119

Mexico, 203

Middle East, The, 93, 140, 189, 195, 199

Mill, J. S., 169

Milne, Duncan Grinnell, 142, 144

Milne, George (later Lord), 72

Milner, Lord, 191

Ministries; Economic Warfare, 9; Defence, 41, 43, 50, 207; Health, 138, 179

Mr. Churchill, see Guedalla

Missolonghi, 49

Moments of Memory, see Asquith

Monarchy, *see* The Crown

Monck, George, 1st Duke of Albemarle, 67

Monmouth, Duke of, 120

Monroe doctrine, 92

Monroe, President, 92(n)

Montaigne, 157

Montesquieu, 157

Montgomery, F/M Viscount, 11, 16, 46;

his pedestal, 90, 91; on leadership, 125, 127; feud with Auchinleck, 127–8, 129–30; his generalship, 127–8; Alamein, 127, 129, 131

Montgomery/Morgan Overlord, *see* Overlord

Monty, *see* Montgomery

Moonlight Sonata, The, 182

Moore, Gen. Sir John (1751–1809), 40

More, St. Thomas, 140

Morgan, Gen., 16, 63, 105

Morgenthau, Henry, 16, 45, 51, 93, 180; *Secrets of the Bosphorus*, 180(n)

Morley, Lord, 16, 67, 94, 106, 107, 108

Morning Post, The, 25, 166, 200

Morrison, Herbert, 1st Viscount, 16, 25

Morton, Major Sir Desmond; in Secret Intelligence, 9, 26; work for I.I.C., 9–10, 24, 27–8, 29; Roskill's estimate of, 9–11; A.D.C. to Haig, 20, 173(n), 186; collaboration with Hankey, 10, 24; house on Kew Green, 10, 22–3, 29; association with Churchill, 9–11, 20–21, 27–8, 80–1; his understanding of Churchill, 11–12, 24, 26, 28, 162–3; on the assessment of Churchill, 33–4; summary of career, 19–23, 29; Churchill's tribute to, 20; his sense of humour, 22, 23, 24, 26, 65; avoidance of limelight, 23, 25, 27; the quality of his letters, 25; taste for theological discussion, 27; his advice on writing, 37, 45, 52, 61–2, 107–9, 135; his estimate of O'Gowan, 45, 49, 50, 57–9; criticism of Churchill's strategy, 47–9; his view of Eden, 49; on emotional slogans, 49, 56; Churchill's capacity for 'basic toil', 53–4; appraisal of Liddell Hart, 59, 67–8, 69, 71–4, 86; admiration for Alexander, 61; on the fashion for denigration, 77–8, 90; Bomber Harris, 86; on the writing of history, 58, 99–100, 205; Churchill's great mistake, 101, 103–4, 123; Churchill–Roosevelt–Stalin, 101–4; discusses significance of Industrial Revolution, 107–8, 116–7; and the origin of war, 111–3, 117; Churchill's attitude to 'authority', 117–9; Churchill's unconquerable spirit, 121–2; defines 'politician', 135–6; the problem of Churchill, 144–5, 148–9; Churchill and Franco, 159–60; Churchill as a leader in war, 160; on dreams,

166–7, 169; discusses 'hubris', 170–1; his reaction to Churchill's treatment of Wavell, 174–5; politicians, diplomats and ordinary people, 186–8; on Churchill's alleged fatalism, 197–8; a lunch with Churchill, 203. *See also* Letters

Moscow, 103, 188

Mountbatten, Earl, 16, 42, 47, 181

Mount Street, 172

Munich, 63

Mussolini, 35, 37, 115; his invasion of Greece, 119

Myitkina, 182

Naked and the Dead, The, 121

Nanny, the English, 134

Napoleon I, the Emperor, 108, 136, 141

Napoleonic Wars, 10

Nascissism, 154, 202

'Narsees' (Nahzees), 88, 194

Nation; development of the, 111–2

Natural Compost Farming, 129

Navy, the Royal, 42, 65–6; the Netherlands, 65–6

Neilson, Francis, 63, 64q, 70, 85, 144; his career, 64–5; view of Churchill, 64, 65, 76, 82; Liddell Hart's caution on, 66, 84; his book, 82, 165; libellous information from, 165–6, 167–8

Nelson, Lord, 134

Netherlands, The; a delegation, 66; *see also* Navy

Newport (Salop), 65

New York, 36(n), 183

Nicholas I, Czar, 94, 192

Nicky, *see* Nicholas, Czar

Nicolson, Harold, 196

Nightingale, Florence, 194

Normandy, Campaign in, 127

North, Major John, 51; collaboration with Alexander, 127–8, 129, 131, 137

North Africa, *see* Africa North

Norway, the campaign in, 10, 72–3, 89, 115, 178, 180

Norwich, Viscount, *see* Cooper, Duff, Sir A.

Nye, Lt. Gen. Sir Archibald, 16, 25

Observer, The, 108, 110, 134, 150, 153, 196

O'Connor, Gen. Sir Richard; his N. African campaign, 40–1, 93

Oedipus complex, 157

O'Gowan, Maj. Gen. Eric, 16, 27, 40, 64,

67, 84, 127, 128, 171, 189; a lecture by, 32, 40, 41; information to the author, 33, 36, 39, 46, 62, 63; compares Churchill with Cromwell; 33, 35, 40; letters to Paget, 39, 40–1, 45, 49–50; on Churchill's attitude to army commanders, 40–3, 55–6, 58; a 'Ulysses Grant war', 46–7; Churchill and staff work; 51–2, 57–8; 115, 171; a letter to Liddell Hart, 57–9; his dismissal, 185(n). *See also* Letters
Old Bailey, The, 207(n)
'Old Man of the Sea', 185
Oliver, F. S., 16, 93, 96
Omdurman, Battle of, 115
Onassis, 76, 86, 141, 142
Once and Future King, The, 206
Ophelia, 88, 89
Organised Man, The, 203
Oriel College, Oxford, 22
Ouija board, 122
'Overlord', 46, 63, 182
Oxford, 95

Pacific (theatre of war), 16, 91, 92, 95, 121, 181, 185
Paget, Gen. Sir Bernard, 16, 38, 46, 48, 63, 131; his assistance to the author, 36, 39; O'Gowan's letter to, 40–3; letter to O'Gowan, 43–5, 49; criticisms of Churchill, 44; death, 125
Pantellaria, 42
Paris, 93, 184; Peace Conference (1919), 13, 14, 75, 176, 201
Parliament; Churchill's respect for, 118–9, 120, 148
Parliament Bill, The, 182
Pauling, Dr. Linus, 207
Peace Conference (1919), The, *see* Paris
Pearl Harbour, 92, 95
Peck, Sir John, 16; his knowledge of Morton, 26–7
Perkins, Frances, 75
Persian War, The, 120
Phillipopolis, 184
Pink gin, 36
Pitt (the Elder), 10
Planchette, 122
Playfair, Maj. Gen. I. S. O., 54; *Middle East* (H.M.S.O.), 52, 54, 98
Pogue, Forrest, 140
Poland, 10
Politicians, 135–6, 156, 188, 191; Haig's

dislike of, 53; their responsibility for war, 113, 116; monarchs and, 182, 186; and Privilege, 183–4
Politics; in military history, 59; party, 193–4
Polo, 94
Port Arthur, 94
Portal, Viscount, Marshal of R.A.F., 16, 44
Powell, Rt. Hon. Enoch, M.P., 153, 158
Power; its nature, 136, 150, 152; the lust for, 153–4
President, The U.S., *see* Roosevelt, Eisenhower, Kennedy, Monroe, Wilson
'Presidents and Prime Ministers', *see* Beloff
Press, The, 99, 100, 102; foreign, 186
Pretoria, 169; Churchill's escape from, 82, 85, 159, 166, 167
Priestley, J. B., 161
Prime Ministers, 197; British attitude towards, 57
Prince, The (Machiavelli), 136
Princeton, 178
Privilege, 183–4
'Prof.', The, *see* Charwell, Lord
Psychiatrists, 126
Psychology, 126, 156–7, 167; in the study of history, 58
Public Record Office, 28
Punjab, The, 188
Purgatory, 142

Quadragesimo Anno, *see* Encyclicals
Quebec, Conference, 177

R., *see* Rommel
Radar, 16
Rand Foundation, The, 178
Read, Herbert, 169
Red Indians, 121
'Reg', *see* Dorman Smith, Sir Reginald
Revelation, The Book of the, 153
Revolutionary War (U.S.), The, 56
Richard III, King, 145, 146
River War, The, see Churchill, W. S.
Road to Mandalay, The (Masters), 181
Roberts, F/M Earl, 89, 106, 150, 166, 168, 171
Rockefeller Foundation, The, 76
Roebeck, Adm. Sir John de, 180, 184
'Rogers, N. W.', 165
Roman Catholic Church, The, 23
'Roman Policier', The, 130

Rommel, Gen., 92, 131, 140
Roosevelt, Mrs. Eleanor, 54
Roosevelt, President F. D., 35, 70(n), 94, 144, 152; and 'Unconditional Surrender', 12, 87–8; dealing with Churchill, 44, 48, 52, 54, 56, 64, 65, 67, 69, 74, 81, 87, 96, 101–2, 142, 150, 181; his reticence, 54; concern for U.S. interests, 65, 175–6; as commander-in-chief, 74; at Yalta, 74, 75; dislike of de Gaulle, 96, 142, 154; relations with Stalin, 101–4, 159
Rosebery, Rt. Hon. Earl, 67, 94, 106, 107, 108
Roskill, Capt. Stephen, 16; Foreword by, 9–12; impression of Morton, 9–12, 23; Man of Secrets (Hankey), 10, 16, 25; assessment of Thompson–Morton letters, 11–12
Roumania, 184
Royal Air Force, 10, 71; as an independent service, 40, 43; bombing strategy, 40, 72; T. E. Lawrence in, 199
Royal Field Artillery, 20
Royal House Artillery, 20
Royal Society, The, 63
Royal United Services Institution, 40, 41, 46, 51, 64; Quarterly, 98(n)
R.U.S.I., see Royal United Services Institution
Russell, Bertrand, 143, 207; and C.N.D., 207(n)
Russia, 143; Czarist expansionist policies, 104, 105; German advance into, 119. See also U.S.S.R.

Sackville, see Germain
St. George and the Dragon, 196
Salisbury, Marchioness of, 169
Sardinia, 59
Sartre, J. P., 150; comment by Morton, 153
Savage Club, The; a party at, 34–5, 36
Savinkov, Boris, 67
Schadenfreude, 156
Schiller, 144
Scholasticism, 164
Science and Government, see Snow, C. P.
Screwtape Letters, The, 133
Second Front, The, 91, 98
Second International, The, 193
Second World War, The, see Churchill, W. S.

Secrets of the Bosphorus, 180(n)
Selborne, the Earl of, 170
Serbia, 184
Seven Years War, The, 10
Shakespeare, W., 191q, 202
Shaw, G. B., 47, 143
Shelley, P. B., 134
Sherwood, Robert, 69, 70(n)
Sicily, 42, 59
Sidi Barrani, 40
Sikhs, 188
Singapore, 41, 89
'Skyscraper', 16, 44, 46, 63
Slessor, Marshal of R. A. F., Sir John, 128
Slim, F/M Viscount, 12, 16, 179; comment on strategy, 101; in Burma, 181; views on Churchill, 181–2; Churchill's dislike of, 181
Smith, F. E. (1st Earl of Birkenhead), 55
Smith, Heckstall, Anthony, 140
Smuts, Gen., 159, 166, 194
Snow, C. P., Science and Government, 131, 137; Morton's comment on, 133; his novels, 134
Socialism, 108, 170, 193
S.O.E., see Special Operations Executive
Solomon, King, 200
Somaliland, 175
South Africa, 194
South African War, 61, 89, 166–9, 191
South America, 25
South-East Asia, 42
Spain, 92(n), 93, 97; see also Civil War
Spanish Civil War, The (Thomas), 159–60
Special Operations Executive, 26, 28
Spitfires, 59
S.T., see Sunday Times
Staff College, The, 180
Staff officers, 51, 53–4; see also Chiefs of Staff
Stalin, 35, 38, 76, 78, 94, 110, 115, 159, 178, 195; Stalin-Roosevelt-Churchill, 101–4, 105, 145, 152
Stalinism, 102–4
Stamfordham, Lord, 186
Stephenson, Adm.; an anecdote, 65–6
Stern, Albert, 192
Stilwell, U.S. Gen., 179; in Burma, 181–2
Stopford, Gen. Sir Montagu, 16, 181
Strategy, British School of, 42
Suez, 43
Summit Conferences, 177

Sunday Times, The; Alexander articles in, 127, 128, 131
Supreme Command, The, see Hankey
Sussex Square, 198
Sweden, 72, 180
Sydney Street, 82, 198
'Syntax diffusion', 131, 132
Syphilis, 158, 162, 165

Tacitus, 40, 131
Tammany Hall, 124
Tanks, The (Liddell Hart), 70, 74
Taylor, A. J. P., 134–5, 137, 139; *Origins of the Second World War*, 139
Teheran, 104, 150, 178
Television, 67, 121
Thomas, Hugh, 159
Thomas, Rt. Hon. J. H., 199
Thompson, Mrs., 31, 47, 83, 121, 127, 149, 157, 170, 178, 200; first impressions of Morton, 29–30; as teacher of Latin, 36, 40, 46, 64, 131, 204
Thompson, R. W. (the Author), his search for Churchill, 19, 25, 76–7, 109, 137, 189; first meeting with Morton, 22, 25; the 'Yankee Marlborough' theory, 33, 34, 77, 105, 115, 121, 122; the central problem, Churchill–Roosevelt, 56, 64, 67; a conversation with General Fuller, 75; on 'bogus maleness', 82, 85–6, 88, 145, 148; Churchill soldier–adventurer–journalist, 88–9, 105; Churchill and Vichy, 93, 96–7, 98; the power of Churchill's personality, 98, 99, 100–1; Churchill–Roosevelt–Stalin, 104–5; debates significance of Industrial Revolution, 106, 109–10; the outsider's view of Churchill, 123–4; criticism of Montgomery, 127–8; Churchill as perpetual child, 116, 144, 145–7; the problem of Power, 150–2; on the reading of many books, 157–8; reflects on politicians and privilege, 183–4; Churchill's mediocrity in peace, 196; the travail of writing, 188–9, 201, 203–4, 205–6; desire to become a French citizen, 207; Writings; *The Yankee Marlborough*, 25, 26, 37, 38; *Cry Korea*, 25, 37, 62; *The Price of Victory*, 25, 26, 33, 36, 39, 46, 98, 99, 114, 206; *War was my Peace* (projected), 114
Timbuktu, 89
Times, The, 10, 121, 134

Times Literary Supplement, The, 78, 92
Tizard, Sir Henry, 16–17, 63; his struggles with Cherwell, 131, 133, 134; character, 135
Tizard Memorial Lecture, 63
Tizard Committee, 16
T.L.S., *see Times Literary Supplement*
Tobruk, 43
Today (weekly), 169
Tojo, 38, 39
Tokyo, 89
'Tom Tiddler's Ground', 94
'Torch' (operation), 92
Tory party, 85, 97, 170, 192, 193, 196; Churchill and the, 172, 198
Tovey, Adm. Sir John, 12
Toynbee, Arnold, 104
Trafalgar, Battle of, 108
Treasury, The, 22
Triumph of Integrity, The (Milne), 142
Trondheim, 44, 47
Trotsky, 67
Tschiffely, 36
Tschiffely's Ride, 36(n)
Turkey, 14, 16, 97, 180; ambassadors in, 180
Tynan, K., 158

'Unconditional Surrender', 12, 44, 48, 84, 87–8, 89, 90, 107, 114, 123
United Service Institution of India, 32(n)
'Urchin', *see* Hedgehogs
U.S.A., 30, 42, 110, 121, 143; industrial policy of, 32, 59, 73; pre-war unemployment in, 64, 65; entry into the war, 74, 95, 201, 202; Chiefs of Staff, 74, 92; police, 183; and the Bomb, 207. *See also* Churchill, W. S., Roosevelt
U.S.S.R., 20, 99, 103, 104, 121; post-war domination of Europe, 84; Churchill and, 87, 91; relations with U.S.A., 90–1; 1917 revolution, 97, 192; economic expansion of, 105, 107. *See also* Stalin, Communism

Valona, 189
Vansittart, Sir Robert (later 1st Baron), 199
Vergil, 40
Vichy, 93, 96–7, 98
Victoria, Queen, 108; a biography of, 62
View from the West (C. Cockburn), 189
'Vinegar Joe', *see* Stilwell

'Voice', The, 115–6
Von Sanders, Gen. Liman, 14
Von Speer, 193
Von Thoma, Gen., 131

W. (Winston), see Churchill, W. S.
Wall Street, 124
War; origin and causes of, 111–3; and the nation state, 111; and the gentleman, 111–3, 115; religion and, 112; the rules of, 112; and the politicians, 113, 116–7; fear and discontent as causes of, 113, 115, 117, 121; modern technology in, 116–7. See also Civil War, World War I
War Aim, The, 114
War Cabinet, The, 10, 15, 17, 24, 41
War Games, 17, 24
War Office, The, 28, 42, 46
Warwick, Tom of, 206
Washington, U.S.A., 13, 92
Waterloo, Battle of, 40(n)
Watts, Col. R. P., 206
Wavell, F/M Earl, 12, 17, 56, 128, 173; Churchill's treatment of, 11, 56, 173–5, 178; and the campaign in Greece, 49
Wavell, Portrait of a Soldier (Ferguson), 173
'Wehrwirtschaft', 59
Wellesley, Sir Arthur, see Wellington
Wei Hai Wei, 94
Wellington, The 1st Duke of, 40; a letter quoted, 62
Wells, H. G., 197
Westminster Cathedral, 21
Wheatley, Dennis, 17, 26; inventor of

'War Games', 24; meets author, 26–7; see also Letters
Whigs, The, 170
White House Papers of Harry L. Hopkins, The, 70
White, T. H., 206(n)
Who's Who, 24, 64
Wigram, Ralph, 17
Wilhelm II, Kaiser, 94, 115, 144, 187
William the Conqueror, 77
Williamson, Henry, 36
Willingdon, First Marquis of, 199
'Willy', see Wilhelm II
'Willy-Nicky' letters, 94, 106
Wilson, President Woodrow, 75
Wingate, Gen. Orde, 179, 181; Churchill's admiration of, 11, 42, 47, 185; the 'Clive of Burma', 181
Winston Churchill and the Second Front, see Higgins
Women's Suffrage, 178
World War I, 191; origins of, 183, 187; and World War II, 115

Yalta, Conference at, 12, 150; its significance, 68, 69, 74, 76, 84
Yankee Marlborough, The, see Thompson, R. W.
Yorick, 76
Young, Francis Brett, 132

Zagreb, 184
Zeebrugge, 89
Zulu language, 145
Zulu War, The, 115